THE MARKETING PROBLEM SOLVER

WILEY SERIES ON BUSINESS STRATEGY
William A. Cohen, Editor

Direct Marketing Success: What Works and Why
  Freeman F. Gosden, Jr.

Winning on the Marketing Front: A Corporate Manager's Game Plan
  William A. Cohen

Public Sector Marketing: A Guide for Practitioners
  Larry L. Coffman

The Marketing Problem Solver
  J. Donald Weinrauch

THE MARKETING PROBLEM SOLVER

J. Donald Weinrauch

JOHN WILEY & SONS
New York • Chichester • Brisbane • Toronto • Singapore

Copyright © 1987 by John Wiley & Sons, Inc.

All rights reserved. Published simultaneously in Canada.

Reproduction or translation of any part of this work beyond that permitted by Section 107 or 108 of the 1976 United States Copyright Act without the permission of the copyright owner is unlawful. Requests for permission or further information should be addressed to the Permissions Department, John Wiley & Sons, Inc.

This publication is designed to provide accurate and authoritative information in regard to the subject matter covered. It is sold with the understanding that the publisher is not engaged in rendering legal, accounting, or other professional service. If legal advice or other expert assistance is required, the services of a competent professional person should be sought. *From a Declaration of Principles jointly adopted by a Committee of the American Bar Association and a Committee of Publishers.*

Library of Congress Cataloging-in-Publication Data

Weinrauch, J. Donald, 1942-
   The marketing problem solver.

   Bibliography: p.
   Includes Index.
   1. Marketing. I. Title

HF5415.W366 1987   658.8   86-15971
ISBN 0-471-81309-5

Printed in the United States of America

10 9 8 7 6 5 4 3 2 1

*To my loving family
Rosemary, Karen, and William*

Series Preface

Peter Drucker said, "The future will not just happen if one wishes hard enough. It requires decision—now. It imposes risk—now. It requires action—now. It demands allocation of resources, and above all, human resources—now." The Wiley Series on Business Strategy is published to assist managers with the task of creating the future in their organizations.

Creation of the future requires application of the art and science of strategy. Strategy comes from the Greek word "strategia," which means generalship. It has clear military roots, defining how a general deployed the available forces and resources to achieve military objectives. But business and military strategy, though similar, are not identical. Business strategy is the allocation of resources to achieve a differential advantage at the time and place of decisive importance. "Resources" may be human, financial, promotional; they may have to do with unique know-how; they may have a psychological emphasis. But to be effective, these resources must be concentrated where they count. This achievement is the essence of any successful business strategy and the theme of the series.

The series will investigate strategy in all of its many facets in business, including marketing, management, planning, finance, communications, promotional activities, leadership, corporate culture—to note only those topics under preparation or planned. Its aim is to equip the

practicing manager with the techniques and tools he or she will need for the most competitive and exciting period in business of all time.

WILLIAM A. COHEN
Series Editor

Preface

Countless books about marketing have been published. Many are theoretical, "textbookish," merely descriptive, "dictionaryish," or superficial. They fail to offer sound or significant marketing ideas and guidelines that can positively influence their readers.

Practicing executives need answers to a variety of marketing problems or concerns. In their search for solutions they may buy and read a number of specialized books on marketing, and may eventually amass a large library on such vital areas as selling, advertising, product development, pricing, and the like. The search may be time consuming, costly, and frustrating. In fact, an executive may need only a few questions answered in each area. Why isn't there a good, readable reference book on marketing?

This book is intended to fill the gap. It identifies and discusses a number of major marketing areas and gives suggestions, tips, and recommendations that can be used to promote the well-being of a business. The book consists of both strategic and tactical concepts that stimulate interest while possibly preventing a few major business problems and/or correcting some current marketing errors.

As a former marketing manager and now a consultant/marketing professor, I have often heard people fuss that marketing is too abstract. Active business people and those studying part-time for an MBA complain that marketing seems too nebulous. "There appear to be no marketing rules, procedures, or consistent guidelines." After thinking about these criticisms, I realized that numerous practical decision-making

tips and suggestions for marketing can indeed be identified. They may not have been fully developed previously, or perhaps they've been presented in academic jargon. I decided to *collect* and *synthesize* the many marketing rules, procedures, and recommendations that might be helpful to executives and students of marketing and present them in a body. Hence this book.

Many authors warn in their preface that they will avoid lists, rules, or a cookbook approach. From my experiences, however, I believe that busy executives welcome the "cookbook" approach: helpful lists, problem statements, guidelines, summary charts, "quick and dirty" rules, and tabulated advice for decison making. They don't want authors to be evasive, cute, or academically safe by hedging or skirting tough problems or challenges inherent in the subject material. They prefer authors to make decisions and take a stand. As intelligent readers they can then decide on the relevance and usefulness of the written material.

The guidelines and suggestions covered in this book give fruitful input and encouragement for making crucial marketing decisions. Marketing is not a pure science. But certain principles do apply to it. These principles, if applied, can help executives avoid bad marketing decisions or even colossal blunders.

Some of the many attractive features of this book are enumerated here (the first list):

- The book is a quick, practical reference guide about marketing.
- The book has a handy reference index so specific topics about major marketing issues or problems can be easily located.
- The book offers step-by-step guidelines on implementing specific marketing strategies, tactics, or functions (e.g., a turnaround strategy, pricing of goods and services).
- The book contains numerous lists which identify standards and criteria for judging particular marketing strategies and tactics. These give a good basis for comparison of company operations with what a successful marketing program should entail.
- The book gives helpful advice and information of immediate value. These provide a sound foundation for implementing useful ideas.
- The book contains numerous real-life examples, personal experiences, quotes, vignettes, situations, and illustrations to buttress key points and increase understanding.
- The book includes marketing topics and tips that deal with both age-old and future challenges and opportunities.
- The book will serve both novice and experienced marketing exec-

utives. The book's content and format will be useful to readers who know little about marketing but demand a sound orientation. The great detail of coverage of some marketing areas will be extremely useful to more experienced marketers.
- The book gives advice based on my own experiences, careful research, studies (formal study for over 11 years), and practice of marketing for over 25 years (I am still learning about this fascinating field).

In short, my recipes for success should give the reader a basis for successful marketing strategies and sound decisions. The process of planning, researching, and writing this book included the impossible task of finding a title. At times I almost settled on *The Only Marketing Guide You'll Ever Need*. But I was too afraid that critics would call this presumptuous and naive. I suspect that some academic purists will even "flog" me for trying to codify marketing rules and offering a cookbook approach to marketing. However, this really is a minor risk compared to the opportunities of giving you a practical, helpful, and meaningful book. I realize that there are some essential marketing procedures and rules that managers and business people ought to know that can make a vital difference in their own situation. Let us then begin together on reading and pinpointing those rules and procedures that may best meet your own needs and interests.

Organization of the Book and How to Use It

This book has been written to serve the reader, and is thus organized for readability and convenience. Its suggestions are applicable to:

- Large and small businesses
- For-profit and nonprofit organizations
- Marketers and nonmarketers
- Top and middle level executives
- Organizations that sell a physical product, a service, or both

Therefore, the content and material of the book are arranged by traditional marketing topics and issues instead of by type of organization or by management level and field of expertise.

The book has five major parts and 21 chapters.

Part 1 deals with the marketing management setting and the ever-present search for excellence in marketing. The four chapters cover the essential concerns of developing a favorable marketing climate, locating the best marketing people, appreciating competitive challenges, and avoiding classic marketing mistakes. The overriding theme of Part 1 is that successful marketing requires the right philosophy, attitude, commitment, and qualified people. This first part is essential for organizations new to the marketing arena. The four chapters give a solid foundation for developing a positive organizational climate.

The two chapters of *Part 2* emphasize the importance of the strategic and annual planning process and the financial support needed for marketing. They cover new opportunities for accountability and controls in the area of marketing.

Part 3 contains a number of suggestions and recommendations for a better understanding of the marketplace. Chapter 7 gives fresh insight on dissecting opportunities in the marketplace. Chapters 8 and 9 offer specific rules and ideas for analyzing and researching consumers. The marketing research and test marketing chapters should be of interest to both novices and more sophisticated marketers.

Part 4 is the longest section of the book and is perhaps the most important for the reader who wants specific marketing advice or reference on marketing mix variables. It contains various strategies, tactics, and suggestions for product development, product mix decisions, customer service, pricing, advertising, personal selling, sales promotion, and physical distribution. This section is organized to reflect the major topics of the marketing mix. It also provides special chapter coverage on direct marketing, including telemarketing, and trade show strategies. Many how-to or reference books on marketing give scant coverage of these new but progressive techniques. Although some of these chapters are quite long, such as Chapter 14 on advertising, the reader can constantly refer back to material by using the appendix or index. The material in some of these longer chapters will appeal to the executive who must *carry out* the steps or the manager who must see if the tasks are being done *correctly*.

Part 5 has two chapters. The first chapter deals with the whole concept of change, which is so common in marketing. Advice is given on how to plan marketing strategies under various economic conditions. The end of the chapter examines forecasting techniques and improving forecasting approaches. The last chapter of the book is the shortest one. It merely tries to inspire all of us—including myself—to apply the numerous principles, strategies, and recommendations that are discussed in the book. Hopefully, the very last chapter serves as a small motiva-

tional tool to constantly refer to this reference book. It also gives a feeling of closure and summary to the book.

A thorough, extensive index is available at the back of the book. It is organized to steer the reader quickly to the subjects covered in the book.

All titles mentioned in the text are fully referenced at the end of the book.

The *table of contents* provides a quick scan of the major topics and how the book is organized. The chapters are mutually exclusive and don't necessarily build on each other, so they can be read in any order. The book is organized, however, to be read from beginning to end. The reader can thus use it in either way.

J. DONALD WEINRAUCH

Cookeville, Tennessee
October 1986

CONTENTS

PART ONE: Background for Making Marketing Decisions

1. Creating a Positive Marketing Climate — 3
2. Finding the Best Marketers — 13
3. Knowing and Analyzing the Competition — 17
4. The Ten Most Colossal Marketing Mistakes — 25

PART TWO: Planning and Productivity

5. Developing a Strategic Marketing Plan and an Annual Marketing Plan — 31
6. Enhancing the Bottom Line — 41

PART THREE: The Marketplace and Marketing Intelligence

7. Taking a Microscopic View of the Market: Rules of Market Segmentation — 51
8. Formulating a Good Marketing Intelligence System — 61
9. Test Marketing: A Mandatory Folklore — 79

PART FOUR: A Sound Marketing Mix Program

10. Winning the Risky but Rewarding Innovation Game — 85

xv

11. Improving Product-Related Decisions in the Organization: Tennis Balls or Eggs? **101**

12. Enhancing Customer Service: Post Product Sales Are Not an Epitaph but a Beginning **131**

13. Developing Sound Pricing Strategies: Dollars and Sense **145**

14. Getting Big Results from Advertising Strategy **165**

15. Developing and Managing a Sound Sales Force **199**

16. Encouraging Better Results Through Sales Promotion Techniques **229**

17. Avoiding the Common, Nasty Trade Show Blues: Boondoggles, Bathing Beauties, and Managerial Blunders **241**

18. Exploring and Improving Opportunities for Direct Marketing **255**

19. Developing Guidelines for Successful Distribution **273**

PART FIVE: A Changing Environment and Being Prepared

20. Succeeding in a State of Flux: Etc., Etc. **291**

21. Epilogue: Lessons to Be Learned **309**

Selected Bibliography **311**

Index **313**

PART ONE
BACKGROUND FOR MAKING MARKETING DECISIONS

1
Creating a Positive Marketing Climate

Every business organization, whether for-profit, nonprofit, or a government agency, has a culture. Terrance Deal and Allen Kennedy, in *Corporate Culture*,* described this culture as an environment that prescribes procedures for carrying out the business of doing business.

The strengths and weaknesses of a firm's culture are largely dictated by the pervasive role of marketing. To be effective, marketing must be a two-way function: It communicates to management the needs and reactions of customers and society, and it promotes to current and prospective purchasers the goods and services of the organization. To paraphrase Peter Drucker in *The Practice of Management*, marketing is the unique function of a business. An organization in which marketing is absent or incidental is operating on the "dark side." It is not being run as a true business.

Some companies have been accused of lacking a marketing perspective. For instance, according to some critics Chrysler and Texas Instruments were once very weak marketers. Marketing people had little say in the planning and operations of either company; engineers were believed to dominate both. In short, the firms were out of touch with their customers. Following are the basic principles to maintain informed and relevant customer contact.

---

*Titles referred to in this text are fully referenced at the end of the book.

▶ Marketers Must Have Systematic and Formalized Input when Vital Strategic Plans, Policies, and Operations Are Developed

This rule does not necessarily mean that the president or CEO must have marketing experience or be biased toward the field, but top marketing executives should report to a top corporate-level executive. Marketing should not be subservient to such areas as production, finance, and personnel. When Chrysler was reorganized, an executive position aimed at long-term market planning was created. Marketing is now an integral corporate function at Chrysler.

▶ Top Executives Must Take an Active Interest in, and Even at Times Become a Part of, the Marketing Process

When successful organizations are analyzed, one characteristic stands out. Top management appreciates the opportunities, challenges, and potential contributions of marketing. When professional service firms are having a difficult time marketing their services, the major causes are often that (1) their personnel do not fully understand the role and scope of marketing and (2) the marketing responsibilities are given to a junior executive who has little status or formal authority. To motivate managers to push marketing ideas, a distinguished and respected executive in the firm should formally assume the marketing tasks. Managers at the lower levels will then see that top management is serious about marketing.

▶ Marketing Must Be Marketed Within the Organization

Ironically, some outstanding marketing people who do an excellent job of marketing their firm's multitude of products or services externally fail miserably when trying to apply the same concepts and tools internally. They are often in conflict with accountants, production managers, engineers, and others. Perhaps these marketers lose credibility because they fail to identify the needs, concerns, and objectives of their company peers. They neglect marketing research or fail to make use of an effective management information system (MIS). Marketing personnel are thus handicapped in communicating and promoting the wishes of the marketplace to other company managers.

▶ Marketers Must Skillfully Balance Consumer Demands with Organization Objectives

Marketing people are sometimes so busy advocating customer satisfaction at all costs that they forget about organization objectives. In the short run there can be conflict between satisfying consumer expectations and fulfilling profit goals. High market share and sales volume objectives, despite the costs, may indeed hurt bottom-line profits. Marketers must be careful to balance the environmental challenges of competition, government, channel members, customers, and even their own peers within the organization.

Decentralized decision making is sometimes mandatory, but marketing executives still must make decisions within the guidelines, policies/procedures, and strategic plans set by top management.

▶ Managers Must Move Beyond the Promotional Bias

Some executives with marketing problems automatically think that the solution is to increase advertising or personal selling efforts. This "quick fix" tactic is perceived as a means to a strong marketing program, especially in industrial manufacturers, nonprofit organizations, and professional service firms to whom marketing is new. They ignore the other aspects of marketing that should be addressed first: reorganization, marketing research, planning, and pricing.

▶ The Organization Must Learn How to Listen and How to Anticipate the Marketplace

Safeway Stores, a large supermarket chain, has gone through a major transformation. Through management changes, innovation, store design changes, marketing research, and newer merchandising concepts, Safeway is learning how to monitor the marketplace more effectively. Management is becoming a better listener by finding out what consumers want and then developing desirable products and services. In this way, Safeway management will be able to improve their predictions of future consumer trends.

▶ The Organization Must Be Able to Respond Quickly in the Marketplace

Rapid market changes and surprises are realities to all companies, even when they have a good track record of predictions. No matter how successful their schemes have been in the past, corporations must still encourage feedback from their marketing people and be ready to act fast in the tumultuous marketplace. For instance, Campbell Soup recently reorganized its four divisions into 50 major groups. Each group manager has responsibilities for marketing, manufacturing, and profit/loss for his or her own unit. This structure enables group managers to act expeditiously in the marketplace.

▶ Top Management Should Expect Marketing Personnel to Be Leaders in Innovation and New Ideas

Executives should have many opportunities to interact with internal and external marketing groups to enhance the innovation process.

Since it is difficult to pinpoint consumer trends and to quantify successful marketing decisions, a credibility problem often surfaces with chief executives. For example, how can one measure the productivity of a marketing researcher who may have astutely noticed something in focus interviews that results in a highly profitable product 5 to 10 years later?

Theodore Levitt, in an excellent and well-known article entitled "Marketing Myopia," noted that top management can be responsible for the decay and decline of a company. Shortsighted managers become myopically loyal to obsolete products or manufacturing processes. The focus of their business is the product instead of the benefits to and the needs and satisfactions of the consumer. Eventually consumers find substitutes that provide greater satisfaction, sometimes even at a lower price.

▶ Marketing Must Be Part of the Strategic Planning Process

Marketing people are sometimes overlooked in the strategic planning process. And organizational problems may take precedence over consumer problems. Acquisition of a certain company, for example, may

look financially appealing, but the acquired company can become an albatross if marketing realities are ignored. New competition, changing channels, product/technology obsolescence, poor synergism with product lines, or diminishing market potential are possible problems.

▶ Marketers Must Be Given Authority to Make Decisions and Act Like Entrepreneurs

In *The Decentralized Company,* Robert Levinson, former owner of Steelcraft Manufacturing, noted that corporate managers have become mechanical robots. To overcome this stagnation, marketing people need freedom to adjust to rapid changes in the market. They need a creative climate that provides ample opportunities to take the initiative and make decisions that reflect the wishes of local markets and special market segments. Most marketers are not afraid to be held accountable if they are wrong. Taking good calculated risks is exciting, and having real authority inspires their ingenuity at playing the game.

▶ The Organization Should Strive to Be a Marketing Leader in Its Industry

Management should constantly "think" and "talk" marketing. IBM, Taylor Wine, Levi Strauss, Southwestern Airlines, Philip Morris, and Coca-Cola—all have outmarketed their competition. They all applied basic marketing ideas, such as market segmentation, brand management, product planning, and product positioning, to industries that were slow to appreciate creative marketing strategy and tactics. Philip Morris, for example, used its packaged-goods techniques and "tobacco marketing approach" to develop and sell Miller Lite Beer. In doing so, it revolutionized the marketing approach to the brewery industry.

▶ Long-Term Strategic Objectives and Considerations Must Be Carefully Evaluated and Appreciated

A good company does not allow short-run concerns to outweigh its long-term plan. Poor quarterly reports or unexpected downturns in sales should not adversely affect a sound strategic plan. A firm with a solid

marketing function learns how to balance short-term performance standards with long-term expectations. Sound contingency planning, which assumes different strategies for various scenarios, enables marketers to chart a steady course in the changing and rough seas of the marketplace. An equitable reward system, strategic objectives and priorities, corporate planning teams for different business units, and a stable environment give managers confidence that the firm is committed to them over the long haul. A clear sense of direction and purpose breeds loyalty.

▶ Marketing Research and a Management Information System Used by Marketers Must Be Vital Functions to the Firm

For its firm to be classified as a good marketing organization, management should do extensive research on the behavior of consumers, channel members, competitors, suppliers, and other "publics" that interact with the firm. Opportunities and challenges should then be noted via an effective MIS. A sound marketing intelligence system results in better planning and new products/services that satisfy unmet needs while giving outstanding profits. The marketing research function should not be viewed as a one-shot project: It is performed on a timely and continuous basis to anticipate and prevent potential problems. An ailing organization is often one that has ignored marketing research—or used it only to overcome such catastrophes as declining sales, lower profits, or loss of market share. In such a firm the MIS is devoted almost entirely to bookkeeping, accounting, and/or financial concerns. Hence it does not serve the entire organization.

▶ Management Must Search for the Organization's Niche

When developing marketing strategies, marketers should identify and develop the company's strengths in the marketplace. Management must search for differentiation that will offer the firm valuable competitive advantages. A "me too" approach does not give consumers a reason to patronize a business. Good marketers try to enhance their position by seeking such competitive advantages as favorable reputation; product quality; lower prices; exceptional customer service, or unique location, technology, promotion, or packaging. By "listening" to consumers and observing the competition, marketers can identify voids in the market that the company can fill.

▶ Top Management Must Appreciate the Wonderful World of Marketing Synergism

In looking at new corporate business opportunities, managers must identify their current marketing strengths, technology, and distribution structure. Good opportunities for natural expansion can come about through horizontal or vertical integration. For instance, many consumer food packaging companies, such as General Foods, Procter and Gamble, and General Mills, develop new businesses or acquire firms that fit in nicely with their current business goals or services. Not only do the new businesses complement existing business units, but the synergistic impact enables the firm to achieve further economies of scale (e.g., delivery routes, trucks, and a sales force may be already established) and substantially increases revenues at little additional cost. New business units—including those gained by acquisition or merger—may enhance the overall prestige of the firm. By carefully developing the synergistic effect, top management can cultivate a balanced and effective symbiosis of the many parts of the corporation.

▶ The Organizational Structure and Ideas of the Company Must Coincide with Market Realities

A corollary to synergism is the idea of adjusting to the traditions and realistic norms of the market. When Smith Kline began selling its services in laboratory medical testing, it simply expanded its sales approach for pharmaceuticals. However, even though its representatives were already calling on doctors, Smith Kline found that the selling of lab work was quite different from the selling of pills. Different ideas, organization structure, and commitment were needed. Smith Kline had to modify its selling strategy. It was now trying to take lab business away from other suppliers, some of whom had strong local ties that even helped doctors with patient referrals. Smith Kline was asking these doctors to switch their loyalty to a distant and impersonal lab testing chain.

▶ Marketers Must Be Held Accountable Through Progressive and Objective Performance Standards

Much has been written about improving productivity in the factory. However, the cost of marketing a product or service is often greater than the cost of production. Thus it is vital for top managers to observe the

level of marketing efficiency. Specific marketing people, such as product managers and sales personnel, must be answerable for the generation of direct costs versus revenue. A good marketing organization must be able to plan and implement budgeting and control procedures. In functions such as advertising, marketing research, and planning, whose bottom-line contributions are hard to measure, a solid marketing company tries to develop criteria for evaluating performance.

To implement various control procedures, companies like General Foods, R. J. Reynolds, Johnson & Johnson, and Du Pont have even created the career slot of marketing controller: a manager who appreciates the role and contributions of marketing personnel while controlling wasteful marketing expenditures and overseeing productivity. Rewarding effective marketers gives incentive to others.

▶ Top Executives Should Demand Periodic Evaluations of the Entire Marketing Operation of Their Firm

Marketing is a dynamic field. Successful products, businesses, practices, and strategies can quickly become obsolete. Therefore, management should regularly schedule systematic marketing audits that examine the entire marketing program. These audits help identify the firm's strengths and weaknesses, the changing environment, and future marketing opportunites. The audit should be perceived as both diagnostic and prescriptive.

Audits need not be done on a yearly basis if management annually reviews the performance of subunits, such as advertising and product development functions. However, a complete marketing audit may be necessary every 3, 5, or 10 years. Environmental circumstances should dictate the time frame.

▶ A Sound Marketing Organization Distinguishes Between Bad Symptoms (Omens) and Real Problems in Its Marketing Operations

A weak marketing firm wrongly treats symptoms instead of the disease itself. For instance, an organization may assume that creating new products will automatically overcome declining sales and loss of market share.

Column 1 in Figure 1.1 highlights the conditions that often drive management to discover the importance of marketing. Ideally, ailing companies should discover and use marketing before these adverse conditions surface. The figure also summarizes characteristics that exemplify marketing excellence.

Figure 1.1. The development of excellence in marketing

Factors that Precipitate Discovery of Marketing

- Loss of market share
- Sales decline
- Slow growth
- Increase in marketing costs
- Decrease in profits
- Changing trends
- Turbulent markets
- New/Increasing competition
- Massive product recalls
- Government regulation or deregulation
- Economic uncertainty

→ New active participation →

Top Management Marketing Functions

- Planning
- Organizing
- Staffing
- Coordinating
- Evaluating

→ Positive outcome →

Having Marketing Muscle Means:

- Being able to make quick decisions
- Having a bias for action
- Listening to consumers
- Identifying purpose of the business
- Being entrepreneurial in marketing
- Rewarding risk takers
- Interfacing marketers with top management
- Adapting quickly
- Understanding and respecting competition
- Balancing long-term and short-term goals
- Avoiding excessive layers of marketers
- Having marketers who work well with other departments
- Performing marketing audits
- Basing strategy on market segmentation
- Using marketing research/MIS
- Monitoring environmental trends
- Having self-confident, creative marketers responsive to the competitive environment

2

Finding the Best Marketers

The field of marketing is so broad that generalizing on the best ways to find and reward qualified marketers is difficult. A variety of marketing positions and careers are available in both the business and nonbusiness environment. Marketing attracts people with all types of backgrounds, personalities, and lifestyles. Despite the lack of a general ideal model for staffing the marketing function, a few guidelines are still feasible.

▶ Marketing Personnel Must Accept and Understand the Role and Scope of Marketing

To be effective, an organization must have a spokesperson committed to the philosophical core of marketing—the marketing concept. A business will seriously suffer in the long run if it does not have a leader who teaches management to "listen" to the marketplace.

▶ A Marketer's Attitudes, Communication, Interests, and Professional Development Must Be Eclectic

Marketers have multidimensional responsibilities and must interact with all types of groups within and outside the organization. Marketing is a people-oriented profession.

A good marketer must therefore have the ability to acquire knowledge about and empathy for a variety of corporate functions, customer targets, and environmental sectors. He or she must be flexible, since the marketing field is in a constant state of evolution. Management must avoid hiring a marketer who is narrow in scope, a poor communicator, or too dogmatic.

▶ Proper Planning, Analysis, and Matching of Job Requirements, Job Specifications, and Available Marketing Candidates Are Vital

Every business must try to develop its own profile of a successful marketer. If the industry is new to marketing and there are no track records from which to create a profile, management must borrow ideas and/or hire talent from a related industry.

▶ Marketers Should Know the Marketing Process or the Industry, or Both

Marketers must know how to find out what consumers want and then determine whether the organization can provide it. This capability may require experience and expertise in market analysis, research, product development, price formulation, distribution planning, channel management, and promotion strategies. In some industries, management is willing to pay a premium for people who have been successful in marketing. In others, experience in the industry itself is considered more important than formal marketing education. People with industry experience may offer key contacts among customers, suppliers, channel members, associations, and even competitors.

▶ Excellent Marketers Have a Thirst for Formal Marketing Education and Development

Successful marketers learn continuously. By studying marketing theory and classic marketing mistakes and successes, professionals learn how to be effective. They should know how to keep up in the field and should welcome opportunities for taking management development programs and pursuing self-study.

Through formal and informal marketing education, marketers achieve the continual energy, creativity, and cleansing needed for the marketing function. The following shows a few of the characteristics of a successful marketer. Such a person:

- Is innovative and entrepreneurial in thought and action
- Appreciates the financial dimensions of marketing actions
- Knows how to promote products and services under various conditions
- Is mentally agile, adaptable, and technically competent
- Appreciates the multitude of relevant factors that affect pricing decisions
- Is able to monitor and predict necessary channel changes
- Knows how to plan and implement the strategic and tactical elements of a marketing program
- Can predict future trends, such as sales, costs, and consumer interests, with reasonable accuracy
- Attempts to understand and appreciate consumer behavior
- Looks constantly for ways to improve the marketing intelligence system within the organization

3

Knowing and Analyzing the Competition

Every for-profit and nonprofit organization is vulnerable to the competitive forces of society. Even old and seemingly stable industries and companies have experienced turbulent times. The emerging economic and social environment of the 1980s is quite different from previous, more peaceful eras. No one can predict where an organization or industry will encounter competition. Consequently, progressive executives—especially marketers—must stay abreast of changes that promote competition.

▶ Marketers Must Study and Analyze Competitors' Product Performance and How Consumers Perceive It

Strong companies initiate regular and formal evaluations of their own products in comparison with those of the competition. Marketers and quality-control personnel (e.g., engineers, production managers, lab technicians) should have input into the development and measurement of variables that rank the firm's products.

In addition, marketing people, especially the sales force, customer representatives, marketing researchers, and channel members, should determine how consumers rate product performance. A common mistake is to believe that the company product is much better than that of the competition and that consumers see it in the same way. Even if the product is indeed superior, the consumer may not be aware of this su-

periority. In this case promotional personnel must educate the public by highlighting and differentiating the features that are better.

For example, many consumers strongly believe that the Japanese produce better and stronger cars than the American automotive industry. Whether this is true or not, it means that Detroit marketers must overcome any automotive performance problems and at the same time deal with consumer perception problems.

▶ When Feasible, the Company Should Go Through a Product Teardown of Competitors' Products

Ford Motor Company breaks down competitors' products to identify various components, determine the materials used, observe how the product is produced, and calculate likely costs. Other companies can learn from Ford's five-step sequence:

Step 1: Purchase the product.

Step 2: Tear the product down, including unscrewing or unbolting removable components, undoing rivets, and breaking spot welds.

Step 3: Reverse-engineer the product. Assemble a parts list while analyzing the entire production process.

Step 4: Determine the cost of manufacturing the various parts. Analyze labor requirements and estimate overheads.

Step 5. Establish economies of scale, break-even, and profit projections.

When individual cost elements have been defined, a bottom-up approach can be used to estimate the feasibility of matching or improving on competitors' products.

▶ Marketers Should Regularly and Systematically Utilize Numerous Sources for Competitive Evaluations

Marketing people should gather pertinent information to monitor current competition and anticipate new competition. Sources of data might be:

- Trade shows
- Trade associations
- Government publications
- Suppliers
- Trade magazines
- Local government officials
- Channel members, retailers, wholesalers
- Related business contacts, advertising agencies, bankers, lawyers, accountants, consultants
- Professional service and social clubs or organizations
- Previous employees of competitors
- The organization's own employees, such as purchasing managers, engineers, field personnel
- Syndicated commercial auditing reports, such as those by A. C. Nielsen, Market Research Corporation of America, National Purchasing Diary Panel

If use of any of these sources appears to invite unethical behavior, the source should be avoided. Some sources will offer general suggestions about future competition. For example, at one time if a firm hired the Boston Consulting Group it was almost certain that that firm would adopt specific approaches, portfolio management, and certain actions for a strategic management plan. This allowed competitors to anticipate decisions that might impact their own plans.

Other sources of competitive information include:

- Customer warranty information
- Patent/copyright filings
- Product announcements
- Annual reports (10 Ks)
- Government papers from grants on specific industry trends
- Brokerage analyses of specific industries
- Advertising campaigns
- Technical product specifications, manuals, brochures, training literature

By developing competitive profiles and analyses from various data sources over time, the effective marketer will discover which sources have the highest reliability and validity.

Figure 3.1. Competitive profile: Identifying strengths and weaknesses in marketing

Key Marketing Variables	Major Competing Companies[a]					Evaluator	Additional Comments
	A	B	C	D	E		
Market share							
Sales force							
Distribution							
Technological strengths							
Profitability							
Financial status							
Consumer loyalty							
Product quality							
Advertising							
Trade allowances							
Key managerial personnel							
Pricing policies/procedures							
Services/warranties							
Future market strength							

[a] Each company could be rated excellent, good, fair, poor, or very poor for each variable.

▶ A Formalized Framework and Checklist Should Be Used to Enhance Analysis of the Competition

Marketing people must be sensitive to common marketing-related variables that can influence the company's competitive strengths and weaknesses. Figure 3.1 lists the critical marketing factors that must be weighed when intercompetitive comparisons are made for specific products within certain market segments. It also provides a format for doing so. Additional factors may be important depending on specific circumstances.

▶ Representatives from Every Department Should Be Involved in Pinpointing Key Competitive Strengths, Weaknesses, and Resources

Widespread participation contributes to a comprehensive analysis and united front when marketing strategy is formulated to meet the competition. A person in manufacturing, for instance, might be able to pinpoint major product weaknesses in the competition on which salespeople can capitalize when meeting prospective customers.

▶ Marketers Must Be Trained to Listen for Complaints about or Subtle Vulnerabilities in the Competition

Field personnel must be encouraged to observe and communicate back to the home office the following competitor problems:

- Consumer complaints about products, services, pricing, delivery, and so on
- Reseller concerns and dissatisfactions
- Government investigations about the conduct of business
- High turnover of personnel
- Labor strikes
- Product shortages
- Class-action lawsuits by licensees or franchisees
- Supplier-related problems
- Financial shortcomings
- Obsolete technology causing inferior quality control
- Poor productivity results
- Increasing shareholder complaints

Company marketers who are familiar with these problems can develop a sound marketing program of their own.

▶ Marketing Managers Should Help Develop Ethical and Legal Barriers that Impede New Competition

Without violating government antitrust or anticompetition statutes, marketers can legally and ethically discourage competition from becoming industry entrants. For example, to develop a competitive advantage marketing people can seek strong patents, copyrights, and trademarks, or develop solid brand loyalty among consumers.

▶ Marketing Personnel Should Clearly Decide Where the Company and Products Will Be Positioned Within the Competitive Environment

A good example of this positioning challenge is in the soft drink industry. Both Dr. Pepper and Philip Morris (7-Up) had to decide how to com-

pete with the two cola giants, Coca-Cola and Pepsi-Cola. They used various positioning tactics to emphasize how their products differed from colas (e.g., lemon-lime flavor, no caffeine, the "uncola" image). Additionally, to minimize direct confrontation and huge start-up costs in distribution, both beverage companies piggybacked on the Coke and Pepsi bottlers, who felt they needed a full line of beverages to sell to consumers.

▶ Management Must Answer Certain Key Questions Periodically to Stay Competitive

No organization is an island unto itself. It must have a keen awareness of current and future competitive changes. A handy checklist of questions can serve as a basic reference scheme for managers.

> Who are our stiffest competitors? Are they becoming stronger? Weaker?
>
> Do we recognize the limits of our own competitive position?
>
> In what markets or product categories are we gaining market share? Losing market share?
>
> How can we exploit our competitors' vulnerabilites? Which specific firms provide us with additional selling opportunities? What will be the costs and resulting profits if we take share away from them?
>
> How can we overcome our own competitive weaknesses? Are any firms exploiting our weaknesses?
>
> What competitive defensive and offensive strategies provide the greatest opportunities? Do the targeted consumers know about our competitive strengths?
>
> Are new competitive entrants, including foreign ones, on the horizon?
>
> Are many competitors leaving the industry?
>
> How attractive is the industry outlook?
>
> Does our remaining in a certain industry or product category coincide with our strategic plan?

In conclusion, marketing executives need to become fully cognizant of the competition. Many new and challenging forces, such as government deregulation, industry crossovers, foreign competition, acquisitions/mergers, and high technology advancements, have blurred

competitive demarcations. It is no longer a simple task to determine where competition lies. A prime example is the consumer financial services market—competition exists among banks, stockbrokers, savings and loan companies, insurance firms, retail chains, and so on. A formal approach to analyzing the competition is a major obligation for marketers.

4

The Ten Most Colossal Marketing Mistakes

No marketer or company is ever immune from making blunders. Well-known companies have gone bankrupt, while others, in spite of grievous errors, have become turnaround success stories. All executives appreciate the challenge of making successful business decisions and the risk of making wrong ones.

Three outstanding books give examples and histories of marketing gaffes. They are: *Big Business Blunders,* by David A. Ricks; *Marketing Mistakes,* by Robert F. Hartley; and *Case Histories of Marketing Misfires,* by Thomas I. Berg. These books provide interesting anecdotes and allow in-depth study of this topic.

By studying marketing history, marketers can learn common errors to anticipate and avoid. Of course people learn the most from their *own* experience. But eventually companies run out of money to pay for managerial mistakes. Thus it is useful for managers to know hypothetically the most common errors made in marketing. The following list is based on my experiences as a marketer, active consultant, researcher, professor, and student of marketing. The entrants represent what I consider the ten *major* marketing mistakes.

▶ Failure to Understand and Appreciate Trends in the Marketplace

Consumer lifestyles and the accompanying competitive forces change frequently and quickly. Marketing inertia results in obsolete marketing programs.

▶ Lack of a Continuous and Efficient Marketing Intelligence System

Both commercial and nonprofit firms need to gather pertinent primary and secondary information. A company cannot afford to ignore feedback from key sources. The excuse of being too small, too inexperienced, or not wealthy enough to accomplish this does not suffice. The cost of information gathering need not be large.

▶ Failure to Understand Buyer Behavior Differences Among Market Segments

Marketing personnel should know the various factors that cause consumers, including industrial buyers, to behave in a certain manner when buying and consuming goods or services. Consumer behavior is a complex phenomenon. Only by attempting to understand it can marketers develop an effective marketing program.

▶ Indifference to Sound Budgeting Techniques

Marketing managers often do not plan or control the budgeting process; instead they spend on a day-to-day basis. Hence specific marketing objectives are not matched with cash outflow. This problem is common with advertising expenditures.

▶ Poor Integration Between Strategic Marketing Planning and Short-term Marketing Plans

Quite often executives are unable or are not encouraged to see the impact of their day-to-day decisions on the long-run vitality of the organization. Although an evaluation and reward system is difficult to design and implement, it encourages marketers to think strategically. Marketers must move beyond the mere question of how to sell the product. A company cannot afford to sacrifice long-run opportunities for short-run gains.

▶ Lack of Coordination of Product Offerings with Market Targets and the Organization's Own Capabilities

A number of product considerations must be recognized by management. For instance, products can quickly become obsolete, and therefore a line-up of new products in the organizational pipeline is a necessity. Marginal products are a cash drain and may waste excessive time and corporate resources.

▶ Indifference to Market Realities and Company Objectives with Regard to Pricing

If top management ignores the challenges and complexities of setting pricing policies, procedures, and individual prices, the company becomes

- Too cost oriented
- Too stagnant to capitalize on a changing environment
- Indifferent about competitive prices
- Lazy about regularly reviewing and analyzing prices (the responsibility of chief marketing executives)

▶ Indifference to the Interface Between Physical Distribution of Products or Services and Channel Management

When a company can't get the right goods to the right place at the right time, it may alienate interested parties, customers, or channel members. Today's marketers must recognize that their profits and survival depend on cooperation with the middlemen or suppliers who are partners in moving their goods or services through the channels of distribution.

▶ Failure to Plan, Coordinate, and Evaluate a Total Organizational Communication Program

To do a good job of promoting a product or service, marketers must appreciate the sales devices that work. Balance is needed among the

advertising, personal selling, sales promotion, and public relations functions. All must be cohesive and persuasive to get different market targets to buy the product.

▶ Neglect in Answering a Vital Question: What Makes an Effective Marketing Person in Our Industry?

Many managers are unable to identify the key traits needed to market their firm's products and services successfully. They don't know how to match the person with the job requirements and challenges. An experienced and successful marketer is aware of the common marketing blunders and knows exactly what an organization must do to develop a good marketing program. However, if top management has not defined its own preferences for the marketing department, bitterness, misunderstandings, and lack of commitment may become prevalent. This last mistake could be the most significant of all.

Do's and Don'ts for Managing Mistakes

Do's	Don'ts
Recognize the limitations of marketing—it cannot create demand or perform overnight miracles.	Allow "managment by crisis" in trying to overcome blunders; it can breed additional mistakes.
Keep a sense of humor—by staying loose, marketers can retain their objectivity and seek solutions to their misfortunes.	Forget that one mistake can result in a vicious circle culminating in more mistakes.
Analyze why mistakes were made to avoid making the same ones again.	Forget that a failure can be relative—it is not always absolute.
Remember that bad news travels fast, while daily decisions and successes may be forgotten.	Threaten marketers or create a hostile environment if an error is made.
Communicate and listen across channels of communication—openness and honesty often result in a forgiving climate.	
Recognize that a competitor may want top management in other firms to think its own marketers erred, thus opening up an opportunity for the competitor.	

PART TWO
PLANNING AND PRODUCTIVITY

5
Developing a Strategic Marketing Plan and an Annual Marketing Plan

Haphazard policies, inconsistent actions, and uncontrolled expenditures can cause havoc within the marketing function. For a successful program, a formal planning process is mandatory. The preparation of a strategic marketing plan and an annual marketing plan is one of the most important and challenging responsibilities of marketers. These plans serve as vital guidelines to charting a course of action, and they give the personnel reinforcement as to what is expected of them. The basic differences between a strategic marketing plan and an annual marketing plan are shown in Figure 5.1. In short, the strategic plan has a long-range focus, while the annual plan gives short-term direction integrating market targets with appropriate marketing strategy and the accompanying budgets and tactics.

Figure 5.1. Comparison of strategic and annual marketing plans

Strategic	Annual
Time frame: Covers more than one year	Covers one year or less
Management's emphasis: Top management	Middle management
Approach: Long-term objectives/strategy	Short-term operational strategy/tactics
Financial emphasis: General allocation of monies by major strategic business units	Specific estimate of marketing revenue and expenditures for operational units

▶ Coordination and Communication Are Needed Between Top and Middle Managers to Mesh the Long-Range and Short-Range Plans

To achieve a marriage of the strategic marketing plan and the annual marketing plan, managers need input ("bottom-up" approach) and feedback from lower-level personnel, including the marketers. Not only will all of the lower-level managers then be more committed, but they will better understand the role and scope of the annual short-term marketing plans. Although they may have some disagreements with and questions about top management's strategic plan, marketers will know that at least some of their ideas have either been considered or incorporated into the long-term mission of the firm.

▶ A Strategic Plan Should Include Major Components Pertinent to Both the Environment and the Resources of the Firm

Any good strategic plan should consist of these minimum basics:

1. *Corporate Mission.* What business are we in? What businesses should we be in?
2. *Competitive Threats and Opportunities.* What are the current and future long-term strengths and weaknesses of the competition? Who might be our future competition? What can be done to improve our future competitive position?
3. *Environmental Conditions.* How will changing economic, political, technological, cultural, and social conditions affect the business? Will the future climate be positive or negative for our business?
4. *Company Resources and Cultural Climate.* What are the strengths and weaknesses of the organization? Does the company have the resources and commitment to meet future challenges and opportunities?
5. *Long-Term Company Objectives and Strategies.* After recognizing our resources and limitations, how can we match our strengths with future business opportunities? What should be our long-term objectives? What type of strategies would be most effective?

These are the five basic decision areas that must be considered and analyzed. For example, strategic planning decisions may include such

major and publicized by-products as acquisitions, mergers, divestments, overseas expansion, and vertical or horizontal integration.

▶ The Usefulness of the Strategic Plan Is a Function of the Information Provided by Marketing

Strategic planning is a demanding task that requires pertinent information to maximize opportunities and minimize risks. Marketers are in an excellent position to keep top managers abreast of competition, emerging industries, and new technology.

▶ The Limitations of Strategic Planning Must Be Understood

A strategic plan is not a guarantee of future success. Mistakes can still be made, and tough decisions will be needed to overcome them, especially decisions to write off millions of dollars.

▶ Management Should Be Prepared for Problems During the Planning Process

Planning provides a means to an end. A number of challenges and problems can occur during the planning process. The following are typical:

1. Unavailability of complete and perfect information. Decisions must be made on the best information obtainable, especially with time and cost constraints.

2. Impossibility of predicting future events. Errors will often be made in forecasting sales, market growth opportunities, expenditures, and so on.

3. Lack of commitment by top or middle level executives. Perceptions of merely going through the motions may make plans useless or superficial.

4. Need to balance time, costs, and personnel priorities. Daily tasks and budgetary expectations must be met while planning is also being done.

5. Need to coordinate creativity with realism. Good planning should not discourage creativity and sound risk taking. Managers should realize that planning does not *prevent* all mistakes, and the plan should not be perceived as threatening. Unrealistic objectives, goals, and expectations are catastrophic to morale. The planning process will become a feared and dreaded undertaking.

6. Conflict between strategic and operational decisions. Marketing people are expected to make decisions for short-term opportunities while still contributing to the long-term strategic plan. Given limited allocated resources, the two may not always coincide, and juggling the demands of both may become a tedious task. Overemphasis on either strategic or operating decisions can adversely influence the organization.

▶ Strategic Planning Offers a Number of Benefits that Should Culminate in Payoffs

As noted, strategic planning is the domain of top managers. It affords them the opportunity to analyze strategic alternatives and then try to capitalize on the most attractive options.

The numerous benefits of good strategic planning are that it:

- Encourages and facilitates exchange of ideas and analysis.
- Defines direction with established priorities.
- Highlights potential trouble spots while emphasizing strengths.
- Attempts to allocate resources objectively and to set timetables.
- Clarifies roles and responsibilities of managers and the divisions within the firm.
- Facilitates an integrated systems approach by dictating total company objectives among the strategic profit-center units.
- Requires executives to think ahead and anticipate potential problems.
- Gives operating managers guidelines for developing their own annual marketing plans.
- Serves as a vehicle for all levels of managers and the various divisions to interact with each other.

Probably the greatest benefit of the strategic planning process is the chance for management to critically and thoroughly examine itself and

the organization. In doing so, it may uncover a number of exciting strategic alternatives. Chief executives learn a great deal about the organization and its environment during this period.

▶ Strategic Plans Require Periodic Review, Update, and Modification

Because of the long time parameters involved in the strategic plan, a number of changes will be needed. Since accurate forecasting of future events is not possible, managers must often make new decisions in light of new developments. Even the best plans will have to be altered to reflect dynamic and ongoing changes in the marketplace.

▶ Management Must Not Forget the Important Step of Implementation

Many companies hire consulting firms to help develop their strategic plan. On paper the plan may seem to possess sound logic and may generate much excitement about the future outlook. Unfortunately, follow-up and implementation may never be achieved. Top managers then become disillusioned with the whole process.

▶ The Annual Marketing Plan Should Be Developed After the Strategic Plan Has Been or Is Nearly Completed

Marketing people can use the strategic plan or the preliminary ideas for this plan handed down by top management to formulate their annual marketing plan. This top-down approach is useful in defining short-term marketing tactics, the required budgets, and the annual goals and quotas. In preparing the annual plan, marketers should ask and answer the following vital questions: (1) Where have we been? (2) Where are we now? (3) Where do we want to go? (4) How do we get there?

▶ A Good Annual Marketing Plan Should Contain Certain Elements

Although the planning process varies among organizations (some taking a highly structured approach, others setting up only general guide-

lines), the final plan should include identification and analysis of the following:

- Brief marketing and sales history
- Short assessment of where the company, division, or product stands in the marketplace
- Specific and measurable marketing objectives and goals, including an ordering of priorities
- Target markets and customer analysis
- Marketing strategy and tactics (courses of action in product/service mix, pricing, promotional activities, physical distribution interface, and channel management)
- Implementation steps (timetable, budgets, quotas, and assignment of various tasks to different marketing people) (In my experience this step is one of the most overlooked aspects of marketing planning, a major oversight that ruins the entire annual planning process)
- A formalized way to evaluate how well the plan has worked at the end of the operating period

▶ Marketing Planning Must Allow for the Probable Actions of Competitors

Marketing personnel must try to project themselves into their competitors' environment. Admittedly, marketers are not clairvoyant. Yet penetrating analyses of current and potential competitive events helps the company to anticipate pressure areas instead of constantly reacting after the fact to acts of competitors. Marketers must have different tactics ready from which to choose. Advance preparation gives a marvelous advantage. In Chapter 3 are concrete and useful ideas on monitoring the competition.

▶ Objective Controls Are Needed to Determine Whether the Company Has Been Successful in Establishing a Marketing Plan

These controls should relate to the marketing objectives that were developed in the plan. The controls would consist of evaluation of such specific results as (1) profit, sales, and/or cost breakdowns by different

marketing units, (2) job tasks actually completed, (3) consumer- and market-related achievements (e.g., a decrease in number of customer complaints, product recalls, or achieved market share), and (4) overall contributions to the organization. The transmission of the control reports should be *timely* and *accurate*.

▶ The Marketing Plans Should Be Put in Writing

The planning process requires analytical thought. An informal and casual approach merely results in glib, weak strategies and guidelines and possibly in confusion, misconceptions, and misdirections. Even small and medium-sized businesses should take the time to develop comprehensive and systematic *written* plans. The writing process forces sharpening and disciplining of creative thoughts.

▶ Planners Should Understand and Utilize Common Techniques and Aids for Creating the Plans

A few popular and/or helpful planning aids and techniques related to marketing are briefly highlighted in the following.

Planning Aids in Marketing

Technique	Brief Description
Portfolio analysis	Examination of composition and value of business units/products and their relationship to current and future profits, risks, and growth opportunities. Originally financial tool whereby management searched for best mix of current and future securities. Three planning portfolio marketing analysis tools are (1) market growth/relative market matrix (also known as product portfolio matrix), (2) industry attractiveness/company strength matrix, and (3) directional policy matrix
Brainstorming sessions	Formalized "think tank" approach that encourages free thinking and

Planning Aids in Marketing (continued)

Technique	Brief Description
	promotion of new ideas or novel concepts. Strategic and operational ideas are evaluated later
Market research and marketing intelligence system	Systematic process of compiling and analyzing pertinent data related to marketing activities (including experimentation, surveying, and test marketing)
Product life cycle	Investigation of products' sales, profits, customers, competitors, market potential, and marketing strategy from beginning to end
Profit impact of marketing strategies (PIMS)	Ongoing study that analyzes various environmental, company, and marketing variables on profitability and return on investment (ROI)
Marketing simulation models	Creation of complex models that resemble real process, system, or marketplace
Forecasting techniques	Use of different quantitative and qualitative methods for predicting future events for both sales and company-related concerns
Business screen	Combination of interplay between financial concerns (e.g., cash flow, ROI, capital budgeting, financial objectives) and strategic marketing opportunities and risks
Checklists and published forms	Use of criteria or questions that need to be performed or considered before and/or during planning process

▶ Excuses Given for not Formulating Strategic and Annual Marketing Plans Are Usually Feeble

Reasons for escaping the complex planning process are easy to find. Common excuses are:

- Plans are too abstract.
- The benefits of planning to decision making and profits are questionable.
- Formulation of plans is very time consuming.
- The cost of planning outweighs the benefits.
- It is too difficult to predict future.
- Today is what counts.
- We lack the data-gathering capabilities.
- Plans create a bureaucratic nightmare.
- We're too small.
- The planning process is confusing.
- Planning is too much work.
- We're doing just fine without plans.

However, a progressive business can not afford the luxury of operating on a day-to-day basis. The business environment is too dynamic and competitive. Why would a company foresake the multitude of advantages incurred from the planning process? Just about anything worthwhile or advantageous to the future demands hard work and dramatic effort. Nothing in life is simple.

Do's and Don'ts for Preparing Strategic and Marketing Plans

Do's	Don'ts
Include all facts, assumptions, and pertinent data, but be concise.	Be afraid to make strategy revisions if the desired financial and marketing results are not met.
Set timetables, budget figures, and specific goals/tasks for planners.	Be overly concerned with petty details and create a nightmare in paper work.
Encourage candid comments and feedback on proposed plans.	Use the plan as a "straitjacket" or "club" for marketers.
Emphasize the learning opportunities during the planning process.	Forget some type of mechanism to evaluate current and future plans.
Consider yearly bottom-line objectives with long-term implications.	
Integrate marketing strategy into the strategic plan.	
Encourage a management information system that incorporates environmental, market, and competitive information.	

Do's and Don'ts for Preparing Strategic and Marketing Plans (*cont.*)

Do's	Don'ts
Allow enough time for brainstorming and thinking about strategic alternatives while plans are being developed and written.	
Clearly define authority and responsibility for creating and carrying out strategic and marketing plans.	
Allow enough time and support to formulate and write the plans.	
Study previous plans and how well the objectives and strategies were met.	

6

Enhancing the Bottom Line

The contributions and costs of marketing can no longer be ignored. Given the pervasive role of marketing in any for-profit or nonprofit organization, financial and economic accountability is essential in (to quote Abraham Lincoln) "knowing where we are and whither we are tending." A continuous effort is needed to measure and evaluate marketing performance. A search for greater marketing productivity is becoming the norm in today's competitive milieu.

▶ Marketing Productivity Is Improved by Having as Few Levels of Management as Possible and Facilitating Direct Communication Among Them

Shrinkage of middle management (personnel earning between $25,000 and $80,000 annually) is occurring throughout the corporate world. Only the leanest and fittest companies will survive the future competitive environment. Such companies as Brunswick, Xerox, Aluminum Company of North America, NCR, and Emerson Electric have either been examining and revamping their organization chart or giving specific guidelines to improve white-collar productivity. Companies sometimes find that reducing the number of middle managers enables marketers to respond more quickly to the market. Marketers can now consult computers for data about the market, price quotations, inventory, and so on.

▶ Marketers Must Understand and Predict the Various Costs of Doing Business

Marketers are directly responsible for two major tasks: generating revenue and controlling costs. Theirs is the only operational function directly accountable for sales. Managers in other departments sometimes complain—at times rightly—that marketing people have an insatiable appetite to spend but do not monitor expenditures. To overcome such criticism and enhance their marketing efficiency, marketers can use various schemes. For example, an analysis of the following may be fruitful:

- Incremental revenues from versus incremental costs for new products, markets, warehouses, and so on
- Contribution margin approach
- Cost/benefit techniques
- Capital budgeting measurements
- New profit center structures

The progressive marketer can not afford to ignore the essential field of financial and accounting management.

▶ Traditional Natural Costs Must Periodically Be Reclassified into Functional Costs

Accountants compile expenditure data on the income statement by the "object of expenditure costs," such as rent, salaries, supplies, taxes, depreciation, and cost of goods sold. The object category is pertinent to external reporting to shareholders, the Securities and Exchange Commission, the Internal Revenue Service, and other interested parties. For marketing decision making, however, gathering and analyzing cost information by functional costs, that is, costs according to the purpose, is sometimes helpful. In this case costs are broken down into single marketing activities—such as marketing research, storage, advertising, and product development—that are mutually exclusive. Functional costs are then allocated to specific marketing units (customers, services/products, territories, type of industries, sales force, and so on). After the cost data are classified (with the help of cost accountants), management can observe if any marketing units are spending too much.

One lumber mill wholesaler made some startling discoveries after he developed a functional cost scheme. He found that some product groups were too costly to carry. They not only were a financial drain but did

not help increase sales for the other product lines. He was thus able to see the necessity of eliminating them. This action helped lower his inventory carrying costs while improving profits. Development of this new cost system allowed the wholesaler to concentrate on fewer product groups while still satisfying customers.

▶ The Analysis of Marketing Cost Data Should Include Segment Contribution-Margin Classifications

In short, analysis should allow managers to highlight and separate costs into variable and fixed categories. A particular marketing segment can then be judged by the contribution it makes to overhead (i.e., fixed costs). Depending on available courses of action, operating capacity, and opportunity costs, management might even decide to keep marginal products, customers, warehouses, and the like. The questionable marketing segments may be covering all of their variable costs and also making a contribution to corporate overhead. Hence keeping them increases total business profits.

Some executives argue that preparing cost data by the contribution-margin approach is expensive and time consuming. Others advocate a full costing approach—allocation of overhead to various segments—on the grounds that this approach forces managers to recognize that all costs are pertinent and makes them more sensitive to keeping costs down.

Despite these arguments, the segment contribution-margin approach is an excellent managerial marketing tool for internal planning and control. The fact that fixed costs are not arbitrarily allocated to various marketing units improves decisions on questions such as adding or dropping products, warehouses, geographic markets, and so on. Use of contribution-margin income statements thus should be encouraged by management for aiding internal marketing decisions.

▶ Even if a Marketing Segment Shows a Weak Contribution Margin, Keeping the Segment May Still Be Prudent

Any of the following circumstances and exceptions may apply:

1. The product (or customer) has had inadequate marketing attention.
2. The product is in its growth stage.

3. The customer shows promising sales potential.
4. The product did not receive enough financial support.
5. The product complements the company's "bread and butter" products.
6. The product is needed by the supplier so that the supplier can offer all products needed by its customers ("one-stop shopping" for customer convenience).

▶ Careful Measurement and Analysis Are Needed of Incremental Revenues Compared with Incremental Costs

"Incremental" is defined simply as the difference in cost or in revenue that occurs when a new course of marketing action is adopted. For example, a company may have the option to add more warehouses, products, sales personnel, advertising, retail outlets, and the like. Management must decide which of these, if any, will bring in enough revenue to compensate for the additional costs. The increase in revenue should exceed the costs of implementing the option.

▶ Marketers Should Understand the Potential Opportunities Provided by the Experience-Cost Curve Effect

In simple terms, unit costs decline as experience and knowledge are gained with cumulative volume. The decrease in costs is the result of economies of scale, labor efficiency acquired by experience, fine tuning of technological advances, and use of capital-labor substitutions. The experience-cost curve concept has had a major impact on marketing strategy in such firms as Texas Instruments, Du Pont, Hewlett-Packard, Black & Decker, and Briggs & Stratton. Sometimes the cost-volume relationship has caused companies to pursue a price-cutting strategy or to expand operations by increasing direct expenses, since the advantages of increased volume are very large.

However, the experience cost-curve effect may not always apply. The following are exceptions:

Caveat: Rapid Product or Process Innovations Can Create a Complete New Experience-Cost Curve

Marketers must not assume that the advantages obtained from previous experience and additional production volume will give them a competitive

advantage forever. For example, new technology and processes in the automotive and telecommunications industries caused dormant competitors to leapfrog past industry leaders.

Caveat: *If Competitors Can Easily Discover Technical Advances by Copying or Buying Them, They May Eventually Enjoy a Cost Advantage over Former Leaders*

Quite often newer companies are not burdened with the huge investments and fixed costs incurred in the development of equipment, a technology, or a product. They might copy or merely purchase the newest equipment or technology. They have more discretionary funds for operations, unlike product founders, who must pay off fixed costs. (If the technology, process, or product can be kept proprietary, that is, patented, the experience-cost curve advantage remains intact.)

Caveat: *The Marketplace May Be Indifferent to the Cost Advantages Realized from the Experience-Cost Curve*

Consumers may not care who has the lowest price or costs structure. They may place a higher premium on other factors, such as personalized service, favorable delivery terms, customized product specifications, or geographic market niche. It would then be foolhardy to encourage a price war or to increase market share at the expense of decreasing profit margins.

▶ Marketers Must Appreciate and Utilize the Total Cost Concept

In many marketing situations a marketer is confronted with trade-offs of interrelated costs. For example, the elimination of a few warehouses may increase transportation or inventory carrying costs. Some companies choose to ship by air, although rates are higher, since the faster travel time saves them expenses in warehousing, insurance, loan interest, and taxes. Thus marketing and distribution, as well as other aspects of the business, must be viewed as a total entity.

▶ Marketers Must Try to Pinpoint Opportunity Costs

Opportunity costs are revenues that are lost in changing a marketing strategy. The marketplace is not static. For example, to save costs managers may decide to ignore a new market or product line or to cut back on the number of middlemen, sales forces, warehouses, or customer service representatives. But this could result in canceled orders, lost sales, poor image, and other, more subtle problems. Through experimenta-

tion, market surveys, historical analysis, and use of other marketing intelligence devices, marketers must try to estimate and predict opportunity costs.

▶ Sunk-in Marketing Costs Are Not Relevant to Decisions about the Future

This rule is one of the hardest to follow. Many executives believe that if they have already spent a great deal of money on a project, such as developing a new product, they cannot afford to drop the project. They thus sometimes merely throw good money after bad.

▶ A Break-even Point Should Be Ascertained to Determine the Wisdom of Developing New Products or Services

At the break-even point, total costs are met. Above the break-even point a profit is made; below it money is lost. By knowing the break-even point, management can determine whether a particular marketing venture is prudent. The most desirable venture would be one with a large sales forecast over the required break-even volume. A number of bankruptcies among entrepreneurs could have been avoided by calculation of general break-even figures.

▶ To Improve Marketing Productivity, Marketers Must Ask Basic Questions

Marketing personnel need to ask themselves certain basic questions to determine whether their activities are effective and how they might be improved. These questions are:

How do our marketing costs compare with those of our competition?
Where are the greatest opportunities to lower costs without hurting profits?
What factors might give our competition major marketing cost advantages or disadvantages?
What are marketing costs-to-sales ratios by various categories? For example, by product lines, salespeople, customers, middlemen?
Which marketing areas have positive or negative trends for controlling costs?

Can anything be done to decrease marketing costs without hurting sales?

Who should be responsible for establishing cost planning, analysis, and control procedures? Product managers? Marketing managers? Marketing controllers?

How can we get field personnel—the sales force, customer service reps, product managers, and middlemen—to give the feedback we need for compiling and analyzing key expenditures?

How much do our standard or predicted marketing costs differ from our realized costs? Are there unusual variables during the period under examination?

What is the relationship between a change in costs within a marketing function/unit and revenue? Do we improve revenues and profits by increasing expenditures?

When and how often should we collect and examine revenue and cost data?

What role can managerial accounting and MIS play in planning and controlling marketing expenditures?

Do's and Don'ts for Improving Marketing Productivity

Do's	Don'ts
Consider subcontracting certain marketing projects. Subcontractors often have the special expertise and capital to do them cheaper.	Assume that previous marketing budgets and cost areas are sacred cows. Too often some marketing costs become institutionalized and managers automatically include them in the budget.
Ensure that someone is held accountable for finding ways to measure and improve marketing productivity.	Be afraid to adopt capital budgeting techniques, such as payback and internal rate of return methods, to strategic marketing areas.
Analyze revenue, budget, and cost trends over a period of time and make an earnest attempt to forecast future revenues and costs.	Forget to make vital budget and costs comparisons with industry norms.
Integrate marketing objectives with budget plans and time deadlines.	
Whenever possible try to quantify the impact that a marketing unit or course of action has on revenue and costs. A continuous and formal process of cost/benefit analysis must be encouraged.	

PART THREE
THE MARKETPLACE AND MARKETING INTELLIGENCE

7

Taking a Microscopic View of the Market: Rules of Market Segmentation

Successful marketers realize that the mass market is heterogeneous. A firm that tries to please everyone makes a grave mistake. The "shotgun approach" is too costly and inefficient; to be successful the company must find its market niche.

▶ One of the Most Important Marketing Universals Is the Need for Market Segmentation

In market segmentation, the total or mass market is divided into small groups of actual or potential consumers who share common characteristics. Breaking down a total complex market into smaller and distinct submarkets allows a company to better serve the needs of the submarkets and to pinpoint business opportunities in each.

There are two broad categories of consumer markets. They are (1) ultimate or household consumers (who buy things for their own or household use) and (2) intermediate/industrial consumers (who purchase offerings for use in their organization, the government is included). Many firms sell the same item to both markets. Since the behavioral traits, practices, and procedures of the two groups are different, a company needs two distinct marketing programs. Further, the company usually needs separate marketing strategies for the various market segments within the two broad consumer classifications.

▶ There Are Different Ways to Break Down Household and Intermediate Markets

The following summarizes characteristics by means of which consumers can be classified and analyzed.

Basis for Market Segmentation

Household Consumer Market	Intermediate Markets
Demographics (e.g., age, sex, income, education, religion, occupation)	Standard industrial classification (by industry categories)
Geographic location	Geographic location
Method (cash versus credit) and timing of purchase	Amount of purchase
	New versus repeat business
Size of market	Type of middlemen
Purchasing influences (e.g., family members)	For-profit or nonprofit organization
	If government: local, state, or federal
Personality	Application of product
Benefits received from product	
Psychographics, which includes demographics, personality, and lifestyle variables	

With these characteristics in mind, marketers can better go through the steps involved in targeting their best markets.

Step 1: Define the total market and industry in question. Which industries and product lines are to be considered? Will the household market be served, the intermediate market, or both? Is it possible to clearly pinpoint distinct industry groups? This may be difficult in certain industries, such as high technology. For example, the distinction between telecommunications and computers is becoming somewhat fuzzy. On the other hand, the total beer market, cigarette market, or health care consumer products (such as toothpaste) are obviously a one mass market for one industry.

Step 2: Divide the total mass market or generic product market into specific groups of customers. This second step requires analysis of the entire buyer behavior process. Target customers in the household market might be examined and selected on the basis of common physiological, psychological, demographic, or lifestyle variables. The inter-

mediate market might be evaluated on the basis of specific problems, needs, and concerns of the particular industries involved. This step requires a good ongoing marketing intelligence system that encompasses insight and feedback from marketing field personnel.

Step 3: Match the company's products with the preferred market targets. A major requirement for success is being in the right markets with the right business. Even the best management cannot overcome a poor product-market fit. The individual strengths of the product must meet the needs and wishes of the predetermined market. Sometimes the costs of attracting a particular consumer group are not commensurate with the payoff.

Step 4: Plan and implement marketing strategy to go after a particular target market. The consumer group that is targeted will influence the strategy. After recognizing and studying market segments, marketers can make better decisions on such things as pricing, product offerings, distribution, and promotion. A firm should have different strategies for each unique market segment. One of the most common marketing mistakes is to apply an approach that is successful in one market to another market. For example, Southwestern Airlines was extremely effective with its no-frills low-price strategy for the consumer passenger. But the same pricing strategy was not effective with the business traveler, who may be more concerned with other variables. Selective pricing strategy was needed for two separate market targets.

Step 5: Monitor and measure the successes and failures of serving various market segments. Marketers must know who they are serving and how successful they are with their various market segments. Whenever feasible, the profitability of serving each group of consumers should be analyzed. Sometimes a market is too costly to serve. On the other hand, management may be surprised to find out that a particular group of consumers is making a significant margin contribution to the entire organization.

Step 6: Aim marketing strategies at special consumer segments of the future. Marketers cannot wait around passively for their strategy to catch anyone who happens to appear. Target marketing is a prerequisite to an effective marketing program.

Step 7: Estimate how well alternative market targets will meet the strategic marketing objectives and goals. A managerial evaluation is

needed to predict the feasibility of achieving objectives among the market target options. Obviously, the market targeting process must be integrated with the strategic plan of top management. The strategic objectives serve as a useful guideline for targeting.

▶ To Qualify as a Market Target, a Group of Consumers Should Meet Important Conditions

For any group regarded as a potential market target, the following questions should be asked:

> Will the group satisfy our *profit objectives?*
> Is it apt to *grow?*
> How *stable* is the market?
> Can we accurately *measure* the size and purchasing power of the target?
> Will we be able to *reach* the target with our promotion?
> Do we *have the resources* to serve the proposed targeted market?
> Are the homogeneous consumers within the possible segment *influential?* Will their purchases cause other groups to buy the products?
> Can we *identify* the consumers so that we can know where and how to appeal to them?
> How strong is our *competition* in this target market? Are there any competitive opportunities for us?

Many market segments will not meet the above requirements. For instance, a certain group may not have promising growth potential, yet it may offer stable and profitable business forces.

▶ A Current Customer Profile Is Helpful in Forecasting Who to Serve in the Future

Good marketers examine who they are attracting and why. Answers to consumer-oriented questions that begin with who, why, how, when, and where help executives reach good conclusions on future consumer groups.

Figure 7.1. Perceptual mapping of services of several motor freight carriers

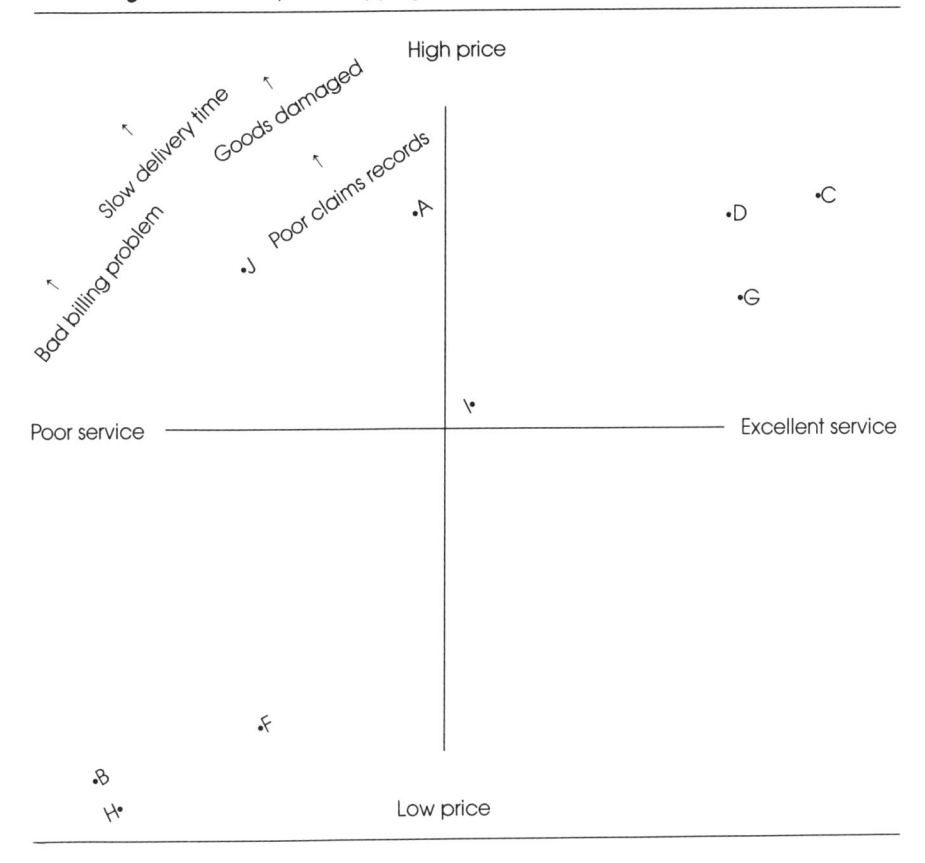

```
                        High price
        ↑       ↑
  Slow delivery time  Goods damaged
    ↑                    ↑
  Bad billing problem  Poor claims records
   ↑         •J         •A          •D    •C
                                     •G

                         •I
Poor service ─────────────┼───────────── Excellent service



                   •F
           •B
           H•           Low price
```

A corollary to development of a current customer profile is to match consumers' perceptions of the product with their perception of either competing products or the hypothetical ideal organization. Based on consumer perceptions, management can then observe where there might be a void and therefore an opportunity in the marketplace. Sophisticated marketers may resort to the perceptual mapping (also known as multidimensional selling) technique. This method gives respondents' perceptions and preferences as points on a map or graph. Figure 7.1 shows hypothetical mapping of consumers' beliefs after several motor freight carriers. Motor carrier J is very inefficient and is probably in trouble in the market. Company I offers no market or product niche. Which company enjoys the best market niche?

▶ The Entire Industry May Encounter Direct Competition from Secondary or Substitute Industries

For example, banks realize that they must now compete with thrifts, brokerage firms, credit unions, insurance firms, mutual firms, retail chains, and the like for deposit and lending services. The point? A decision maker looking at a perceptual map of different bankers cannot forget the other industries that may directly or indirectly affect business with substitute products or services.

▶ Marketers Must Attempt to "Position" the Organization and Products to Their Selected Market Targets

In *Positioning: The Battle For Your Mind*, Al Ries and Jack Trout pointed out that marketing people must create the perception of company and product uniqueness. Through the tools of advertising, personal selling, sales promotion, and public relations, they can communicate a reference point for their market targets.

A product or company's positioning relative to that of the competition is what influences consumers. Marketers must try to get their product ranked first by the relevant target markets. Often there is little actual difference between competing products, yet consumers tend to prefer one over all the others. Hence marketers are interested in encouraging a psychological positioning of their product over that of the competition. For example, even though they may be unable to taste any difference, consumers often seek a certain brand of canned soup, frozen vegetable, beer, or ice cream—solely because of its marketing image.

▶ Repositioning an Existing Product Can Enhance Sales and Extend the Product's Life Cycle

Arm and Hammer repositioned its baking soda for the California swimming pool market. While still promoting the traditional applications of the baking soda, executives repositioned the product as a good remedy for red, stinging eyes that have been exposed to chlorine. The strategy paid off in a surge of sales.

▶ The 20–80 80–20 Rule

This classic marketing principle states that a minority of customers (20 percent) often accounts for the largest percentage of sales (80 percent).

The rest of the customers (80 percent) account for only a small number of sales (20 percent). What is the management implication? Marketing budgets and efforts should reflect the current and future sales/profit contributions of the different market targets. An example of use of this guideline is the implementation of key account or national account service. In other words, major customers get individual attention in the form of a marketing executive and/or national account sales rep assigned to their account.

▶ Every Organization Has a Strategic Mission that Appeals to a Core Market

Organizations must be extremely careful when they decide to penetrate outlying fringe markets. Such an attempt could backfire by confusing or alienating their core market.

Sears, for instance, had a solid core market with "middle America." To expand into new markets, management decided to go into fashion merchandising for the more affluent customer. The strategy bombed, since the higher-income market was unresponsive and Sears' core customers were not satisfied with the higher price-tag inventory. Chrysler also alienated its core market of older, traditional, conservative buyers. Chrysler tried to attract people of a more youthful lifestyle with the Dodge Rebellion theme. The strategy was unsuccessful, and in the meantime many repeat Chrysler buyers decided that the new cars no longer satisfied their self-concept and personality.

Does this mean an organization should not move beyond its core market? No. All managers may have to take risks for the purpose of penetrating new markets. But they should not forget to measure the possible impact of the new strategy on their "bread and butter" markets. If the new strategy poses potential problems, the firm could develop a new brand or even start a *different* organization to serve its new target consumers. The company could then continue to cater to the core segments.

▶ Product & Service Specifications Must Match Market Needs

Sometimes a firm—especially in high technology develops an engineering or R&D breakthrough, and management becomes enamored of the innovation. The market for the product, however, may be a "ghost." There may simply be no need or demand for the ingenious product, and it becomes a failure and a disappointment to management.

Gould faced this problem with a computer printer. The R&D people were excited and optimistic about the printer. But industrial consumers had no desire for the faster printer and its unique product specs that had been developed in the laboratory. In short, product development must be driven by market needs, not by technological advances.

▶ Companies Must Search for the Differentiation that Will Appeal to Their Market Targets

At one time in the New York-Washington market, Eastern Airlines was caught between a cut-rate carrier (People Express) and regular carriers (TWA and Pan Am) that were charging premium prices for luxury service and wider seats. Eastern had no distinct competitive advantage. It was in the middle.

▶ Use of Demographics Is a Good Beginning for Market Targeting in the Consumer Market

Demographic divisions are easy to observe, and many secondary data sources—especially government related, like census data—classify consumers in this way. Thus market segmentation analysis should begin with various demographic traits. Although showing relationships between purchase of a product and the buyer's age, sex, marital status, occupation, and so on may be difficult, collating the buyer's personal characteristics provides a good basis for breaking down the population with more advanced concepts. Combinations of influencing variables, such as personality, attitudes, motivations, desired benefits, usage patterns, geographic location, and frequency of use, can be examined.

▶ A Good Starting Point for Targeting in the Intermediate Market Is the Standard Industrial Classification (SIC) System

This system allows marketers to match products and services to different industrial market groups. Segmenting markets by industries is perhaps the most popular method of trying to categorize prospective intermediate customers.

Effective industrial marketers appreciate the complexities and checks and balances that apply among organizational buyers. The buyers expect marketers to help solve their problems and provide meaning-

ful advice in meeting their organizational objectives. The business-to-business market has other demands of particular significance to sellers:

1. Marketing people may need to be highly technical and scientifically trained.

2. Successful salespeople must be adequately rewarded for the long time needed to develop the groundwork for a sale (it may be many months).

3. Committee selling and marketing should be cultivated; field people often need backup support.

4. Marketing research must help sellers identify all the individuals and groups involved in a purchasing decision within the target organization.

5. All professional personnel within the seller's organization must help instill confidence, loyalty, and mutual trust in a prospective industrial buyer.

6. Catalogs, brochures, product specification sheets, and trade shows should be based on sound marketing concepts. (As a consultant to industrial firms, including the robotics industry, I find that marketing opportunities are widely overlooked. Sellers become so enamored with their technical product that they neglect to explain how it might benefit buyers.)

7. Formal contracts must often be worded specifically, to avoid misunderstandings about the obligations of the seller.

8. Negotiating a price on major industrial transactions is a tough function for field people. They often need advice and moral support from the corporate office. Smooth communication helps to overcome potential disappointments or shocking surprises for field representatives.

9. Industrial marketers need to do a better job of marketing the function of marketing itself within their own organization. Household marketers tend to be somewhat ahead of their industrial counterparts in this respect.

▶ Market Targeting Has Important but Overlooked Subtleties

A successful marketer must sometimes go beyond the obvious considerations when segmenting a population or industry.

1. A number of firms segment their markets by income. Why not also include net worth? A former client who owned a small rural bank decided that income was a poor marketing classification for retirees who were moving into a popular Sunbelt retirement community. If he relied only on their current income, these potential customers (many of them affluent) would be ignored in target marketing.

2. Consumers must have a positive attitude before they will buy an offering, but this is only part of the picture. Many other variables are also relevant and must be considered.

3. Nonprofit organizations must include the many "publics" in their segmentation plan. Frequently, a not-for-profit business has both clients they serve and donors (especially volunteers and financial contributors) who help provide support. I have seen administrators diligently classify clients into various segments while neglecting to do the same with donors. Frequently these administrators have trouble finding enough volunteers or financial supporters. Target marketing procedures and concepts should be applied to all the "publics" of a nonprofit organization. In fund raising, the 80–20 20–80 rule often applies. Hence, fund-raising efforts must focus on key donor groups.

4. Giving buyers too many choices can cause confusion and be costly for the marketing firm. How much segmentation is enough for a firm? There are more than 69,000 possible permutations and combinations of options for the 1984 Ford Thunderbird. Clearly, some industries may go too far in segmenting their markets. Marketers must decide what product differences the consumer will pay for and which ones are too expensive or are not critical to target audiences.

5. Too often marketing research surveys the individuals who do the actual buying while ignoring other parties who help make the decisions. Joint decision making is common in the buying of cars, homes, appliances, and vacation packages. Interplay and exchange between the joint decision makers may themselves create a unifying trait that can be used to direct marketing efforts.

6. In marketing to middlemen or wholesalers, marketers must look beyond the immediate customers and study their customers' customers. The demand for many goods and services really depends on the demand for other products. Sales of lumber, cement, glass, appliances, aluminum, and nails are dependent on the number of new homes built. Hence marketers must appreciate the sales patterns of the final consumer product.

8
Formulating a Good Marketing Intelligence System

The good old days of simplicity have vanished. How to promote our business is now only one small piece of the marketing puzzle. We must now recognize all the other pieces of the puzzle and know the mechanics of putting them all together. The solution to the puzzle lies in a viable marketing intelligence system.

The core of this system is the marketing research function and a usable management information system (MIS). Without these, executives operate with a severe handicap—they try to make decisions with incomplete information. (I have been both a supplier of marketing research and a manager and user who had to make decisions based on marketing research provided by someone else and thus can view the problem from both sides.)

▶ An Analytical Budgeting Process Should Be Used to Ascertain the Costs Versus Benefits of Marketing Research

As a general rule, companies spend less than 1 percent of sales for marketing research. Given the tremendous demand for information to help in decision making, many researchers complain that the budgeted amount is a pittance.

It should be emphasized that good research does cost money. I have

seen managers who balked at paying $20,000 to $100,000 for a marketing or feasibility study but who quite arbitrarily spent millions of dollars on the manufacturing or the "brick and mortar" for a new concept. Every decision maker must often ask: Is marketing research a good buy? How do I know if it is worth the money? What contributions will it make to decision making and "the bottom line"?

The following questions are helpful in measuring the usefulness of marketing research personnel, whether employees of the company or outside research suppliers/consultants.

- Do the researchers challenge management to think? To raise the level of creativity?
- Do they help the firm anticipate problems, or do they merely react to problems?
- How well do they interact with other departments?
- Do they keep up on trends in the marketplace? On the latest marketing research techniques?
- Do they know where to find vital information at reasonable costs?
- How relevant are their marketing research efforts to decision making?
- Are their marketing research reports timely? Are deadlines and budget constraints met?
- Do they follow sound scientific and research methods?
- Do they make recommendations that have an impact on formulating new, effective marketing strategy? Are new ideas abundant for product development, market growth, advertising planning, and the like?
- Are they well acquainted with the best sources of suppliers for marketing research and consulting?
- Do they appreciate the role and scope of marketing research to the marketing program and to the overall mission of the organization?

Top management must help make marketing research a good buy. Chief executives can take an active interest in the function. In fact, many marketing research departments are asked to do broader types of studies whose results influence strategic planning. Furthermore, regular measurement of marketing research performance helps create better visibility and rewards for successful researchers.

▶ Certain Steps Can Be Taken to Get the Most for the Research Dollar*

The following suggestions are aids to keeping research expenditures reasonable while still obtaining full benefits:

1. Try a pilot study first to see if a major study is needed.
2. Study only that which is pertinent to the research objectives, extra "interesting" information is too expensive.
3. Establish research priorities so that decision-making tasks can be ranked.
4. Try pooling investigations with those of other organizations, such as trade associations.
5. Examine cheaper secondary data before gathering primary data.
6. Develop a sound MIS framework to record and keep track of previous research efforts; develop a marketing data bank.
7. Develop the research design with care. Who must be part of the universe? Part of the sample? Why?
8. If the study is a random type and management wants only a general idea as a result, lower the required level-of-confidence percent and consequently the required sample size.
9. Carefully examine questionnaires and tie them in with the research objectives; eliminate superfluous questions.
10. Make sure the questionnaire design is meticulously precoded to save tabulation costs later.
11. Whenever possible, avoid expensive cities where personal interviewing costs can be exorbitant.
12. See if studies with the same data-collection procedures can be consolidated.
13. Be careful in selecting, hiring, and developing the interviewing staff—about a third of the study costs could occur in the interviewing stage.
14. Consider using the telephone or a mailed questionnaire in place of the personal interview approach to data collection.

---

*Many suggestions taken from J. Donald Weinrauch and William Piland, *Applied Marketing Principles* (Englewood Cliffs, N.J.: Prentice-Hall, 1979), p. 108.

15. Follow up on nonrespondents; the small incremental cost is well worth it for the higher rate of cooperation.
16. Use sophisticated and expensive statistical techniques only if they are necessary.
17. Anticipate the results—will the collected data really aid managerial decision making? How will the data impact management's course of action, including status quo?
18. Don't waste time making out voluminous reports.

If management contracts research to outside suppliers, it should not buy on price alone. From my experience there is no correlation between quality received and fees charged, yet management sometimes has the notion that if a project isn't expensive, it must be of little worth. The marketing research function must be a cost center with all applicable sound managerial accounting principles.

▶ Decision Makers Must Work Closely with Marketing Researchers to Create an Effective Marketing Intelligence System

While this rule may seem axiomatic, one of the most significant problems of industry is poor interaction between executives and researchers. Conflict sometimes takes place over:

- Financial support
- Staffing
- Role and scope within the organization
- Assignments and deadlines
- Use of research results
- Reporting process
- Expectations
- Cooperation and communication
- Future agreeable objectives

The partnership must be carefully orchestrated. My feeling is that marketing researchers must take the initiative. They should appreciate the needs of managers and then formulate efforts to fulfill these needs. Research must zero in on pragmatic, decision-oriented results.

▶ Marketing Researchers Need Good Communication and Problem-Solving Salesmanship Skills

Researchers need effective communication skills when dealing with executives. They must know how to encourage managers to seek advice at the beginning of a project. Further, during work on the project and after it is finished, they must be able to communicate easily about the impact of the project. Follow-up analysis by researchers and users helps to overcome or prevent interdepartmental conflicts.

I believe that researchers must actively and creatively sell their work. In trying to maintain an atmosphere of objectivity, some researchers merely present the data and "let the numbers speak for themselves." This passive and detached role may only alienate users. Decision makers want researchers to share their wisdom, interpretations, analyses, and recommendations.

A research project is not an end but a means—research is an ongoing supplement to the decision-making process. An aloof "objective" presentation of results may only backfire. Researchers need not prostitute their results, but they do need to become involved with the decision-making dynamics. Why should managers put their careers on the line with research results when the marketing researchers will not back up their own efforts?

▶ Execution of the Marketing Research Project Is an Important Part

One of my most frustrating experiences was a project I did for a medium-sized electrical distributor. The data showed that top management would have to restructure their marketing department and take a different approach if they wished to penetrate some key industrial markets. The study was well received by top managers and they were very excited about the marketing suggestions. Despite their enthusiasm and my follow-ups, the recommendations of the study were never implemented and the new markets were never tapped. Surprisingly, a year later at a social function, the president admitted that the cause of inaction was inertia. He thought my ideas had merit, but he simply got involved in other things. In this case there was no materialization within the marketing research process.

▶ Marketing Research Is Worthwhile Even if It Reinforces Management Thinking

Executives might complain that the research effort has merely told them what they already knew. Hence the effort seems to have been a waste of valuable time and money. This is not necessarily so. If anything, such a result may make users even more committed to a course of action they had considered but needed the motivation to carry out.

▶ Marketing Research Should Not Be Used as an Explicit or Implicit Device to Threaten Executives

Sometimes a manager will use a marketing investigation to harass certain personnel or departments. At the start of one of my assignments, the client encountered the charge (unknown to me) that the marketing research data were going to be used against the chief administrator. Consequently there was an ugly split within the board and negative opinions of the survey among the administrator's own supporters. They felt that the collected data were a tool to get their man fired. The chairman of the Board of Directors emphasized that the study had been commissioned to detect strategic strengths and weaknesses, not as a political tool. Interestingly, the completed investigation did show that different capabilities and qualifications were essential for the administrative position. But owing to the innuendos from both sides, neither side wanted to examine the potential applications of the study. Discussion centered around personalities. The study was never used, the chairman resigned, and bad feelings spread through the organization.

Top management and marketing researchers thus must create a cooperative, positive climate when a research study is commissioned. This environment will make managers, especially at the mid-level, more supportive of and excited about the research. Fear is sometimes a natural response when marketing research is first being introduced. Assurances must be given—and kept—that the data collection process is to aid decision makers, not replace them.

▶ Management Should Be Extremely Careful about Releasing Marketing Research Data Outside the Organization

Once in a while management may feel that the data collected will help to promote a social/political cause, sell products or services, or raise

monies. Public release of private information should be done with extreme care. Competitors, government agencies, consumer groups, opposing political groups, customers, and other interested parties will thoroughly scrutinize the information. If only parts of a study are released, specialized interest groups may demand to see the entire study.

I am aware of a newspaper chain (selling advertising space against competing media), a political candidate (trying to raise money), and a consumer packaging firm (testifying in congressional hearings) that regret the release of some marketing research data.

▶ Completion Dates for Marketing Research Projects Should Be Coordinated with Decision Deadlines

Effective marketing researchers must plan their work so that it is completed within the time constraints of the decision makers. Managers become frustrated when a study is not ready or when it is received after the decision is made. Executives must be fair and realistic in allowing enough time for the investigation. In some cases unexpected outside forces—such as new competition or economic changes—may require a decision before the set completion date.

▶ Steps in the Marketing Research Study Are Interrelated and Interdependent

One poorly executed step in research can be devastating to the entire study. Management must therefore be aware of the steps and plan a smooth transition between them. The steps are as follows:

Step 1: Work with management on identification of problems and purposes of specific studies.

Step 2: Define the research objectives.

Step 3: Gather internal secondary data.

Step 4: Collect external secondary data.

Step 5: Decide whether primary data will be needed, and if so, how it will be gathered.

Step 6: Collect primary data.

Step 7: Summarize and analyze data.

Step 8: Prepare conclusions and/or recommendations.

Step 9: Present findings to management.

Step 10: Follow up to measure impact.

The researcher must consider each of these steps and decide on the ramifications it will have on a specific decision.

▶ The Problems, Purposes, and Objectives of the Marketing Research Study Must Be Clearly Defined at the Outset

One common mistake in doing market research is to first develop an instrument/questionnaire, gather the data, and then attempt to figure out what part of the collected data is worthwhile. This trial-and-error procedure is time consuming and costly.

A top executive of a previous client of mine stated that doing a survey was really a simple task. All that was needed was to list a few questions on a postcard or sheet of paper and mail it to residents in the community. What was all the fuss about doing a study? Marketing researchers wish it were that easy.

A good researcher should ask probing questions. I am often amazed about how many preliminary meetings with decision makers are needed before a study can begin. These meetings begin with a discussion of certain symptoms or of a particular problem marketing area, either of which may end up being relatively insignificant to the study. After further thought it becomes apparent that other aspects of marketing ought to be analyzed first. A good professional investigator helps management ask the right questions and develop appropriate objectives.

The researcher should not assume that the executives have accurately pinpointed the questions, problems, or issues that must be addressed. If the study turns out to be superfluous and costly, it is the marketing researcher's career that is at risk. This professional is trained and paid to *find the right things to study.* Training should include the interrelationship of continuous marketing research and decision mak-

ing. For the most part, business executives welcome the researcher's expertise and insight on formulating the purpose and objectives of a particular study.

The following questions offer a useful checklist to enhance this important part of the research process:

Are the objectives clearly stated?

Can specific objectives be tied to particular decision areas?

Do we have the necessary facts/assumptions to undertake the study?

What will be the strategic opportunities associated with the objectives?

Are the research objectives consistent with what management hopes to accomplish in terms of marketing and corporate objectives?

Will the purpose/objectives help to predict and anticipate or will they merely describe the market behavior?

Are we concentrating only on immediate problems and "brush fires" rather than long-range and broader issues?

Are the objectives and purpose realistic given the budget and time constraints?

Have we put priorities on what research objectives and problems to study first? (We cannot study everything, due to time and budget constraints.)

Are the research objectives/problems put in the context of information units instead of actual marketing objectives?

Often someone will identify the research objective as an increase in sales, profits, new product development efforts, number of new customers, or the like. These are really marketing objectives. Research objectives should resemble pieces of data. For instance:

- Describe current attitudes among first-time home buyers.
- Trace the progression of "young" new buyers' actions from first thinking about purchasing a home to after-sale behavior.
- Identify influences that contribute to a specific home purchase.
- Measure the degree of influence of interest rates on home buying among new purchasers.
- Predict future marketing challenges in overcoming concerns of new home buyers.

The foregoing are statements that might be incorporated in a formal study. Management sometimes is unsure of research objectives, and in this case an exploratory investigation may be needed to uncover them.

The need for clear objectives may seem self-evident. But isolating problem areas is not always easy. I know of one capital equipment manufacturer who was losing market share. The company changed advertising agencies to correct the "problem." The new agency convinced the company to do marketing research. Eventually it was found that the company had major problems with its distributors and that in fact the previous agency had done a good job of creating product awareness and positive attitudes. With isolation of the real problems the decision makers could then formulate a corrective strategy for dealing with distributors.

▶ Secondary Data Should Be Sought Out and Examined Before Primary Data Are Gathered

Collecting data (already in publishable form) is less expensive and less time consuming than collecting primary data. Sometimes researchers and managers decide to do surveys, experiments, traffic counts, test marketing, and so on before they review secondary data. They spend thousands of dollars in obtaining data that may already be available in-house (e.g., in sales invoices, warranty cards) or from external secondary sources (e.g., the government, trade associations).

Secondary data are often useful in deciding which problems or research objectives to study. The contributions of such data should not be minimized. A wealth of marketing-related data is available that can faciliate decision making. An old questionnaire might even lead to ideas for a new one.

For around $1,000 (less than what might be spent for an all-day staff meeting with marketing field personnel), a library with solid marketing sources might provide access to such publications as:

- *Encyclopedia of Associations*
- *Federal Reserve Bulletin*
- *U.S. Government Manual*
- *Funk and Scott Index*
- *Statistical Abstract of the United States*
- Guides to Special Issues and Indexes of Periodicals (For example, *Business Periodical Index*).

- *Moody's*
- *Sales and Marketing Management's Magazine's* four annual surveys: *Survey of Buying Power, Survey of Buying Power II, Survey of Industrial Purchasing Power,* and *Survey of Selling Costs*
- State directories of manufacturers
- Buyer guide directories
- United States Census Data

▶ Executives Should Expect the Marketing Researcher to Explain Certain Issues Related to Research Design and Primary Data

Management should ask the researcher the following major questions:

Will the research design result in descriptive, diagnostic, or predictive input for decision makers?

Do we need an exploratory, descriptive, or casual study?

Who should be included in the universe we want to study? Why?

Should we gather data through a survey, through observation, or through experimentation?

Is a sample needed? If so, how large a sample? Should we take a random or nonrandom approach? Why?

What is the incremental benefits-versus-costs ratio for increasing the sample size or changing our level of confidence (assuming a random sample)?

How are we minimizing sampling and nonsampling error? Who will actually collect the data and what controls will be used to ensure accuracy? (Surprisingly, the data collection step is often farmed out with few controls. Careless interviewers can ruin the whole study.)

If we do a survey, should we collect the data by mail, personal interviews, phone, or a combination? Why?

How and what should be included in the research instrument? Will we pretest the questionnaire to eliminate any "bugs" in the design and content?

What type of quantitative, qualitative, and analytical analysis will we do with the collected data?

Will the research design and instrument meet the research objectives and the information we need to make sound decisions?

▶ Creative Salesmanship Techniques that Do Not Bias Respondents' Answers Are Needed to Ensure Respondent Participation and Satisfaction

Researchers must remember that they are dependent on respondents' cooperation and willingness to provide information. Respondents have to volunteer their time and perceptions, answer sensitive questions, and/or possibly forego pleasurable activities in order to participate. Since both the general public and professional managers/administrators are being inundated with surveys, the researcher must show why the prospective respondents' involvement is significant to the results of the study. Study participants should not be alienated by being put on the spot, nor should they be expected to be overly enthusiastic.

From my own experiences I have found that prospective respondents who first offer resistance to participating are the ones who eventually become the most cooperative and talkative. But overcoming their objections takes patience and positive selling.

To improve the rate of return in personal interviews, phone surveys, and mailed questionnaires, here are a few helpful tips:

- Have a powerful and dynamic introduction (cover letter in mailed questionnaire) that tells the importance of the respondents' cooperation and how it will benefit them. Create a feeling of interest and excitement.
- Personalize the introduction whenever possible—avoid the "Dear Sir" approach.
- Promise anonymity.
- Keep the questionnaire short and make answering the questions easy.
- Make participating convenient (e.g., offer a self-addressed, stamped envelope).
- If appropriate, provide a monetary incentive for those who cooperate.
- Use persistent follow-ups and reminders for nonrespondents.

I have found the last suggestion to be extremely effective in increasing the rate of return. Many people are forgetful, need urging, or have time pressures. A friendly follow-up or reminder helps respondents who are willing to participate if given the right consistent stimulus.

In conclusion, these tips are relatively inexpensive to incorporate into a marketing research study. Preplanning, then, is essential when creating the study.

Figure 8.1. Advantages, disadvantages, and marketing applications of the focus group interview

Advantages	Disadvantages	Marketing Applications
Helps identify and formulate research objectives for future studies	Expensive; costs per respondents add up quickly	Design of packaging
		Concept testing
		Product development
Allows respondents to express themselves in their own words	Does not lead to quantitative generalizations about total population being studied	Changes for older products
		Planning and development of survey research, such as problem formulation and questionnaire construction
Offers many creative and fresh ideas		
Gives wide range of ideas that can be fine tuned later	Go/no-go decisions are inappropriate with group session results	Generation of ideas and concepts for promotion strategy
		Identification of consumer behavior trends
Provides qualitative input (emotions, perceptions, attitudes) for in-depth consumer behavior issues	If not controlled, informal group member leaders may dominate	Pretesting of research project that is quantitative in nature
	Immediate and measurable contributors to firm not readily seen	Postresearch investigation for clarifying certain results from previous studies
Generates phrases, cues, syntax, and buzz words that could be used in promotional efforts	Validity of results questioned by many	Establishment of research priorities on what must be done in future
May uncover problem areas	Moderator who can blend group dynamics with marketing applications difficult to find	Identification of product positioning opportunities
May result in greater number of concepts than one-on-one interviews		Orientation of in-house marketing personnel or channel members

▶ Researchers Must Grasp the Opportunities, Advantages, Limitations, and Procedures for Conducting Qualitative Marketing Studies in Today's Marketplace

For our discussion, qualitative research is defined as an in-depth, possibly subjective analysis of responses without use of numerical or statistical measurements. In other words, there is no intent to make statistical inferences about the population studied.

The most popular form of qualitative marketing research is the focus group interview. It originated from psychiatrists' work in group therapy, and is nothing more than an unstructured group interview of a small number of people, usually 8 to 12, by a trained moderator/interviewer. The group leader focuses discussion on relevant topics without offering specific directions. Freedom of expression and free-flowing interaction among the group members is encouraged. Figure 8.1 shows

advantages and disadvantages of this popular research approach and identifies ways in which it can be applicable to organizations.

Do's and Don'ts for Using Focus Group Interviews

Do's	Don'ts
Pick a location that offers a relaxed atmosphere.	Make quantitative generalizations (statistical inferences) from focus group interviews; they should not replace quantitative research if such research is needed.
Encourage participation, free flow of ideas, and a high degree of interaction.	
Select group members carefully and make sure they will feel relatively comfortable with each other.	Allow one or two participants to dominate the group discussion.
	Use too small (fewer than 7 or 8) or too large (more than 12 or 13) a group in one session.
Allow enough time in a session so that all members have ample time to speak.	Allow the executives/decision makers (such as brand managers) who might be users or beneficiaries of the results to come in and bias the discussion or group interaction.
Keep an open mind on what might come from the open-ended discussion; avoid preconceived ideas.	
Be cautious in selecting the moderator or group leader; a poor interviewer can ruin the whole purpose of the focus group sessions.	

Minimum prerequisites for the ideal moderator of a focus group interview are

- Prior experience in running focus group sessions
- Understanding of psychology, group interaction, and/or motivational research
- Ability to listen, adjust, and relate to respondents (creation of relaxed atmosphere)
- Knack of gaining respect, confidence, and admiration of people
- Skill to integrate group dynamics with overall marketing purpose of why sessions are being conducted
- Ability to analyze sessions and offer interpretations and conclusions to which management can respond
- Talent for recognizing subtleties and picking up on new group concepts or ideas that could have far-reaching value for marketing opportunities or problems

Often a good discussion leader can uncover information that marketers have not thought of or can pinpoint marketing problems that have gone unnoticed. The moderator should write up observations as soon as possible after a session is over, even if the session was videotaped. There are often little nonverbal behavior cues or other group behavior actions that may be forgotten if observations, interpretations, and conclusions are not quickly recorded.

▶ Marketers Should Make Greater Use of Longitudinal Analysis Through Consumer Panel Groups (Consumer Panels)

As already noted, a sample of a predetermined universe is usually used in a specific survey, experiment, or observation study. After the completion of the project, the sample is not contacted again. Hence the data are pertinent only at a particular time.

Nevertheless, decision makers are interested in trends and changing attitudes or perceptions. At reasonable cost and with proper controls on the scientific method, researchers may choose to develop a group of respondents who can be contacted periodically, for the purpose of spotting trends. A portion of the group (10 to 20 percent) could intermittently be replaced by new participants, to avoid stagnation or the creation of a "professional" (and thus unrepresentative) panel of respondents.

I believe that industry could utilize the panel approach on a wider scale. The panel is an effective marketing research device for recognizing and predicting changes in the marketplace. One small rural bank began a community consumer panel group in its retail banking market. Eventually the bank started to share some of the data with its commercial and small business customers. This gave the managers information about the changing retail market while also creating goodwill among the business market segment.

▶ Decision Makers Should Usually Request a Marketing Research Proposal and Have Specific Criteria for Judging the Merits of the Proposal

A marketing research proposal is a blueprint of how the marketing research investigation will be conducted. A proposal is usually necessary even when the research is to be done by personnel within the organization. Usually, the proposal will pertain to a specific project, although it might include multiple projects and stages to meet the vast infor-

mation needs of decision-making executives. It should contain the following material:

1. Brief background of the topic in question
2. Purpose of the proposed study
3. Research objectives, problems, and/or hypothesis, or, if an exploratory study, the marketing issues and areas that could evolve from the study
4. Research methods including:
   a. Definition of population
   b. The type and size of sample
   c. Method for collecting data, such as a mailed questionnaire or telephone survey
   d. Who will collect the data (I think a buyer/user of research has a right to know if any "subcontracting" will be done)
   e. Quantitative techniques to be used in analysis of the data
5. Data processing and computerized applications
6. Budget and time frame for completion of the project
7. Biographical statements of people who will do the project (if the professionals are outside the firm)
8. Optional: An appendix with any other information that might help the buyer make a go/no-go decision

There is no set length for a marketing proposal. I have written proposals one page long and others that ran to over 50 pages. Sometimes a fee may be negotiated for a lengthy proposal that contains good ideas on attacking major problems and issues.

In fairness to researchers, especially suppliers and consultants, companies should not expect a lengthy exposé on how the study will be performed (including questionnaire). Nor should they expect professional advice to be included within the proposal. Many researchers have been exploited at least once by a buyer who wanted more and more advice in the proposal, subsequent oral conversations, and meetings. The buyer then actually did the study after receiving this "free lunch."

The following are questions to ask when examining proposals:

> How well do the authors understand our industry and the concerns of our own situation? What are their previous experiences and expertise?

Do the researchers encourage interaction and healthy exchange with managers/uses when planning the research project or projects?

Are the research purposes and objectives clear, precise, and useful to decision making? Does the proposal show understanding of the problems and issues?

How sound and logical is the research design?

Will the scientific method be properly used? How detailed is the proposal for specific steps? (Often the proposal will contain schedules, flowcharts, and the like to illustrate the time frame and attention to essential details.)

How creative is the proposal in attacking the issues? Will multiple methods be used to get the job done?

How well do the prospective investigators communicate, both orally and in writing? Is the writing style articulate and concise?

Who will actually conduct the investigation? Will the presenters do the work, or will they hand it over to another team? Are the writers and presenters merely the "sales force" or are they the suppliers of marketing research studies? Will any work be subcontracted to other suppliers?

What type of statistical analysis, computer applications, and software will be used?

Are available facilities spelled out in the proposal?

Is the proposal's time frame for completion realistic? Does the completion date coincide with our time parameters?

What are the proposed costs for the project? What type of safeguards are included if there are expenditure overruns?

Are brief biographical statements included? Do they give insight into
- Formal education
- Writing, analytical, and verbal skills
- Specialized skills and knowledge
- Prior experiences
- Accomplishments and contributions from previous research accomplishments
- Managerial and operations skills
- Awards, honors, and reputation in the industry

Are references included in the proposal? If not, will the presenters give references so that they might be contacted *before a decision is made to accept a specific proposal?*

Managers often have a hard time judging proposals. A few researchers shine in the proposal stage but later are unable to deliver. Too often the powerful cosmetics—in the proposal or even in the actual final write-up of a study—will offset the poor content. Executives must do their homework when judging different proposals.

▶ Marketing Research Should Provide Input and Be an Ongoing Part of an Organization's Management Information System

The MIS function basically (1) stores/retrieves data, (2) monitors the flow and dynamics of information, and (3) helps with interpreting information for decision making. Marketing research personnel use the MIS hardware and software to carry out their tasks. The information system should be designed to receive input from previous and current research projects and studies. Over time, the MIS should accumulate information useful for planning future research endeavors. The point is that aggregate building of marketing research information is much more useful than isolated experiences or one-shot projects. Previous efforts should not be ignored, for they help to build norms and guidelines.

Effective interplay between MIS and marketing research enables an organization to create a productive marketing intelligence system. Such interaction provides the framework for good decision making.

9
Test Marketing: A Mandatory Folklore

Many marketers have a love/hate attitude toward test marketing. Although such marketing be an effective tool in the product development process, it is very expensive and time consuming. If it is done improperly, colossal blunders may occur. Some examples of mistakes that have been made are:

- A dog food that discolored on store shelves
- A pet food brand that gave test animals diarrhea
- A cigarette package that allowed the cigarettes to dry out
- Insufficient glue in packaging material that caused over half of the packages to come apart during transit
- Baby food that separated in a cold climate
- Cans of cherry topping that began exploding because an ingredient was fermenting the cherries

Test marketing thus is essential, simply to give the marketer one last evaluation before a new product is introduced on a full-scale basis. Test marketing can serve any of the following purposes:

1. Trade acceptance of the proposed new product can be gauged. Are middlemen excited about the product?
2. Sales forecasts can be made.

3. Marketing strategy, such as advertising, packaging, pricing, channel management, and personal selling concepts, can be monitored and evaluated.

▶ The Number of Strategic Alternatives to Be Examined Should Be Minimized Before Test Marketing Is Done

A product that has many "variables" may have several testing points. Market tests thus will be costly. Through the use of other marketing research techniques (for example, concept testing, surveying, and focus group interviews), marketing personnel may need to actually test only two or three strategic/tactical marketing ideas.

▶ Consumers' Needs and Interests Should Be Identified Before the Product Reaches the Test Market Stage

Marketing personnel should first adopt certain studies, such as a consumer survey, before they reach this final and expensive stage called test marketing. Further, they must make sure the company has the resources and commitment to produce the product according to specifications of the market target. For example, a few new computer manufacturers decided to develop models that competed head-on with IBMs and Apples. The marketplace, however, was looking for reliability, reputation, and steady suppliers. Before even beginning to develop a specific computer model, the marketing people of the new companies should have asked themselves if they really had the resources to succeed against those established firms.

▶ The Budget for Planning and Implementing the Test Market Program Must Be Realistic

An overzealous manager may try to push a new product through by means of excessive marketing expenditures. The product risks failure because the firm cannot afford the higher costs to market it on a national level. To illustrate, in test marketing a new consumer catsup product, marketing personnel at Smuckers spent more on advertising in the test markets than the normal budgeted amount. They then based their national market sales projections on the test market results, thereby creating false hopes and slanted sales data.

▶ A Comprehensive, Coordinated Marketing Plan Must Be Created

Successful test marketing is dependent on the cooperation of key channel members, sales representatives, media personnel, and suppliers of raw materials and components. The marketing program must be orchestrated with these groups in mind.

▶ Competitive Reactions and Counterattacks to a Test-Marketed Product Must Be Carefully Scrutinized

The test market can become a battlefield with the competition. For instance, General Mills tried test marketing a liquid batter coating for chicken, called "Crisp'N Tender." General Foods, which had 90 percent market share with "Shake'N Bake," jumped in with a liquid called "Batter'N Bake." After the potential benefits of "Crisp'N Tender" were duplicated with the liquid "Batter'N Bake," General Mills decided to remove the product. Having eliminated its competition, General Foods withdrew its product as well.

Another example is provided by the tactics of Ralston Purina, which had a reputation for finding out about a competitor's test-marketed product and counterattacking by flooding the test cities with thousands of coupons, discounts, and free samples of its own competing product. Certain large companies, such as Procter & Gamble, just wait out counterattacks, but smaller companies do not have the resources to do this. Awareness of the problem, however, may help smaller firms to analyze the situation sooner and decide on the next marketing action.

▶ Marketing People Must Follow the Ground Rules for Picking Test Market Cities

Several rules should be followed in choosing test market sites to ensure objective results. They are:

1. The cities must not be overtested and should represent a "typical" market for the proposed product.
2. The cities should represent an average promotional situation.
3. One industry should not dominate in the area, so that cyclical events in this industry do not create a bias in results.
4. The cities should have a normal historical development. Rapid or deteriorating growth may bias test results.

5. The costs to test market in the city should be similar to marketing/physical distribution costs in nontest cities.

▶ The Test Should Be Long Enough to Allow Repeat Purchases

The test marketing period generally ranges from 6 to 24 months, but is a function of numerous variables. Too brief a period may prompt mistaken optimism. Many consumers are willing to try a new product once. But will they be satisfied and purchase the product on a *regular basis?* On the other hand, too long a period may allow the competition to expedite its own efforts and become first with a similar product.

▶ All Sales Results and Market Behavior Should Be Carefully Monitored

Sales auditing and research services should be carefully planned and implemented. At this stage a company must avoid misleading results—it must be *objective* in examining its test market data. Wishful thinking or acceptance of inaccurate data can be catastrophic.

Do's and Don'ts in Making Predictions from Test Marketing Data

Do's	Don'ts
Consider all angles when projecting test market data to the total market data.	Forget the geographic differences and seasonal nature of the product when making projections.
Allow test market periods to be long enough so that predictive purchase patterns can be examined.	Merely average data across test markets, since the markets are never equal.
Appreciate the potential problems of extraneous and uncontrollable factors, such as weather, economic, or political conditions, when forecasting from test cities.	Ignore feedback from salespeople and channel members when forecasting test market data.
Obtain precise test market sales data by using various projectable and trend audits, such as factory shipments, warehouse withdrawals, retail store audits, or consumer panels in selected test cities.	Assume that the competitive environment will stay the same if the new product is launched nationally.

PART FOUR
A SOUND MARKETING MIX PROGRAM

10
Winning the Risky but Rewarding Innovation Game

Development of new products and services is one of the most difficult marketing tasks. Yet for an organization to survive, grow, and prosper, it must have a systematic, comprehensive program for creating new offerings, technology, and processes. Interestingly, high employee morale seems to coincide with companies that have a high incidence of innovations.

Many diverse policies and procedures are available for spawning and marketing new products and services. They range from very sophisticated to highly unsophisticated techniques—that is, the "seat of the pants" approach. Many different statistics are available for the rate of new product/service failures. The discrepancies are due partly to lack of a universal definition for "failure" in this context. Evidence does demonstrate, however, that new offerings are rife with disturbing and treacherous problems, obstacles, and failures.

Even though dangerous, the development of new products, concepts, services, and processes if the most rewarding activity in today's business environment. Figure 10.1 lists generalizations that can be made about product development.

▶ Top Management Must Create and Cultivate a Climate that Encourages New Company Offerings

Positive rewards and ample financial and personnel support are basic attributes of a climate favorable for innovations. New offerings should be perceived as an investment rather than as a necessary and expensive

Figure 10.1. Generalizations about product development

Recessions discourage new product development.
Changing lifestyles present new opportunities for innovative concepts.
Expenditures per innovation decline as the firm's number of new products in the marketplace increases.
Unlimited promotion will not make a faulty new offering a success.
Market timing is critical.
No organization can afford inertia when trying to develop new offerings.
An innovative organizational climate attracts creative people.
Product development is often necessary to ensure organizational growth.
Important new product ideas are often in short supply.
Innovation and new competition frequently occurs from companies who are from other industries.
Marketing of new concepts has high risks but is necessary for company survival and growth.

evil. (Chapter 1 gives precepts for perpetuating a positive marketing climate.)

Most new product ideas originate inside the corporation. Outside sources, such as customers, distributors, suppliers, competitors, inventors, and consultants, can also be helpful, however. The majority of new offerings are extensions, modifications, or improvements of existing offerings.

Since finding usable and marketable offerings, even from a host of ideas, is difficult, management should adopt and encourage an innovative organizational climate. It should:

1. Schedule creativity/brainstorming sessions in which people from all functions and levels of management can participate. The groups should be of reasonable size and the differing personalities of group members appreciated. It may be prudent at times to not include supervisors in the sessions. Group members may feel inhibited or may merely agree with their supervisor.

2. Schedule problem-solving staff meetings with executives from different functions.

3. Organize companywide meetings with licensees, distributors, retailers, suppliers, and the like, to collect ideas on future innovations.

4. Place a high premium on the hiring, training, promoting, and transferring of creative personnel. (Creativity is a learned trait that can thereby be encouraged throughout the firm.)

Figure 10.2. *Guidelines for becoming more creative*

Study and adopt the positive traits of individuals that you identify as being creative.
Learn to seek out and listen to creative people.
Be a generalist and periodically investigate other fields.
Allow time for brainstorming sessions with yourself.
Learn to be receptive to unusual thoughts from your peers.
Welcome constructive nonconformity and individual differences.
Translate imagination into realities.
Interact socially and professionally with a variety of people.
Avoid detailed planning, time pressures, trivial patterns, and burdensome administration when brainstorming.
Avoid the urge to evaluate your new concepts immediately.
Study the process of and thinking on creativity by reading published literature on the subject.
Appreciate the interdisciplinary approach, especially in bridging technical fields with the commerce field.
Learn how to think by sometimes getting away from the job and avoiding the daily political pressures.
Most of all, remember that creativity is a *learned* behavior that can become a way of life and an ongoing process.

5. Design formal and informal meetings to promote the cross-fertilization of ideas from different fields of business. (One small industrial marketer requested that mid-managers from each of the various corporate functions/departments have a weekly business lunch. According to the mid-managers, these meetings were extremely useful in stimulating new ideas for attacking common problems and creating new product concepts.)

6. Establish a continuous, sound, and comprehensive marketing intelligence system. Marketers should be the conduit for generating and channeling new ideas.

It should be noted that 50 to 100 new ideas may be needed before even one new offering is successfully marketed.

Besides encouraging the total organization to be innovative, top management can also help *individuals* to become more creative. The important point is that creativity is a learned trait. Figure 10.2 offers practical tips for enhancing personal creativity. Progressive organizations place a high premium on people who are creative—especially when creativity results in successful new products in the marketplace.

▶ For Follow-Through on New Ideas, the Organizational Structure Must Be Explicit

Some alternative structures include new-product committees, new-product departments, product management, venture teams, and top management product-planning groups. The structure chosen will depend on the managers' resources, objectives, and philosophies. For success, three rules should be followed:

1. A specific person or department must be accountable for generating new offerings.
2. The high status given to innovation must be explicit and reflected within the organizational structure.
3. Proper strategic planning, coordination, and managerial control must be achieved.

▶ A Consistent Systematic Process for Evaluation of New Ideas Is Needed

Policies, procedures, and useful forms can be established that will save time and costs. Every organization needs its own customized manuals or forms that expedite screening and evaluation of new offerings.

Written policies and procedures inform mid-managers about the criteria that are desirable to top management. They also prevent the costly "reinvention of the wheel" each time a new idea is tossed around.

I have prepared policies and procedures manuals for companies that wanted to enhance their product development process. The manuals allowed managers to evaluate new ideas quickly and efficiently. Furthermore, executives in the organization quickly realized what factors were to be considered and how to go through the screening process. The manuals prevented the common problem of each new idea (often from upper management) being analyzed in a haphazard and unique way.

Usually, financial and market potential factors are the most specific and rigid of all factors that must be evaluated. The financial criteria for evaluating proposals are expected return on investment, estimated payback period, net present value, and forecasted profit margins. Prepared customized checklists (see Figure 10.3) help facilitate the screening process, even if data are not available for all the points enumerated.

Figure 10.3. Criteria for evaluating and rating new offering proposals

Area[a]	Rating Scale[b]		
	Excellent	Fair	Poor
Product criteria			
Element of newness		X	
Fit with existing facilities and skills	X		
Differentiation (competitive advantage)	X		
Servicing requirements		X	
Technical feasibility		X	
Legal constraints		X	
Organizational support	X		
Product positioning	X		
Market criteria			
Market size and unexpected company share	X		
Market growth potential		X	
Market positioning and segmentation	X		
Impact on existing product lines	X		
Competitive status		X	
Distribution requirements		X	
Financial criteria			
Potential profit contribution		X	
Return on investment		X	
Total investment requirement		X	
Impact on cash flow		X	
Accessory income possibilities	X		
Impact on costs		X	
Profit margin		X	
Distribution criteria			
Impact on current channels	X		
Transportation requirements	X		
Inventory requirements		X	
Potential acceptance by channel members		X	

[a] Except for distribution criteria, specific decision areas for setting standards are found in Patrick McGuire, *Evaluating New-Product Proposals*, (New York: The Conference Board, 1973).
[b] The rating can be in any form. For example, it could be a 5- or 10-point scale.

After a majority of new ideas have been eliminated by means of the checklist, the various stages of integration of the physical properties of the offering (engineering/production of product or service) with the market target can be addressed. Integration encompasses such techniques as concept testing, surveying, and test marketing. (Since these topics are mentioned in other parts of this book, I will not discuss them further here.)

Caveat: *Using Survey-of-Buyer-Intention to Evaluate the Marketability of a New Offering*

Many marketers frequently ask consumers about their purchasing plans for a potential new product. On the surface this method has sound logic. Why not go directly to the source and ask people if they would buy this innovation if it were made available? The company can then evaluate the probable success rate (and sales) of the new product. Although this technique is quite popular, the following qualifications and limitations should be kept in mind:

1. Can potential buyers who would need and want the new offering be identified?
2. How many potential buyers are there? Can all of them be contacted? If not, will a random sample be possible?
3. Do buyers know what their plans are without trying the new concept? Do they have specific intentions?
4. Will buyers overstate their buying intention?
5. Will the competitive and economic environment change from the date of the survey to actual commercialization of the new product?

Be careful when the brand manager or someone else is excited simply because a survey shows favorable buyer expectations and planned purchases for the new product.

▶ The Company Must Be Careful Not to Create False Expectations About the Features of a New Product

A good example of a company that had problems living up to product expectations is Coleco. Management promoted the new Adam computer as a complete and effective system with an inexpensive mass market price. Coleco marketers kept assuring the marketplace that the company could produce the type of system that was promised. Yet management had actually overestimated company capabilities to build the type of computer and provide the attractive accompanying software that had been proclaimed. Even now it is hard to measure the negative impact of the Adam computer fiasco on Coleco's image.

▶ A New Product or Service Should Be Carefully Tested and Evaluated Before Selling Begins

In the highly competitive marketplace, marketing people sometimes rush the product development process. For numerous reasons—such as

to beat competition, motivate the sales force, satisfy channel members, or impress top management—marketers may prematurely take a faulty product to consumers. Quite often this hasty action results in damage to the company's image and reduced sales of the company's other products.

Texscan, a cable television equipment maker, once took sweep generator prototypes to a German trade show. Visiting engineers examined the inner parts of the prototype and found boxes of messy soldering, tangled pimper wires, and other evidence of poor workmanship. According to Texscan's founder and chairman of the board, this was the marketing mistake of his life. It was almost the company's downfall in Europe.

Interestingly, Texscan's competitors, Oak Industry and Scientific Atlanta, have also rushed new product offerings. They impetuously introduced addressable converters before having eliminated the bugs, and then suffered customer displeasure because of poor workmanship.

Countless numbers of other well-known companies have fallen into the trap of rushing a product into the marketplace before it was perfected. A company president once told me, "The marketing people are always trying to rush R&D." He further noted that sometimes salesmen are already taking orders before the lab people have perfected the product, in fact, sometimes before the product is even technologically feasible!

▶ Rewards Reaped by Innovators May Not Necessarily Be Shared by Followers Who Adopt Similar Marketing Practices

Numerous companies have hesitated to introduce a new product only to see the competition go ahead with it. Consequently their competitors are the first in the market and receive the publicity, accolades, and lion's share of the market.

The various financial service industries are a prime case in which followers had to fight to increase sales or market share. Some financial companies, who were slow with ATM's (Automated Teller Machines), money market accounts, NOW accounts, discount brokerage services, estate planning services, and/or personal financial planning advice wanted to avoid what they perceived as increased costs of offering these new products. Later they had to introduce these products as a *defensive* measure to keep what they already had in terms of market share, customers, sales, and so on. Their payoff then was negligible compared with that of the innovators who were first in the market.

In short, marketers who are first with innovative marketing strategy and new product concepts can reap large rewards. Consequently, management must seek out innovative risk takers in marketing. In light of earlier cautions about premature marketing, timing clearly is of the essence. Marketers must be neither too early nor too late with their new-product ventures.

▶ If Patents Are a Characteristic of the Company Industry, a Comprehensive System for Patent Analysis Must Be Implemented

Patent analysis can help executives observe the technological leaders, followers, and losers in particular product lines. By studying the number of patents obtained, the years left on the patents, and the concentration of patents within various industries marketers are better equipped to decide whether they should enter, remain, or leave a certain technological area. They can also partly observe and evaluate the competition's strategy and future plans.

A good starting point for a sound patent analysis is the U.S. Patent and Trademark office, Washington, D.C. This office publishes a huge amount of information about patents. An organization may wish to develop a patent team. This group could consist of professional managers who have expertise in such critical areas as legal marketing, research and development, capital budgeting, science and engineering, or production. Since the study of patents is a complex endeavor, the staff or advisory committee must include individuals who can make unique contributions to the total group.

▶ A Proposed New Product Can Cannibalize Sales of Existing Products

Osborne, which had to declare Chapter 11 bankruptcy, learned the importance of this rule when it was planning to introduce a new executive portable computer. Although the new computer was not meant to compete against the original Osborne 1 computer, customers and dealers decided to postpone purchases of the Osborne 1 when they heard a new product was in the pipeline. The marketing miscalculations created bad cash flow problems for a company already overleveraged.

Management must always appreciate the impact that a new product may have on existing products. For example, a new product that is poorly received can hurt sales of the firm's established products. This

situation is amplified when the company markets both new and older products under one brand name.

▶ The Company Must Have Assurance of Adequate Supplies and Raw Materials Before Deciding to Market a New Product

Before Wendy's, McDonald's, or Burger King decides to try a new food item, it makes sure that it can find enough suppliers. Launching a new product nationally and then dropping the item because of inadequate supplies would be calamitous. We can easily imagine the huge amounts of chicken needed for the introduction of chicken McNuggets.

The logistics of receiving the raw materials and supplies and of shipping the finished goods are also crucial in the product development process. Strategic logistical planning becomes especially important in high sales volume industries.

▶ When Introducing a New Product or Service, the Company Must Carefully Coordinate Publicity and Promotional Efforts

Management at Apple Computer made a colossal mistake when it brought out its high-priced Lisa model. The company failed to capitalize on the publicity and promotion surrounding Lisa's introduction. It did not ship the product for six to nine months after it made widespread public announcements. Excitement among the press and consumers had evaporated by the time Lisa finally reached dealers' shelves. Considering that Apple spent $50 million in developing Lisa, this is quite a costly marketing oversight!

Apple Computer learned its lesson, however. When it released the Macintosh computer, management did a beautiful job of courting the press and getting everyone excited.

▶ Management Must Think Strategically When Developing New Products, Services, or Technological Innovations

This rule may seem obvious, but I would be remiss if I did not make a special point about integrating innovation with a strategic perspective. Managers in every organization must ascertain the impact that a new concept will have on (1) the other components within the organization and (2) the well being of the firm in the years to come. For the most

part, new offerings are not created overnight, and there is plenty of time to evaluate how the product will affect future company well being. There have been cases in which one new concept either caused the organization to fail or saved it from extinction. The odds for a successful outcome are improved when the new offering has a nice corporate fit (synergism) with the other products and resources of the firm.

Marketers are able to capitalize on the experience-cost curve effect. Costs may be kept low by such favorable factors as:

- Economies of scale
- Ready access to distribution channels
- Built-in customer loyalty
- An established sales and promotional network (e.g., routes, sales force, point-of-purchase displays)
- Availability of physical distribution facilities and infrastructure
- Technical plus managerial expertise within the product/market fit

A new concept can still be successful even if it is completely new to the firm and lacks synergistic advantage. The innovative or technological breakthrough may fill a nice void in the marketplace. However, the potential profits can be dramatic and the risks less when that new offering fits the firm like a glove and meets the overall purpose of the business.

▶ Once a New Product or Service Is Introduced, the Company Must Set Quantitative and Financial Objectives for It

Often a new product or service does not fulfill the expectations and excitement of its sponsors. A tough decision must then be made as to how long to leave the new offering in the market and what criteria will determine its success.

To help answer difficult questions, managers must formulate expected financial objectives. These may include return on investment (the most common one for a new offering), market share, unit profit contribution, and contribution to cash flow.

Executives should also identify nonnumerical criteria with which to evaluate the new offering (for example, image, educational value, middlemen reaction, and completion of a product line). An organization that has not formulated and does not periodically evaluate its cri-

teria for defining success or failure for a new offering has a weak product development system.

The television industry has recently come under attack in this area. Marketing critics argue that programming decisions for new shows are emotional, with little scientific basis. They contend that Nielsen TV ratings are only one tool for new show development or old show withdrawal decisions. In response, marketers in the industry are trying to adopt additional techniques for evaluating programs.

▶ The Aesthetics and Marketability of the Package Should Be Considered when Designing the New Product

A package can enhance sales of a new product. Consumer product marketers have appreciated the importance of careful package design for years. Lately, marketers in the home computer industry have also begun to acknowledge this critical rule. They are now designing attractive, furniture-compatible computers. A good package may be the difference between success and failure for a new product.

A new product sometimes needs different concepts and designs to appeal to various channels or markets. The assumption that only one type of package is needed can be erroneous. For example, attractive point-of-purchase racks, displays, and packages may be needed for sale of new cosmetics in self-service retail outlets. In specialty shops and full-service department stores, however, a different, more sophisticated packaging approach can be used.

▶ The Power and Impact of Product Positioning and Advertising Strategy Should Not Be Underestimated when Introducing New Offerings

The promotional strategy for new product or service must develop a distinctive positive image in the minds of consumers. The company wants its market targets to mentally rank the new product or service first in the buying process. For instance, some brand marketers of beer, jeans, perfume, and cigarettes privately admit that their new offering does not differ from products of the competition. Nevertheless, they try to sell a positive image, partly through product positioning, that will enhance new sales.

Decisions behind product positioning should be dictated by prior

marketing research and competitive analysis. Voids and unmet consumer needs in specific market sectors will often be found. This vacuum provides opportunities to position the product in this sector.

No matter how strong the attributes are for a new product or service, a poor promotion program will cause failure in the positioning process. To ensure some success, marketers should adhere to the following minimum rules:

1. Present uniqueness and benefits of the new offering to consumers.
2. To avoid confusing consumers, don't mention too many benefits.
3. Position product clearly and concisely.
4. Set sights on a specific and identifiable market target.
5. Repeat and reinforce the new offering's name or brand frequently.
6. Pretest the message and the accompanying people, props, devices, and the like.
7. Develop a consistent and overall theme in the advertising.
8. Avoid trying too much with too few advertising dollars.
9. Constantly monitor the impact of the advertising approach.
10. Be prepared with a contingency advertising program in case positioning problems occur.

▶ Marketers Must Understand Two Important Concepts: The Consumer Adoption Process and Diffusion of Innovations

These two concepts have profound implications in the planning and implementation of marketing strategy for new innovations. They are vital marketing principles for product and service development.

Consumer adoption is defined as a decision-making process in which an individual passes from hearing about a new offering to buying it on a regular basis. According to Everett Rogers in his widely respected book on the subject, *Diffusion of Innovations*, a person normally goes through five stages: (1) awareness, (2) interest, (3) evaluation, (4) trial, and (5) adoption. Thus, in marketing the new product or service, the marketer must know where prospective buyers are in the consumer adoption process. For instance, free samples may be needed to move them beyond the interest or evaluation stage. Many consumer food conglomerates have found that they must make a clear distinction between

trial and adoption. Frequently consumers will try a new product a few times but will not purchase it on a regular basis. The company is misled by the high initial sales into thinking it has a winner. This potential problem has a strong impact on how long test marketing of a new concept should last before full-scale commercialization begins.

The diffusion-of-innovations theory states that the rate of acceptance of a new product varies among different consumers. Some consumers are more likely to try a new drug, while others may quickly adopt the latest clothing fashions. The different rates of acceptance have resulted in identification of five adopter categories: (1) innovators, (2) early adopters, (3) early majority, (4) late majority, and (5) laggards. Knowing who the innovators or early adopters are for a particular product line helps in targeting the promotion when the new offering is introduced. Later marketing efforts can be aimed at consumers in the other categories.

It should be emphasized that the market segment characteristics of early adopters vary depending on a host of circumstances. Marketers sometimes make the error of assuming that certain consumers (such as high-income, well-educated people) are the innovators for almost all types of new offerings.

The following elements partly dictate the speed of consumer acceptance of new offerings:

1. *Relative benefits and advantages.* When prospective buyers can easily obtain major pluses from the new offering, they are more likely to buy it immediately. An industrial purchasing manager will be quite excited when the benefits far outweigh the costs of the new office equipment.

2. *Complexity.* Consumers are slow to adopt an offering that is difficult to understand. They are often indifferent to the technical attributes and marvels of the product. They want to visualize how the innovations will meet their own needs and solve their problems. (It took the home computer industry and other high-tech businesses a while to appreciate this fact.) Marketers should not be enamored with the technical aspects of their product while ignoring the task of simplifying its complex features.

3. *Compatibility with current lifestyle or operations.* The new offering should not upset the normal lifestyle or operations of prospective buyers. We are indeed creatures of habit. Although there are cases when an upheaval is desired, the diffusion process will usually take much longer in this case, if it does take place.

4. *Transparency.* The major advantages of a new concept should be easily observable. When buyers can quickly notice the positive opportunities presented by the innovation, they are more likely to buy it regularly. Consumer confusion about the features will slow down the diffusion process. Sales personnel must be able to show exactly how the new product will help consumers.

5. *Degree of risk.* When the new offering presents a high financial, physical, social, or personal risk, consumers may be slow or hesitant to try or adopt it. Marketers must try to minimize the risk or to share in the amount of risk taken by consumers. High risk factors or strong doubt may require marketers to offer a scaled-down version or smaller quantities. Consumers may be willing to take the risk if they can invest a smaller amount of money. Industrial marketers of capital goods frequently build smaller prototypes or allow organizational buyers to try the new item at little cost to them. One robotic manufacturer/distributor is starting to charge a nominal "rental" fee. Prospective buyers can try out the programmable robots in the manufacturing process, to see if the robots do help productivity.

6. *Degree of support among opinion leaders and influencers.* When a new offering has the strong support of respected leaders in a certain marketplace, the acceptance rate is notably increased. Marketers must therefore identify and convince opinion leaders and influencers about the virtues of the new offering.

▶ Before a New Offering Is Introduced into the Marketplace, the Marketing Plan Should Be Well Thought Out

Ironically, an organization may spend months or years on the engineering and production of a product, and then spend just a few days on developing marketing strategy and tactics. A last-minute, poorly developed strategic marketing plan can often doom even the best concepts taken from engineering, research and development, and/or production. A marketing game plan must be interwoven throughout the later stages of development of a particular product or service.

▶ To Avoid New Product or Service Mistakes, Marketers Should Know Common Reasons for Failure

The most common reasons for failure of a new product or service in the marketplace are:

- Poor market analysis
- Market target too small
- Technical product/service defects
- Costs higher than anticipated
- Poor positioning
- Lack of worthwhile differentiation strategy
- Inadequate management support
- Insufficient marketing effort
- Lack of channel support
- Unrealistic forecasts in sales, profits, or return on investment
- Strong competitive reaction
- Bad timing
- Lack of understanding of the buying process
- No real benefit to consumers
- Lack of required organizational resources

Many of these reasons are interrelated and interdependent. No one can perfectly predict future failures and successes, but management can use the diagnostic approach of studying reasons for previous failures.

Do's and Don'ts for Developing New Offerings

Do's	Don'ts
Make sure the new offering ties in with management's desired image and mission of the organization.	Forget to file for patent or copyright protection, if needed.
Study the new product's fit with the needs and preferences of the market.	Neglect continued marketing of current "bread and butter" products while developing the new offering.
Integrate the internal, financial, and technology strengths with the new product plans.	Ignore the legal, social, or political implications of the new product.
Transfer technology and innovation into the operations of the firm; if needed, develop a prototype.	Allow the competition to dictate the developmental process; avoid me-tooism.
Establish concrete financial and marketing objectives for the new offering.	Allow the new offering to cause severe cash flow problems that put the organization in bad financial straits.
Make alternative sales and costs	Forget essential after-sale service requirements.

Do's and Don'ts for Developing New Offerings (*continued*)

Do's	Don'ts
forecasts and analyze possible break-even points.	Allow day-to-day downside sales revenue or short-run pressure to result in premature withdrawal of the product.
Use various capital budgeting techniques to analyze the wisdom of the new innovation objectively.	Allow personnel to become subjectively or emotionally involved with the new concept.
Integrate and monitor the innovative process with a sound marketing intelligence system.	Permit professional marketers to believe the new offering is a win-no win situation in which their career is on the line (such an environment will uphold artificial, weak offerings).
Formalize and integrate the reward system and other executive perks with performance goals for new offerings.	
Encourage a continuous flow and movement of new products or services for strategic growth and organizational vitality.	Forget that employees at all levels of the organization must feel committed to making product/service development a success.

11

Improving Product-Related Decisions in the Organization: Tennis Balls or Eggs?

I am the world's worst salesman; therefore, I must make it easy for people to buy.

—*F. W. Woolworth*

Marketers face the constant challenge of deciding what products, services, or ideas to offer in the marketplace. To use a simple analogy, some products are like tennis balls and others are like eggs. A turbulent economy may take them both down, but when the economy bottoms, tennis balls bounce back while eggs splatter into a nasty marketing mess. Marketers must seek the tennis balls while avoiding the eggs. They need products that give positive results and are resilient.

As indicated by F. W. Woolworth's quote, marketing executives should learn to furnish products that give consumer satisfaction. They must present opportunities that enable consumers to easily meet their own expectations, needs, and wants. To achieve this complex task, marketers are constantly discussing, evaluating, and manipulating product strategies.

This chapter takes a generic and broad-minded view of the word "product." A product is more than a physical, tangible article. It can also be a service (airline travel, motel/hotel bedding), a person (political candidate), a place (world fair), an event (professional sports), an institution (July 4th parade), an organization (volunteer community or civic group), or an idea. Therefore, product decisions may relate to any of these categories.

For example, many sellers of household appliances have expanded their business by offering service maintenance contracts. These contracts provide consumers "peace of mind" in case the appliance fails. Retail salesmen are now trained to sell these profitable contracts while closing the sale of the appliance. Another example is the practice of firms such as General Electric, AT&T, Docutel, Hospital Corporation of America, and Bechtel to sell their managerial expertise in selected consultation services that are an outgrowth of their main product lines. These companies have learned that their core product lines provide a mode of entry for other business services within the same markets.

▶ A Classic but Tough Product Decision Is How to Match Offerings with the Correct Market Segments

The interrelationship between market targets and a firm's offerings is most indicative of (1) the needs and wants of predetermined market targets and (2) the seller's strengths, resources, policies, objectives, and other pertinent internal forces. Management must have the resources, capabilities, and desire to pursue a variety of business opportunities.

The Sears buyout of the Dean Witter Reynolds brokerage firm illustrates this point. Some Wall Street people laughed and thought the acquisition was absurd. They reasoned: "What sane investor would seek financial advice from a retail brokerage company that also marketed such merchandise as overalls and hardware?" Sears executives, however, had noted a major void in financial services for the mid-America market—especially the blue-collar market with two-income families. With Sears' previous retail product mix and the markets it served, management felt that its new business unit would fit in perfectly.

Although time is the best measure of success, the financial centers within some Sears stores are starting to fit like a good glove. Now consumers at Sears may receive financial planning advice, make savings deposits, and acquire securities, insurance policies, and real estate brokerage services.

▶ For Good Decision Making, Marketers Must Understand the Basic Principles of Product Performance

Sometimes executives can observe consistent positive or negative results occurring from the products they sell. Certain generalizations about product performance may therefore prevail. An awareness of

these repetitive conditions may allow for better product related decisions.

1. A small number of products often bring the majority of sales volume and profit.
2. Marginal products drain cash flow.
3. Weak products take excessive management time and expenditures.
4. An increase in management time and resources cannot turn around a product that consumers perceive as defective or inferior.
5. A poor product can tarnish the image of a firm's other products.
6. Management patience is needed with the star products of tomorrow.
7. Product accountability and performance measurability enhance resource allocation decisions for individual products.
8. Modifications and repositioning tactics often extend the life of a product.
9. Competitors are constantly looking for ways to acquire competitive strengths over others' products.
10. Consumer product perceptions may be more significant than the reality of superior or inferior product performance.
11. Very successful products often achieve the lowest cost position in the industry or possess the most superior product qualities compared with competitive products.
12. Faddish, fashionable, or popular products can be like Roman candles—quick to light the skies but faster to fizzle out.

▶ Strategic and Daily Product Decisions Must Support the Overall Company Image Desired by Top Management

The actions of Marketers must be consistent with the formulated company image. A good example of this is provided by Luria & Son, a Florida-based catalog retailer. This company decided not to sell such items as toys, sporting goods, and candy, because these products were thought to detract from the firm's image objective of being a high-quality and better service type of retailer. Management strongly believed that these product lines would impede sales of higher profit margin items such as jewelry and silverware. This strict product mix policy has partly en-

abled Luria to claim an operating profit margin of over 8 percent while other catalog retailers earn around 5 percent.

Another example that buttresses the need to integrate strategic product decisions with desired image is a decision made by Source & Perrier S.A. of France. Perrier executives, marketers of high-quality spring water in the United States, wanted to move from being a one-product marketer to a marketer of several high-quality products. After carefully analyzing product mix alternatives, they decided to become the exclusive U.S. importer for high-quality chocolate products from Switzerland and fruit preserve items from France. Perrier managers believed that their best product niche was high-quality food-related items marketed to small, affluent American market segments.

▶ An Organization Must Determine the Optimal Number of Products that It Can Manage, Market, and Monitor

Many organizations have gone through periods in which they rapidly brought new products to market through research and development, mergers/acquisitions, or product extension strategies. In doing so they not only flooded the market (confusing consumers) but also caused excessive competition for precious shelf space.

Singer, the company once famous for its sewing machines, at one time had a hodge-podge of diverse divisions and product lines. Its business portfolio included a lake, catalog retailing, real estate developing, electronic cash registers, air conditioners, aerospace, defense electronics, and the well-known sewing machines. The rapid product diversification resulted in a financial nightmare. Top management is now making strategic product decisions to reduce the product mix and establish tighter financial and marketing controls.

▶ In Carrying Out Strategic Product Planning Decisions, Marketers Can Use Popular Strategic Planning Tools that Are Related to the Product Concept

These tools enable users to examine variables that are germane to long-range product planning. Their use highlights major criteria for product-related decisions while helping the user integrate decisions with the overall long-term mission and objectives of the organization. Thus, these popular techniques are known as strategic planning tools. They are especially helpful to an organization that has hundreds of prod-

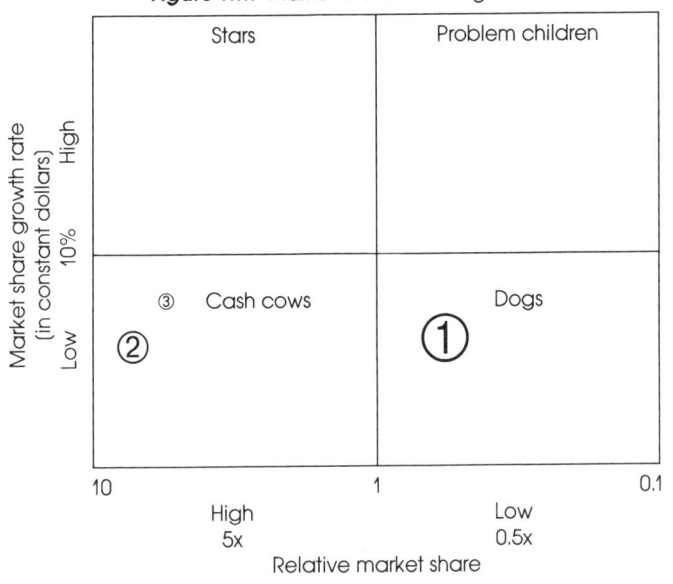

Figure 11.1. Market share/market growth matrix

	Stars	Problem children
	Cash cows ③ ②	Dogs ①

Market share growth rate (in constant dollars): Low — 10% — High

Relative market share: 10 / High 5x / 1 / Low 0.5x / 0.1

ucts—many unrelated—serving vast and diverse markets. Executives in these firms must often make financial, production, and marketing decisions on the allocation of precious resources.

Following are descriptions of a few of these portfolio tools.

Boston Consulting Group's Market Share/Market Growth Matrix

In this model, the product, brand, or strategic business unit (a group of products or collection of related businesses) is assigned to one of four quadrants (see Figure 11.1): stars, cash cows, problem children (or question marks), or dogs.

The four-cell matrix shown in the figure is divided by high and low rankings. On the vertical axis is market growth rate and on the horizontal axis is relative market share. The market share growth axis uses inflation-adjusted dollars to illustrate future dollar sales growth rates. Ten percent is the popular number for distinguishing between high and low growth rates. The relative market share axis, with a logarithmic scale, shows the ratio of a firm's product/strategic business unit sales to sales of the same product/strategic business unit of its largest competitor. Relative market shares of 0.1x and 0.5x mean the firm has only 10 percent and 50 percent, respectively, of the leading competitor's sales volume for two products in question. A market share of 1.0 means the two companies are tied for market share leadership, whereas 5x and 10x indicate 5 times and 10 times the sales leadership of the next strongest competitor in the marketplace. The relative market share is represented in log scale in order to give equal distance between same per-

Figure 11.2. Decision-making scenarios arising from application of market share/market growth matrix

Stars	Problem Children
Money needed because of high growth rate and to deter competitors' challenges	Have high cash demands
	Question of divesting because low relative market share or keeping because high market growth rate
Usually profitable and could become future cash cows as investment needs decline	Having a number of products in this area may mean being spread too thin—should we concentrate on only one or two of these products?
Every organization needs current stars, otherwise no future hope	
Current market growth attractive but new competition will appear because of future positive outlook	Spending more money might make products into stars

Cash Cows	Dogs
Give financial resources to pay bills	Take up excessive management time
Give cash to help other potentially better products grow	Offer poor profitability
	Turnaround question is issue—will sales increase owing to economic issues?
Company image usually associated with this product area because of market leadership	Divestment decisions needed for some dogs
Fight to hold market share	May use short-term cash flow for other product lines (e.g., stars)

centage increases. The size of each circle within the matrix (which can vary by either diameter or area) is proportional to the product/strategic business unit's contribution to total company sales volume. Thus the two largest businesses are represented by circles 1 and 2 in the figure, but product 1 is in the dog category while 2 is in the cash cow quadrant. Figure 11.2 shows how this system can make an impact on product portfolio decisions.

The Boston Consulting Group technique allows integration of market growth, competitive market position, size of product market opportunity, cash flow, and profitability potential. The concept requires allocation plus trade-off decisions among strategic products/business units. Naturally this technique is not a panacea for making product decisions. The user has to be able to apply the model and interpret results. The technique also has potential limitations:

Is there always a positive correlation between profitability and market share?

How well did we forecast future market growth?

Will a divestment decision cause low morale or labor unrest or will it hurt our other product lines?

Will new and larger competitors suddenly make our stars into dogs or problem children?

What type of managerial accounting system will be needed to apply the market share/market growth rate model? Can we always pinpoint cost, profitability, and cash flow when the firm has multiple product lines?

Figure 11.3. General Electric multifactor portfolio matrix

	High	Medium	Low
High (Industry attractiveness)	Invest/grow	Selective growth	Selectivity and earnings
Medium	Selective growth	Selectivity/earnings (look for protected niches)	Harvest
Low	Selectivity	Harvest	Harvest/divest

Business Strengths

Is the model too static?

What do we do with products or industries that may be in only temporary decline or have potential turnaround opportunities?

Could other variables, such as contribution margin, technological potential, and the like, be more critical in evaluating positive product-related features?

General Electric's Multifactor Portfolio Matrix

This too enables comparison of industry attractiveness with company strengths. At one time General Electric used a business assessment display as a classification scheme for products. Figure 11.3 shows nine cells, with the vertical axis representing industry attractiveness. The GE multiple factor list for the industry attractiveness axis may include an evaluation of:

- Market size
- Market growth
- Profitability
- Lack of cyclicality or seasonal opportunities to recover from inflation
- World scope

The horizontal axis depicts the business strengths:

- Technology expertise
- Quality level
- Costs advantages
- Marketing power
- Profitability rating
- Domestic and international market share
- Market share compared with the leader

Figure 11.4. *Directional policy matrix*

	Unattractive	Average	Attractive
Weak	Divestment	Phased withdrawal	Double of quit (full backing for best prospects while abandoning worst prospects)
Average	Phased withdrawal	Custodial (some investment but avoid major commitment)	Try harder
Strong	Cash generation (product near end of life cycle)	Growth	Leader (maintain position and use cash resources)

Company's competitive capabilities (vertical axis)

Prospects for senior profitability (horizontal axis)

The cells represent the nine possible classifications for the industry/business screen. Marketing personnel should supply marketing data and much of the analysis. Like General Electric, other companies can develop a numerical weighted summary of the industry/business attributes listed. After placing the industry/business unit in a particular cell, management can decide on one of three strategies: invest/grow, selectivity/earnings, or harvest/divest.

Directional Policy Matrix

This outstanding portfolio screen, which was created by Shell International Chemical Company, is quite similar to the General Electric system (industry attractiveness is replaced by sector profitability). Figure 11.4 shows the matrix, which consists of the company's competitive capabilities on the vertical axis and the prospects for sector profitability on the horizontal axis.

Sector (product) profitability comprises four variables: market growth rate, market quality, industry situation, and environmental aspects. The company rates each factor with one to five stars. The number of stars given is determined by certain subfactors. For example, market quality is based on profit stability, degree of competitiveness, number of customers, and so on. A numerical score for the product is then determined on the basis of the number of stars given to all four factors.

Stars are also given to the factors for the company's competitive capabilities, which include market position, product research and development, and production capability. The product in question is then given a numerical rating for this category.

The two scores are added and the sum allows placement of the product into one of the nine cells of the directional policy matrix.

Caveat: *Recognizing a Few Limitations of Strategic Product Planning Tools*

In using the various techniques, you might have to make assumptions that may not always be applicable to the situation. Possible problems are as follows:

1. Higher market share is not always positively correlated with profits or return on investment. In many industries profit margins are sometimes higher for companies that have lower market shares than the so-called leader.
2. The experience-cost curve has limitations (see Chapter 6).
3. Organizational objectives, such as production goals, technological opportunities, and environmental challenges, may have a greater impact and significance than the positive product features outlined in the strategic planning tools discussed herein.
4. A question arises as to how the various classification schemes (for example, competitors) that are needed to work the product planning models are set up.
5. Are the costs and time needed to develop and utilize the planning tools greater than the benefits derived from going through the analytical process itself?
6. The models, like most, are static and not dynamic; they merely reflect conditions at a certain point in time.

Be forewarned. These product planning tools are not a cure-all for product decision-making challenges. The models are a means to an end, not an end in itself.

▶ Marketers Must Know and Understand Both the Contributions and Limitations of Product Life-Cycle Analysis

Every product goes through the sales volume phases of introduction, growth, maturity, and decline. Marketers thus must know in which stage each product is. They must also be aware of how long the product will remain in that stage. For example, the life span of a fad may be only a few weeks, while that of a staple product may be many years. Different market factors and the specific life-cycle stage of a product sometimes dictate marketing strategy.

Sales revenue, costs, and profits may influence where a product or service is on the life-cycle curve. Start-up costs are high in the introduction stage, while sales and unit profits climb sharply in the growth phase. Sales may continue to rise in the maturity period, but unit profits may begin to decline. In theory, somewhere in the maturity stage sales and profit volume begin to decrease and then continue downward through the decline stage.

The following gives insight on the positive and negative aspects of using the product life-cycle concept for executive decision making.

Arguments on the Merits of the Product Life-Cycle Concept

Positive	Negative
Most products can be plotted on one of six curves	Many offerings do not fit any of six curves developed by theoreticians
Useful in examining market behavior of general product lines	Difficult to apply in studying market behavior of individual brands
May help to spur product development	May put too much emphasis on product development at expense of current products
Describes strategic marketing of products in distinct product life-cycle stages	Although it is descriptive tool and looks at previous patterns, it does not necessarily help predict future trends
Provides static model that gives useful data at one point in time	
Increased use of computer and mathematical models may show causation and validate the life-cycle analysis	Marketplace is too dynamic to make concept worthwhile for decision making
Can be used as sales forecasting tool by looking at historical sales patterns and estimating length of each cycle stage	So many variables—both controllable and uncontrollable—influence sales behavior that prescribing specific action under different life-cycle stages is difficult
Provides marketers opportunity to structure strategic marketing planning process with capital budgeting decisions; serves as communication medium with top management	Better and more specific sales forecasting techniques can be utilized
	Is outcome rather than cause of strategic marketing decisions. Costs, profits, sales, and length of each cycle are really functions of managerial decisions

Some critics argue that product life-cycle analysis is a meaningless or dangerous tool. The concept is attacked as being a mere explanatory guide and not a predicative force. Some feel that the technique may give false alarms. If a temporary downslide in sales occurs, this barometer could cause a hasty decision in abandoning a product/service or decreasing the support of allocated resources.

The popular product life-cycle principle is not a substitution for decision making. But it does assist in questioning the strengths of the

organization's product mix. By using the technique, marketers may observe that their most important offerings seem to be in the declining stage. This may encourage the management team to develop new products, find new uses for declining products, or modify marketing strategy in some manner. Product life-cycle analysis may thus serve as a catalyst to study the opportunities and threats of the company's product mix in the marketplace. Since the marketing profession has adopted this concept when discussing sales behavior of various products and services, the pros and cons of this technique must be appreciated.

▶ An Excellent Product or Service Is One that Delivers Quality at a Reasonable Price

Good quality has a positive effect on profitability, market share, return on investment, and competing against aggressive marketers. This precept has been well documented in the PIMS research. Marketers of fine products or services have a number of enviable strategic alternatives. They can charge higher prices (within reason), obtain more commitments from channel members, influence sales of other brands within the firm, and maintain good customer loyalty. The objective of trying to improve product quality is therefore a worthy one.

When the firm succeeds in marketing high-quality products, it should be careful not to tamper with the successful formula. Many consumer packaged food marketers have found that their profitable high-quality brands are in the mature stage of the product life cycle. Impatient to create something new, they have caused problems for themselves by modernizing these brands out of existence or by letting them wither through lack of managerial support. Fine products should not be allowed to become poor stepchildren to the new innovations and product dreams of tomorrow.

▶ All Product Specifications Must Be Clearly Recognized, Understood, and Appreciated by Consumers

Marketers can ill afford unpleasant consumer surprises about the specifications and benefits of an offering. The outcome is consumer alienation.

For instance, many investors are unaware of the price volatility of zero-coupon bonds. High risks are involved unless the bonds are held to maturity. If the investor needs sudden cash or if an estate must be

settled, the loss may be extensive. Marketers and financial institutions have not adequately explained the price fluctuations. Eventually consumers will hold these marketers—rather than the issuing corporations—accountable for losses they might incur. These middlemen will lose the trust of their customers for other investment advice as well.

▶ In Trying to Increase or Revitalize Sales of Existing or Mature Products, Marketers Must Be Aware of Certain Product Decision-Making Opportunities and Mistakes

Marketers constantly try to milk mature products for cash flow, dealer loyalty, consumer goodwill, and profits. Extending the life span of an existing product often does reap rewards. But an overzealous marketer can make blunders that are devastating to the organization. The following are frequent mistakes:

1. *Making product changes that alienate consumers.* Schlitz Beer once changed the ingredients and brewing process of its beer. According to loyal Schlitz customers, the alterations adversely affected the taste of the beer. The once-strong number two brewery lost tremendous consumer credibility. It never fully recovered or regained lost market share.

2. *Hanging on to maturing/declining products for too long.* A mature or declining product may drain a company's financial resources. It may also damage the image of other products. And precious financial and managerial resources may be wasted on a dying product. The opportunity costs become exorbitant as profits on alternative products and business ventures are foregone.

3. *Becoming attached to a product or strategy.* Business managers sometimes remain loyal to a product that helped to launch the business. They may fail to observe that marketplace changes are making the product obsolete.

4. *Robbing resources from mature but healthy products for new, faddish concepts.* Balancing the organization's resources between old and new business is a difficult but crucial task. Misallocation of resources can lead to the premature death of healthy, profitable products.

5. *Failing to reinvest profits into mature products.* A product or service may begin to decline in sales or quality because management ignores its upkeep. A good example is provided by White Motor Company. At one time this firm was the number two truck producer. Instead of fine

tuning its trucks with reinvestment, however, it spent money on backward integration with cabs, frames, axles, and engine manufacturing. The strategy eventually deteriorated White's market share while creating higher product costs.

6. *Failing to make positive marketing strategy adjustments to differentiate products from competing products.* The status quo of existing products may need to be altered. Middlemen must remain excited about the goods and emphasize their uniqueness relative to newcomers.

7. *Ignoring new potential market segments.* Apprehension by management and the sales force about exploring new markets can shorten a product's life span. A prime illustration is the concept known as backward inventing. Owing to rapid technological advances and changing consumer lifestyles, demand for an existing product may decline in economically developed countries. This same product, however, may have potential in certain foreign markets where consumer needs and desires match the existing product specifications. Regrettably, some managers are afraid of seeking foreign markets simply because they are intimidated by a different market.

▶ Systematic Marketing Strategies and Procedures Are Needed Even for Discontinuance of a Product

No matter how hard a company tries, a product or service may still fail. It may have to be dropped due to financial/profit disappointments, lack of market demand, or changes in the environment (such as technology, competition, or the economy). A weak product can tax the resources of any firm. It can also disappoint consumers and hurt sales of other product lines. A company in this situation must decide sooner or later what to do with the product or service. Various strategic options are available:

1. The product can be sold to another organization that can more effectively produce and market it. Sales will release limited capital and prevent further deterioration of resources. Some shrewd sellers institute cosmetic changes to "dress up" the product line before trying to sell it. For a short time they devote extra management effort and resources to enhance the product's performance. This strategy is not necessarily unethical; marketers are merely trying to put the product's best features forward. This is more realistic than having a quick fire sale, which results in a lower price.

2. The product line can be ignored and left to linger in the marketplace. I know five industrial marketers in five different industries (oil filters, ball bearings, valves, stamping devices, and machinery) who had a particular model that was in demand among a very small but select market. In all of these cases the marketing people were unexcited about continuing the product line. Even though loyalty was quite strong among a few customers, sales volume and future outlook provided little hope for improvement. Surprisingly, the products are still being offered, with the understanding that they are not given priority in the production, distribution, or marketing cycle of the more profitable product lines. Despite this condition, the few customers are willing to wait longer for the product. Thus, a product line may not need to be completely eliminated if the few loyal customers are notified about new sales and delivery conditions. The customers may be quite understanding and patient about delays. For example, goods might be manufactured only on order and for stock. In fact, the firm may be one of the few suppliers left. This strategic choice is not as drastic as the other alternatives, and a few customers may still be satisfied under the best possible circumstances.

3. The product can be altered. Marketers can often scale back a product or reduce its features. Simplifying the offering may lower its cost. This strategy allows a transitional period of testing the waters before a more extreme course of action is taken. The company may be able to incur higher profit margins while extending the life span of the product.

4. The product can be eliminated from the marketplace. If there are no buyers for a money-losing product, it may have to be dropped completely. Many marketers are reluctant to do this because they are emotionally attached to the product and the personnel who have been associated with it. They may use delaying tactics by scheduling the decision for a future staff meeting or by using a committee process in hopes that no final agreement will be reached. On the other hand, companies naturally want to recoup product-related costs by holding on.

Once the decision to eliminate a product has been made, an orderly and systematic withdrawal must be undertaken. The company does not want to alienate remaining loyal customers, which might damage sales of other offerings. The product or service might be phased out slowly. Manufacturing and distribution may continue until middlemen and customers are able to find alternative sources of supply. Ideally, the company can find an appropriate—perhaps even better—replacement product within its own lines. If not, it must make a diligent attempt to

locate alternative suppliers, even if these are competitors. In the long run, customers will appreciate this effort.

When making product elimination decisions, management must be cautious with the personnel involved with the product. Certain actions may frighten the employees' perceptions of their own careers. Relocation and displacement activities may be one outcome of the decision. When one well-known company decided to drop its large miniframe computers, many excellent professional people left the firm. This exodus had a bad impact on the firm's research and development department. Executives should communicate with the staff and provide encouragement. If staff termination is unavoidable, every effort must be made to help people begin new careers or retire with dignity and economic independence.

▶ Marketers Should Investigate Business Opportunities from Recycling of the Waste or Residue Generated by Their Main Product Lines

In a world with limited resources and nonrenewable raw materials, marketers may make an ecological contribution while still enhancing overall product mix performance. A sharp marketer can sometimes spot a need that is not being met from the public sector. With rapid technological advances, the business of recycling is becoming feasible. A company may find that instead of paying to have product waste removed, it can use the "waste" for new products or even sell the "waste" to a business that can use it. One of my clients made wooden broom handles from his by-products of wooden pallets and crates. Since his business was a small lumber mill supply house and was cyclical, the broom handles served as a steady cash supplement.

To study the merits of marketing waste and residual materials, I have found that marketing target analysis is critical. Through such analysis, one medium-sized company found an immense amount of interest from certain market segments for products made from its recycled materials. Although these products were never the company's biggest sellers, they did have a loyal core market in a group of consumers that was not reached by the traditional product lines. The recycled goods have a nice contribution margin to the firm's fixed costs, which enhanced bottom-line profits.

Interestingly, a new industry dealing with waste is emerging. Companies like Waste Management and Browning-Ferris Industries have found huge profits in the collection, processing, recovery, and disposal

of waste. Such companies may someday take hazardous chemicals and solid waste materials and develop from them new, usable products for consumption or production utilization. One company's garbage may thus be another company's greenbacks.

▶ In Marketing Spin-off Products, Sound Marketing Procedures and Practices Must Be Observed

A spin-off product is one that was originally developed for in-house use only. Once in a while a firm creates a concept, service, or product that will improve its own operations. After carefully getting the bugs out, management may observe that it has a widely marketable product.

For example, many firms develop their own computer software, chemical testing services, sales person training services, marketing research services, or publications of informative documents. They are so meticulous in product development that they create a high-quality product attractive to consumers in the marketplace.

A spin-off product or venture may be encouraged to:

- Fully utilize existing facilities and manpower.
- Generate cash flow or new revenues.
- Motivate personnel who want to try a miniproduct venture for experience.
- Make a contribution to fixed costs.
- Test the waters for selling to new market segments.
- Provide worthwhile managerial experience.
- Enhance product development opportunities in new industries.

Although spin-off products seldom become the primary business units of an organization, they usually give underlying support to the organization's strategic objectives, they can become a nice supplement to the total product portfolio. Management must just be sure to systematically and carefully evaluate the marketability of such products before expanding them.

▶ Marketers Must Stay Abreast of the Constraints and Real Benefits of Patents

A patent offers protection from infringement by other parties on an invention. Protection may cover a new product, method, apparatus, com-

position of matter, or even computer program. A design patent may safeguard the shape and appearance of a product but not necessarily its function. A utility patent covers function; this type is more complex and difficult to attain. A patent, however, is not a fail-safe solution to competitive threats.

A patent holder must often endure the following constraints and challenges:

- Competitors introduce cheap imitations.
- Prospective customers are unaware of buying from copycat competitors. Proprietary ownership is hard to determine and costly to investigate; many buyers assume that a seller is not violating someone else's patent.
- A patent lawsuit is costly and time consuming.
- Court decisions concerning patent enforcement are often inconsistent, which makes management decision making strenuous.
- Competition frequently "invents around" the patent.
- Employees sometimes argue that they legally own their inventions because no ownership agreement—waiver of rights—was obtained.
- Obtaining a patent is time consuming (it can take up to three years).
- Filing a patent with a patent attorney can be costly (perhaps thousands of dollars) for a smaller firm.
- Maintenance fees can be imposing.

Despite the foregoing patents allow a firm some incentives for developing new concepts. A patent may give a monopoly or at least some degree of protection from the ever-present competition. Systematic evaluation of patented inventions is mandatory, since technology or environmental changes may render a product obsolete. As mentioned, competitors may design around the product. Marketers must therefore continually monitor their inventions in the marketplace.

One common snafu is the lack of management preparation for expiration of patent. Sales are sometimes taken for granted during the life of the patent. But once this legal protection runs out, stiff competitive products and generic brands may hit the marketplace. In fact, many competitors will prepare for patent expiration by readying a sound marketing plan. Their strategy may include promotional strategies and loyal middlemen. Thus, the company with the expiring patent must

also have planned its marketing strategy to retain market share and strong industry leadership.

While a company waits for patent approval, it should put "patent pending" on the product and on packaging, fliers, advertising, and other communication media. This may deter competitors from selling a similar product. Although the term "patent pending" is not legally binding, it does convey an image of exclusivity for the product.

In summary, whenever management is contemplating a patent decision, it should consult the U.S. Patent and Trademark Office in Washington, D.C. The federal government provides useful information and published sources about applying for patents and trademarks. (A trademark is words, letters, symbols, or marks that can be legally registered. Approval for trademarks is usually easier to obtain and less costly.) As a starting point, the Government Printing Office has two helpful publications: *General Information Concerning Patents* and *General Information Concerning Trademarks*. The American Patent Law Association in Arlington, Virginia, offers sources of information for both inventors and businesses. Even though the patent process is a complex undertaking, these sources can get the marketing and legal team started.

▶ Any Written, Musical, or Artistic Work Should Be Copyrighted

Copyright security covers products such as video games, board games, and computer software. Product-related concepts are further protected if packages; pamphlets; product manuals; some advertising, operations and sales manuals; and training manuals are copyrighted. In short, a copyright gives the author or originator the legal right to distribute and copy the material in question. Unlike those for patents, the procedures for copyrighting material are somewhat simple and inexpensive. Written material can be registered by filing an application with the Register of Copyrights of the United States Library of Congress. Unlike a trademark, for which the product must be on the market for at least one year, copyright is valid from the moment the original work is created, but the written/artistic work must be registered. After copyright approval, proper notice is given with the symbol "c," the year first made public, and statement of ownership (organization or individual) of the work.

With the advances now being made in information processing and artificial intelligence, more marketers will probably begin to use copyrighting opportunities. This legal tool is an underutilized resource in the marketing arsenal.

▶ A Proper Branding Strategy Can Be a Strong Asset to a Company's Different Product Lines

Some marketers rely heavily on the strong pull of a brand. A solid brand can protect legal ownership while serving as a marketing force.

The brand is anything that identifies a product and distinguishes it from those of the competition. A brand name is the part that can be vocalized, such as Pepsi-Cola, Cheer, Gleem, and Calvin Klein. It is protected by a trademark, which may cover words, letters, numbers, symbols, or pictorial design.

Marketers are beginning to see the managerial role and scope of branding. It is an all-inclusive concept that can instill enormous consumer loyalty while differentiating the product line from its stiff competition.

In today's aggressive marketing environment, potential brands must often be pretested for consumer acceptance and positive connotations. The market targets should tell whether the brand—especially the name—is consistent with the product concept. One of my favorite examples is the La-z-Boy for recliner chairs.

As a starting point, effective focus group or personal individual interviews often give the management team a whole cafeteria of potential brand names and a wide range of branding concepts that may have been excluded. (If the branding decisions and selection process are done only in-house, tunnel vision may create potential adversities with consumers at a later date.) Branding alternatives can then be pruned with the use of quantitative marketing research studies and management intuition. The evaluation step is usually a more difficult process, and a good systematic marketing intelligence system helps.

A brand name should be easy to pronounce, read, recognize, and remember and should be appropriate for both the product and the product's market targets. It should create a positive image that is compatible with current lifestyles, attitudes, and cultural behavior. Serious problems can arise if the brand image is *not* culturally acceptable. In the case of Godfather's Pizza, an organization called the Sons of Italy was upset with the corporate symbol, a man who looked like a gangster, and the use of the name "Godfather" for a pizza chain. Another restaurant chain chose the unfortunate name "Sambo's," which alienated the black population. And "Body by Fisher" caused confusion in some foreign countries where it was translated as "Corpse by Fisher."

A company usually has to make a decision whether to use a family brand or an individual branding approach. With the family brand ap-

proach, the company has one brand for a number of product lines, for example, Sara Lee, General Electric, Smuckers, Heinz, and Campbell. A family brand has its advantages and its risks.

The salient criteria for selecting either the family or the individual branding strategy are the strength of brand loyalty among consumers and the availability of financial resources. A strong brand preference for a company's products may encourage a family branding strategy. The one brand name becomes the entire franchise of the business, a pillar of strength that might be successfully exploited. Coca-Cola has begun to realize this. It is now using the brand and its name in the introduction of new products.

Marketers have also concluded that a family brand may save precious and limited dollars. To survive and compete with larger and more capitalized firms, many executives of small and medium-sized companies have decided to spread their marketing over a number of product lines with a single brand. They simply do not have the financial strength to create a separate brand for each product.

Naturally, generalizations are inappropriate for some industries, due to variations in competition, cost structure, and marketplace. For example, branding is not as crucial in industrial markets as in consumer markets. If brand recognition, preference, or insistence is negligible, family branding may be unwise. A major marketing investment may be required to encourage brand loyalty.

In retrospect, brand insistence is unusual and expensive to achieve. Brand loyalty and sales may be increased at the expense of profits. As one executive told me, "We can get the whole damn market to insist on our brands, but we won't make any money either."

One last area in branding is the trade-off decisions to be made about manufacturer, dealer, and generic brands. Middlemen have to decide whether to have products under their own name (known as dealer, private, or middlemen brands). This strategy usually increases their marketing costs, owing to heavier promotional requirements. But it does give dealers greater control over the marketplace. They are not dependent on carrying certain manufacturers' brands—assuming consumers become loyal to their private brands. Alternatively, many manufacturers decide to sell goods for private labeling because they are not operating at capacity or they need to overcome cyclical problems in their business. Private branding then helps the old nemesis—cash flow. Generic branding (products with no brand names, plain labels, little advertising, and prices usually 15 to 35 percent lower than those of brand products) has enabled some firms to capture certain market segments that are extremely price sensitive. Sales for generic brands often in-

crease during hard economic times. Consumers cannot afford to pay extra for the national brands.

Marketers are starting to pay closer attention to branding decisions. Current business challenges and issues such as consumer perceptions and preferences, positioning, and costs have made branding a boardroom topic. Branding strategy is an integral part of product decisions.

Caveat: *A Strong Brand Loyalty Cannot Always Be Transferred from One Product Line to Another*

Some marketers try to use a successful brand in developing a new product line or appealing to different markets. Sometimes consumers or channel members do not believe the firm has the skills to market the new product line. Sometimes the brand image is so staunchly ingrained that its strengths are associated with only one product line.

To illustrate, Smucker's brand was well known in the jam and jelly market. But this positive brand reputation could not be used for catsup. "What does the Smucker's organization know about catsup," consumers thought. Kraft had the same problem. Its well-recognized brand was associated with outstanding cheese, not catsup.

If you have been "too" successful in communicating positive attributes of your brand with one product line, you may need a different brand for a new, unrelated product line.

▶ A Book (Product) Can Be Judged by Its Cover (Package)

Packaging decisions have become a significant element in the formulation of marketing strategy. Both package and label may be beneficial for:

- Creating customer satisfaction.
- Protecting the contents inside.
- Communicating the product attributes.
- Helping in product handling.
- Identifying brand name and seller.
- Promoting the product with attractive design and colors.
- Keeping costs down.
- Telling the ingredients of the product.
- Offering customer convenience.

A poor package concept can destroy the product's sales. Common consumer annoyances are:

- Leaky milk cartons.
- Loose bottle caps that allow carbonated soft drinks to lose their fizz.
- Oversized bottles that do not fit between the shelves in the refrigerator.
- Tear-off tabs that cut the fingers.
- Boxes that allow the contents to be crushed.

Such situations spawn a bad feeling among consumers and are obviously to be avoided! The following are the most common packaging blunders:

- Defective computer scan code for electronic checkout
- Odd-shaped package that is hard to stack on a shelf
- Fragile package that cannot withstand normal handling
- Ugly and garish design
- Poor visibility of brand or product ingredients
- Big package that takes up too much shelf space
- Use of colors that do not convey the right product image
- Overuse of descriptive words like "natural," best-seller," "fresh"
- Poor resealability after package has been opened

The best way to prevent blunders is to test and research packaging design characteristics during channel distribution, use, and throwaway applications of the product, prior to full production. Following the product from the production process to the garbage can is very helpful. Packaging studies also help in planning and controlling packaging-related costs.

▶ Different Packages Are Often Required for Different Channels and Markets

This rule is particularly important in retailing. With scrambled merchandising, certain retailers may easily be ignored because of a stringent packaging design. The requirements of a specialty shop may differ from those of a discount or self-service retailer. In some cases, a point-of-purchase display kit may necessitate packaging modifications. To meet the challenges of making adjustments for different retailers or markets, a missionary package designer might obtain packaging sug-

gestions from various channel members. These members will examine the packaging concepts before deciding whether to stock the product in question.

▶ A Good Package Can Significantly Contribute to Cost Reduction

With a good industrial package, both company and middlemen may be able to lower shipping costs; lessen pilferage; speed up order processing; reduce warehousing and labor requirements; lower transportation expenditures while still protecting the goods in transit; and reduce waste with raw materials, pallet space, and containerization. Thus, in selling a product to organizational prospects, marketers should make sure the package meets one of their most overriding concerns: cutting their own expenditures.

▶ Marketers Must Use the Product Management System Effectively

The organizational structure of product management was originally started by Procter & Gamble. The management of P&G had a problem with a particular brand of soap. One young executive was given the sole task of turning around the fledgling soap brand. When this organizational arrangement proved successful, P&G made more executives responsible for other individual products.

Other companies, especially consumer packaged food manufacturers, eventually adopted the product management concept. It became extremely popular in consumer goods firms as marketing became an accepted idea in the corporate world during the 1960s and 1970s. Industrial marketers were slower to embrace the product management structure, but the system is becoming more prevalent in this sector also.

Many executives wonder if their organization should utilize the product management system. From my experience, I would say that product management may be feasible when any of these 10 conditions apply to the business, no matter what its size or type:

1. Sales, distribution, or marketing requirements are the same among different products but the products need someone to champion their causes.
2. Different consumer-perceived product specifications and attributes sometimes require unique product marketing approaches within the firm.

3. Individual products are relatively complex, and there is a need for executives to coordinate various tasks to get the products through the marketplace.
4. The span of control and attention needed to handle all product lines is too great for one executive.
5. Individual products are being ignored and becoming orphans because of management indifference.
6. New products need executive advocates to achieve corporate support.
7. Sales of individual products are gaining sufficient volume but are not large enough to justify divisionalization within the product business.
8. The accounting department wants to implement product profitability/segmental analysis, so each product must achieve certain financial goals.
9. Different product lines have different customer groups and thus need separate marketing plans.
10. The traditional marketing management structure or divisional approach is proving ineffective in the multiproduct organization.

In short, the product management concept is most attractive when the multiproduct firm has adequate yearly sales volume for individual products and uses the same marketing, sales, advertising, or manufacturing departments for all. A spokesperson is needed so that some products do not become slighted in the corporate bureaucracy or politics. The product management concept should not be used just because it's popular or the competition has adopted this system.

Marketers face major challenges under the product management system. A classic organization behavioral problem may prevail. Product managers have product responsibility but no authority over specialists who can influence the success or failure of their product. The issue of defining line and staff authority never ends. For instance, should product managers make decisions about their product or should they just offer input or recommendations with regard to merchandising, strategic product planning, pricing, promotion, physical distribution, production planning, and marketing research? Defining a product manager's job is difficult.

Product managers may often suffer job tension owing to interdepartmental conflict, unity of command concerns, lack of role clarity, and high management expectations for certain products. Many executives have, however, adjusted to the challenges of using the product manage-

ment system within their own firm. Top executives who have learned to recognize the limitations of the system formulate realistic and equitable goals for each product manager.

Every marketer who has worked with the product management concept can appreciate some of the problems and mistakes that occur with this organizational arrangement. They may have to work overtime to avoid or overcome such common, nasty product management headaches as the following:

1. Product managers are new MBAs who lack the experience and respect of the other executives. This leads to a credibility problem.

2. Communication is lacking between product managers and line managers, resulting in cost overruns, missed deadlines, missed marketing/sales objectives, and decline in managerial morale.

3. Product managers overreact either by taking too much authority away from line management or by shunning initiative for fear of stepping on toes.

4. Although product managers are urged to handle daily and yearly marketing decisions, they are not consulted about strategic product decisions, such as divestment, market expansion, product acquisitions, and the like.

5. Marketing personnel, especially those in the field, forget to pass on vital information to product managers. Field people are negligent or downright hostile when deciding on the amount and type of data to provide product managers. This situation prevents the managers from collecting vital marketing data, coordinating the proper product strategy, and monitoring the outcome.

6. Other executives become jealous of product managers. If a product is considered successful, the product manager reaps the accolades while others are overlooked. In some firms, product managers are perceived as the kingpins and are handsomely compensated.

7. Job turnover of product managers is high. Successful people are hired away by the competition or professional marketing service companies (advertising, consulting, or marketing research firms). Furthermore, a few firms encourage product management as a career path to upper management, so that product managers seek short-range accomplishments at the expense of sound long-range programs.

8. Limited time exists for strategic planning because of excessive staff meetings, travel demands, committee assignments, and interac-

tion requirements with external marketing groups. Too many daily details consume product managers' time.

9. Some individuals become uneasy with their role as product managers. Due to limited authority, they are unable or unwilling to persuade, cajole, adjust, or compromise. Instead of working with and through people, some would rather work *over* people and exert formal power as executives. If the organization does not have a suitable climate or if individual marketers are misplaced, job dissatisfaction can be a major and disruptive problem.

It is easier to present the challenges and potential problems of the product management system than it is to offer suggestions for improving the organizational arrangement itself. Nevertheless, the system can be very effective for improving product performance. The product management concept is here to stay. It has evolved into a mature state and some of the concerns with it have subsided. With empathy and proper leadership by upper management, product managers serve as useful product advocates and marketing coordinators. They can make significant contributions to advertising, sales promotion, merchandising, and product planning.

Do's and Don'ts for Improving the Product Management Structure

Do's	Don'ts
Remove the "blindfolds" from the product manager--field personnel must pass along marketing data.	Hire inexperienced marketers as product managers; they may suffer creditability problems with their peers.
Have a higher authority who can be a referee for any conflict or major questions between marketing personnel and product managers.	Allow product managers to have tunnel vision by overemphasizing one marketing function.
Define in writing the role, responsibilities, and general working relationships of product managers.	Use the position as a "quick and dirty" pit stop for rising stars or as a place for dead wood.
Provide an orientation and continuing management development program for product managers and for those who interact with them.	Ignore field marketing personnel who have earned the respect of their peers; if they are qualified, reward them with promotion to attractive product management positions.
Spell out the job description, specifications, qualifications, and criteria for performance appraisal of product managers.	Judge performance by product profitability alone, especially when a product manager's authority is extremely limited.

Do's and Don'ts for Improving the Product Management Structure

Do's	Don'ts
Provide adequate financial resources and assistance.	Weaken product management positions by giving them low status in the formal organization hierarchy.
Seriously consider a management-by-objective approach to encourage agreements and mutual understanding.	
Develop procedures, methods, and paper flow—without creating a cumbersome nightmare—to open the channels of communication.	
Encourage visits, meetings, and interaction of product managers with external groups, such as middlemen and advertising agencies.	
Allow product managers to become actively involved with the strategic product planning process.	

APPENDIX
Qualities of a Good Product

1. Gives you a positive cash flow within management's desired time frame.
2. Offers good quality at a "fair" price—fair being defined by the consumers.
3. Coincides with your marketers' perceptions of their market targets.
4. Ties in with your firm's capabilities and resources.
5. Matches the strategic corporate mission and objectives of your top executives.
6. Meets the financial and marketing goals that were predetermined by your management team.
7. Provides a favorable synergistic effect with your other offerings.
8. Fulfills a specific consumer need and may solve a problem for the buyers.
9. Instills a positive image among the many "publics"—including consumers—of your organization.
10. Provides loyalty, confidence, and patriotism among your employees.

Problem Products

Symptoms	Altering Managements Perceptions and Attitudes: Diagnostic Steps	Alternative Strategies for Revitalizing Problem Products
Declining inventory or assigned retail shelf space given by distributors, retailers, or other middlemen Less interest in cooperative advertising by middlemen Loss of market share Turnover of product or brand managers for the good in question Lack of interest by salesmen in pushing the good Excessive number of product recalls High level of consumer complaints about the merchandise Financial indicators—such as profit or contribution margins, return on investment or assets, and direct costs—are decreasing for product. Consumer ill-will for the product is hurting sales of other products.	Recognition and awareness Close attention by management Commitment Patience Follow through Admit defeat if unable to turn it around and move on to other opportunities	Reposition the product by generating new applications, consumer uses or a new image. Increase the amount of promotion—could help to motivate middlemen, product manager, and other concerned parties. Change the media plan or even the advertising agency. Modify the packaging specifications and design. Develop short-run sales promotion tactics such as contests, coupons, to rejuvenate the product. Offer new compensation bonus for the sales force. Reduce price and see if marginal revenue exceeds the smaller profit margins or if competition decides to leave the market and avoid competing on lower prices. Market the unused by-product of the existing product (for example, a lumber mill started making

Problem Products

Symptoms	Altering Managements Perceptions and Attitudes: Diagnostic Steps	Alternative Strategies for Revitalizing Problem Products
		broom handles from their wooden pallets and crates).
		Offer new and better incentives for channel members.
		Find new lean and hungry channel members.
		Move into new or additional domestic or foreign markets.
		Explore feasibility of private branding strategy.
		Capitalize on any new social, cultural, or consumer lifestyle trends.

12

Enhancing Customer Service: Post Product Sales Are Not an Epitaph but a Beginning

A little bit of quality
Will always make 'em smile;
A little bit of courtesy
Will bring 'em in a mile;
A little bit of friendliness
Will tickle 'em 'tis plain—
And a little bit of service
Will bring 'em back again.
   —Source unknown

Important parts of the product function are the type and degree of service that accompany the products being sold. Product function has a broad connotation in this book, covering the selling of intangible items, ideas, professional services, social causes, and the like). Even when a sale has been consummated, marketers must make sure that follow-up is adequate and effective service strategies are provided for the consumer. A sale is not complete until the consumer is fully satisfied with the purchased product.

The customer service function is, therefore, a vital component for (1) helping to close deals, since many smart buyers consider the seller's postsale services, (2) preventing and minimizing consumer doubt or unhappiness, (3) creating a loyal consumer following and repeat business, and (4) possibly generating additional income from extra service ventures. In essence, consumers now view service as an integral part of the

total product. They want the performance of the product to meet their standards throughout the product's life span.

The service area will play an even more significant role for many industries in the future. Household/business consumers are becoming more demanding, and have higher expectations for product performance. Higher educational levels, maturing economies, more corporate accountability to consumers, and technical/sophisticated buyers have also been catalysts to the scrutiny of sellers' presale and postsale service capabilities.

▶ Service Personnel Must Be Carefully Chosen and Trained to Appreciate the Contributions They Can Make to the Organization's Marketing Strategy

Prospective buyers often want to see service personnel and executives before making a purchase. They sometimes recognize the importance of going beyond the sales force to explore in depth such service issues as

- Availability of service personnel
- Quality of repair and maintenance
- Inventory stocking by seller, especially of replacement parts
- Physical distribution
- Availability of technical assistance
- Recycling or disposal options for waste or by-products
- Safety and security
- Potential costs and risks with malfunctions
- Product liability
- Warranties
- Documentation and supportive product literature for buyer's technicians or other employees
- Performance of postsale service functions (does the seller subcontract this out to a third party?)

Salespeople often seek vital assistance from the customer service department. In many markets, service personnel—in addition to their regular responsibilities—are called on to make formal sales presentations by explaining how the service department can help the consumer fully utilize the product.

To take an example, a former client was starting to sell heavy-duty accessory equipment to foreign governments. One transaction entailed millions of dollars. As time progressed, the service manager was asked to make more and more presentations to prospective buyers. Soon he was traveling almost as much as the sales personnel and national account managers. Eventually, top management decided to formalize this additional responsibility by incorporating the service department and its executives into the marketing domain. The department now reports to the chief marketing executive. Many of my client's service personnel were eventually given formal training sessions to help them "think and act like marketers" and make contributions in the formulation of marketing plans. Their input became critical and successful in pinpointing sound marketing strategies.

Although having service people report to a marketing executive on the formal organization chart is not always necessary, making sure that the customer service staff has ample opportunities to participate in the entire marketing process is prudent. Sound service capabilities can be a competitive weapon in promotion campaigns. Whenever appropriate, service centers could be made into showrooms for customers.

▶ The Strengths and Weaknesses of the Customer Service Function Must Be Objectively Monitored and Measured

Marketers must develop the degree and type of services that are desirable in the marketplace. Quick delivery of a product may seem essential, but consumers may place more value on reliability, durability, accuracy, or higher quality.

Creating and monitoring service policies, objectives, and performance standards will enhance the service department. Admittedly, certain intangibles and service variables are difficult to quantify. But those areas that can be measured (such as cost/benefit ratio of adding more service technicians) should be.

The following are key criteria to be considered in an objective service function audit:

- Durability of product
- Reliability of product
- Length of downtime of product sold
- Service support level while product is in use

- Training of seller's service personnel and buyer's employees who are using the product
- Current and future service capabilities (is company keeping up with advanced service technology?)
- Response time to customer calls
- Service support for technicians and dealers
- Number of service outlets, their geographic distribution, and the quality of service representatives
- Level of inventory and number of spare parts for products
- Warranty terms
- Cost versus profit trade-offs between level of services offered and degree of customer satisfaction

Management must further decide if it should treat the service area as a cost or profit center. Corporate demands for profit accountability have opened up new opportunities. Originally, service areas were strictly cost centers. But today many retailers question the wisdom of continuing to offer certain services free of charge. Some are now charging add-on fees or service charges. Many manufacturers and dealers have learned that their service technicians have developed skills that are highly marketable to other channel members or in different industries.

Marketing executives must learn to unbundle the service components and evaluate each one. How does each service component contribute to profits, costs, sales, cash flow, goodwill, loyalty, dealer cooperation, and future growth?

▶ Service Personnel, Like Other Company Personnel, Should Be Rewarded with Schemes

In many firms good service representatives, like good sales people, are now being recognized with prizes, free trips, bonuses, points, and other rewards. Some are also getting commissions for helping to sell lucrative service contracts. Customer service can be used to create new business while still keeping current accounts satisfied, and can thus become a profit contributor instead of a necessary but costly evil. Staffing and training programs may be implemented to teach service personnel effective selling techniques while also updating them on technical aspects related to servicing different product lines. Service technicians

should be troubleshooters, knowing how to repair equipment and also how to handle angry customers.

▶ A Systematic Procedure Should Be Established that Encourages and Makes It Easy for Consumers to Contact Service Personnel

Sometimes salespeople believe they should have complete control over and access to their own accounts. However, an artificial barrier might then be created between the customers and service personnel. Salespeople should let customers know the names of the service representatives in case problems do occur with a product.

Operational and internal/external communication problems should be identified and solved. The flow of information, including consumer complaints should be examined and monitored. The pretransaction, transaction, and posttransaction stages should be evaluated to address potential service errors or determine preventive courses of action.

Good service managers will obtain information to judge how well the product is holding up through various conditions and applications, keeping an eye on previous and current levels of product performance. In addition, channel members must watch other members to ensure that service requirements are being met for the product in question. Lack of scrutiny among channel members is all too common a mistake in distributing customer services. It is too convenient to delegate this responsibility to other channel members and then assume that good service is being maintained.

This system will minimize the problems caused by waiting until a formal complaint is received or a customer becomes distraught. *Numerous dissatisfied customers will not protest to the company, they will simply take their business elsewhere.*

For example, many new car buyers find independent service stations when their warranty expires. Motown is acutely aware of this image problem with customer services, and dealers have made a concerted effort to improve their customer service departments.

As another illustration, some computer manufacturers were initially negligent about controlling the type of dealers who carried their computers and provided postsale services. Sometimes there was little postsale customer service available for the novice household consumers.

When Sears opened its Retail Business Systems Centers, it was cautious about expanding too quickly. It did not want to lose the reputation of giving good postsale service. It also wanted to maintain tight quality and service standards among other channel members as a supplier.

▶ Marketers Should Analyze the Total Value and Associated Risks of Issuing Warranties

More and more executives are starting to see that warranties can be a useful tool in attracting customers, increasing market share, providing a competitive advantage, or achieving differentiation in the marketplace.

Basically, a warranty is a guarantee that the merchandise has been represented accurately and that the seller will stand behind the products. The major types of warranties are

1. Implied warranty, which assumes that the seller guarantees certain conditions and normal operations of the product even though the conditions *may not be spelled out* in the warranty statements.
2. Expressed warranty, which guarantees that the seller will replace the product or refund the purchase price if any predetermined circumstances exist that are *specifically spelled out* in the warranty statements.
3. Promotional warranty, which implies that a product is outstanding by promoting its quality, performance, or life span.
4. Extended warranty, in which the time frame of the product guarantees may be prolonged by mutual agreement between the seller and buyer. Frequently the buyer either pays for this warranty or agrees to purchase the product if the seller includes an extended warranty arrangement.

In developing a warranty program marketers should be aware of the surrounding issues and challenges (see Figure 12.1). It should be noted that many consumers say that, compared with other variables (e.g., price, location, quality, and promotion), warranties are not critical to their purchase decision. Yet marketers are starting to see the light and fully appreciate the potential marketing contributions of warranties.

I believe that one of the best stimuli to public awareness and interest in warranties was the Chrysler five-year or 50,000-mile warranty. This policy did a lot to publicize the opportunities of warranties as a marketing tool. Many companies now offer money-back guarantees if a consumer has any problems. This strategy is extremely effective for penetration of new market segments (See Figure 12.1).

Interestingly, many buyers are willing to pay extra for extended warranties. This add-on service has made the warranty business a potential profit center. It has also required greater interaction between service

Figure 12.1. Challenges of developing a successful warranty program

Costs escalate for servicing the product.
Consumer demands for warranty rights increase.
Competition is aggressively marketing their own warranty programs.
Promotional warranties are a gray area that generates potential legal problems.
Products that become more complicated require an increasing number of parts, retrofits, application aids, and subssemblies; product break-downs are more likely.
Litigation and product liability concerns increase.
Changing state and federal government regulations must be watched.
Products require more precision, reliability, and durability in their functioning.
Some consumers abuse, misuse, or misunderstand the product's applications and take advantage of their rights with warranties.
Getting consumers to carefully read the warranty and properly use the product is difficult.
Fraudulent claims charge manufacturers for work not done by service contractors or repair outlets.
Consumer confusion exists over full and limited warranties, causing dissatisfaction.
Finding, training, and keeping qualified people to handle warranty coverage is difficult.
A good company MIS program is required to keep track of starting and ending dates for all the warranties for all products.
Out-of-court compromises must be made, just to avoid bad publicity on warranty claims.
Measuring the precise incremented advantages of individual warranty programs against the added expenditures is difficult.

people and marketing staff. They must not only sell the concept but make sure the organization does a good job in following through on the extended contract.

Do's and Don'ts for Improving the Warranty Function

Do's	Don'ts
Write the warranty contract in understandable language; buyers are turned off by legal jargon and mumbo jumbo.	Put misleading information in the written warranty; this causes consumer disappointments and/or legal action.
Set up adequate testing and product use in the field. If needed, hire independent labs and consultants to determine future potential product performance; the results can be incorporated into the warranty.	Forget to educate consumers carefully on the most effective applications of the product.
	Forget to update consumers on product-related information that might influence the warranty terms.

Do's and Don'ts for Improving the Warranty Function (*continued*)

Do's	Don'ts
Handle valid warranty claims expeditiously.	Ignore other channel members' responsibilities in upholding the firm's product guarantees.
Make it easy for consumers to contact the firm with warranty questions. Some effective means are toll-free numbers; 24-hour hotlines; adequate number of repair centers and outlets; warranty information printed on the product or in another accessible location; self-addressed stamped envelopes and various warranty-related forms that can be easily mailed; and trained personnel (especially phone operators, receptionists, internal sales staff, service technicians) who know how to handle warranty-related issues.	Attempt to write a warranty document without advice from individuals who have legal expertise in writing warranties.
Have sound internal controls and procedures for requests for warranty information.	
Encourage cross-fertilization between engineering, manufacturing, service staff, and marketing personnel when planning and formulating warranty policies and procedures.	
Compare the warranty to warranties of the competition and try to develop and emphasize a unique, profitable warranty strategy.	
Clearly explain the limits and disclaimers present in the warranty. At a minimum, the wording must include who the warrantor is; who is eligible to receive the guarantee; buyer transferability rights; expiration date or amount of use; specific coverage, terms, and exclusions; and the method for effecting buyer recourse in case of a faulty product.	

Do's and Don'ts for Improving the Warranty Function

Do's	Don'ts
Design the warranty card or form to provide useful information about buyers who use the product. (With a little work and study in questionnaire design, marketers can develop warranty forms that give them good information about consumers).	

A good warranty can increase business while a warranty with vague terms or deceptive wording can cause severe legal and ethical trouble. Consumers have learned to speak out; they want what they have been promised. Dissatisfied consumers can boycott a firm's products or prompt government intervention. Consumers may even demand immediate criminal action against the firm's executives.

▶ To Prevent or Overcome Negative Consumer Reactions, Marketers Must Understand the Macro and Micro Conditions that Breed Consumer Discontent

Recognition of such conditions enables executives to better predict potential consumer unrest and to develop marketing strategy that effectively deals with it.

At the macro level, consumer rancor is often precipitated by a decline in purchasing power and/or when dislocations occur in society. When traditional values—for instance, moral political leadership, religion, ethical behavior, opportunity for education, harmonious family life—are in a state of flux and upheaval, business stakeholders start asking in-depth questions about the role and scope of corporate leadership. How well are executives addressing these basic issues and societal concerns? Furthermore, when consumer buying power, household discretionary income, or industrial purchasing budget declines, consumers begin demanding more and are more vocal about higher product performance and better business behavior. Given their own household/business budgeting problems, consumers scrutinize products more closely and follow up vigorously on purchases that do not meet their expectations.

At the micro level, management is confronted with a multitude of factors that can insidiously induce consumer distrust or discontentment. Potential causes of consumer anger follow:

1. Retailers become bigger, less attentive, and more geared toward mass merchandising (while small retailers fail) and consumers feel that no one is really listening.

2. The marketplace is too complicated and confusing for purchasers, especially in high-tech industries or rapid growth sectors.

3. The technical improvement of product specifications and postsale customer services make it difficult to compare quality, price, product applications, reliability, and so on. Buyers thus have a hard time differentiating among products, and their buying decisions are not always appropriate.

4. Sellers are either in high growth or declining industries, which means either inadequate service levels or a decline in the number of service outlets.

5. Buyers lack experience and know-how in using and maintaining the products. Many consumers are neophytes when using new products or services, and they feel it is the seller's responsibility to teach them.

6. Sales personnel are poorly trained or managed. Salespeople must be able to identify and solve consumers' problems. Incompetent, abrasive, or obtrusive salespeople can have a disastrous effect on consumer relations.

7. Buyers' expectations are unrealistic. The press often excites prospective consumers with product hype. For example, a number of promises and speculations were made about the minicomputer/microcomputer industry. As a result, consumers' expectations were unrealistic and the actual computers did not fulfill them. Technological advancements are exciting, but prospective buyers need practical information and product specifications that are compatible with their specific needs and problems. The fanciest of marketing strategies will fail if this principle is ignored.

In short, the trend of the consumer movement is partly a function of the political, legal, and economic environment. When people are unemployed or worry about their security or basic needs, they may not be as vocal about such popular consumer issues as pollution, ecology, and the like. Executives, however, must think strategically even though such issues are dormant. Too often, managers forget about the challenges presented by increasing consumer awareness.

▶ Marketers Must Take a Proactive Rather than Reactive Approach to Consumer Protest Movements

In the past, many marketers perceived consumer protests as odious threats instead of opportunities for overcoming marketing deficiencies. Now, however, instead of waiting for problems to arise, many companies have learned to develop plans and programs that give consumers positive feelings and impressions. This strategy is designed to prevent consumer complaints before they arise. Good marketers do not want to discourage or limit opportunities for buyers to voice their dissatisfaction: They want to know about major objections or disorders. Without feedback, particularly negative, they cannot take action.

The following are proactive and positive suggestions for overcoming consumer dismay while providing more services to the many "publics" in society.

1. *More gathering of marketing intelligence as it relates to consumer-related concerns.* Everyone, especially service and marketing staff, must develop a keen sense for anticipating and avoiding consumer problems. For instance, marketers at Northwestern Mutual Life Insurance Company conducted nationwide surveys of their policyholders. One disappointing conclusion was that consumers had difficulty understanding the policyowners' insurance notices. In fact, the notices ranked next to last in understandability when compared with other types of forms—barely above the Internal Revenue Service's tax forms. On the basis of the research results, Northwestern redesigned all the routine notices. In follow-up studies, policyholders stated that the notices were easier to understand. Subsequently, many consumer letters even complimented the improved notices. This work took a couple of years and a great deal of research, fine tuning, testing, and retesting. Management, as of this writing, feels the company did a nice job of solving common consumer complaints within the industry.

2. *A systematic educational program for consumers and other general publics.* Sound educational programs can eliminate misunderstandings and misconceptions. Marketing executives should be at the forefront in providing a systematic educational program to the many "publics" and consumers in the marketplace. Parts of the program could come from sales personnel, media advertising, brochures, dealer workshops, sales promotion literature, public relations news releases, and product catalogs. Other less popular but very effective avenues are:

- Newsletters
- Consumer hotlines
- Training programs for sales personnel, repair staff, and service representatives, to enhance customer service
- Classification and expansion of instructional booklets
- Telecommunications with buyers on postsale product services

Above all, the information should be presented in the customer's language, not in the seller's technical vernacular.

To avoid unrealistic expectations or false hopes by consumers, marketers must carefully inform the media. In high-tech industries especially, it is prudent to distinguish between fact and fancy on product performance and its impact on societal lifestyles. Trade associations, chief executives, national or local chambers of commerce, business reporters, editors, writers, and educators could serve as focal points in the dissemination of pertinent and useful information.

In a mature product line or industry, goodwill or advocacy advertising is sometimes necessary to undo the effects of adverse publicity.

3. *Salespersonnel trained to be problem solvers and consultants in the purest form.* Weak order takers, unqualified manufacturer representatives, and unprofessional salespeople who make idle or deceptive promises should be purged from the payroll. A good sales force is vital to improving service performance and creating consumer goodwill.

4. *A proactive role with associations and government agencies.* Such a role aids the reputation and corporate citizenship of the business. For example, the firm may be a leader in formulating and adhering to a code of ethics. As the industry matures or as changes occur in the marketplace, however, the code has to be revised and updated to protect both the vendor and consumers. Self-regulation should be encouraged. This may require that unethical firms be ostracized by their peers. Cooperation and exchange of ideas or information with governmental agencies are also needed. In the long run, a firm must balance the profit motive with the needs of society.

5. *A company ombudsman within the organization.* Some organizations may have a position with a title such as Vice President of Consumer Affairs, Director of Customer Relations, or Manager of Environmental Relations. Whatever the title, the firm needs the position of consumer advocate and watchdog. The person with the title represents consumers' interests within the seller's organization. The

individual can often make meaningful suggestions in formulating policies about consumer issues. In a small business, a top executive or marketing person may have to assume this additional challenge.

6. *Channel members who recognize the significance of cooperating with and coordinating consumer and business demands and needs.* The marketer may have to eliminate businesses in the channel that are not sensitive to consumer service needs and concerns. In many organizations, this decision is made by a wholesaler, service manager, distributor, or purchasing manager who constantly deals with channel members.

7. *Proper management philosophy and organizational climate.* This atmosphere dictates how vigorously managers pursue the goal of addressing consumer issues. Progressive companies are very sensitive and interested in overcoming problems or mistakes that lead to bad publicity and poor consumer relations.

In conclusion, marketers cannot afford an apathetic strategy of ignoring, denying, or combating consumer charges. Businesses that appreciate, understand, and respond to consumer issues are the ones that will survive and prosper.

13

Developing Sound Pricing Strategies: Dollars and Sense

Everyone and everything in this world has a price. This is a trite statement. Besides sounding crass and materialistic, it ignores the challenges involved in establishing a reasonable price for the goods, services, ideas, and other entities that have a value in society. A price is established when both consumers and marketers agree on the consumer benefits versus costs (including profit or other organizational gains) that occur in a transaction. Agreement becomes even more complex when other variables are considered, such as competition and the ways government can influence consumers'/sellers' perceptions of the nonmonetary value of the transaction.

Marketers should be responsible and accountable for the task of developing sound pricing strategies. A marketing executive who cannot make a clear distinction between price and consumers' perceptions of value and benefits of the goods is doomed to failure.

The formulation of pricing policies and strategies has indeed captured the attention of top executives. Previously, pricing decisions were considered a mundane clerical function. A new junior executive (often a lower level accountant) or clerk would mechanically figure the costs and required profit markup for various offerings. This pricing strategy was simple and quick. Even though it was easy when compared with the modern-day aproach, it was done infrequently and was subject to little scrutiny. Too often, prices once set were seldom revised. Current economic, competitive, and consumer challenges have drastically altered this traditional and straightforward approach to pricing decisions.

In fact, many companies believe that pricing may now be the most important factor in marketing strategy. Top managers have taken a keen interest in the pricing function. They may even "meddle" in the marketer's turf and give "friendly advice" on pricing decisions. Furthermore, prices are being reviewed and modified more frequently, since the environment is far more changeable. A stagnant pricing program with few revisions could be a severe marketing blunder.

▶ Marketers Must Learn to Identify and Avoid the Common Mistakes that Prevail in Pricing Decisions

Let the marketer be constantly aware of the following common pricing gaffes:

1. *Basing pricing decisions only on the costs of doing business.* Other influencing factors are ignored, such as competition, the law, the changing culture, and consumers' own attitudes about prices.

2. *Increasing price because of a sudden supply shortage and excessive demand.* Buyers soon feel that they are being gouged and temporarily exploited with this weak position, and they don't forget this shortsighted seller.

3. *Keeping prices constant even when conditions have changed in the marketplace.* The end result is too high or too low a price.

4. *Determining pricing policies and procedures in a vacuum, thus ignoring their impact on the marketplace.* Pricing strategies must coincide with the desired objectives that are sought from the planned marketing strategies. A low price, for example, may damage a company's image as the seller of quality merchandise.

5. *Ignoring communication channels between marketing, finance, and accounting personnel.* Pricing-related decisions dictate interdepartmental interaction and cooperation on a steady basis.

6. *Failing to define authority and responsibility for pricing decisions.* The accountability for pricing actions and associated rewards or reprimands must be pinpointed.

7. *Ignoring the premise that pricing is an art but still requires a systematic, objective approach.* To survive, marketers must try several pricing alternatives under different conditions and then carefully monitor their results within a dynamic environment.

▶ A Successful Pricing Strategy Is Highly Dependent on Tapping Key and Well-Developed Sources of Pricing Information

This became apparent to many executives when deregulation occurred within their industries. The trucking, airline, and banking industries are prime examples of markets that required detailed pricing-related data. Many marketers in airline and trucking firms were unable to evaluate, anticipate, or react to competitive costs and pricing strategies on individual routes. In a few cases they were even unsure of the specifics (weak MIS) that could influence pricing decisions. The same situation occurred in some banks. Bankers lacked particular cost and profit information on individual transactions, product lines, types of accounts, branches, and the like. Their problems surfaced rapidly when they had to compete with low-cost nonbanks that had already garnered highly sophisticated pricing-related information and expertise from their other industries. As the president of a medium-sized bank once told me, "The banking industry is in the horse-and-buggy stage of cost accounting." This situation has changed for the better with the new competitive banking environment. Marketers from the once-regulatory environment must now learn to identify and skillfully utilize pricing information sources.

Deregulation or not, pricing research should become a habit, a natural way of doing business. Components of the research process are study and analysis of financial/cost accounting data, use of public plus proprietary secondary data, and primary data collection techniques relevant to pricing research. Primary research could include experiments, test marketing, focus group interviews, and surveys on consumer pricing perceptions and expectations. Pricing research studies enable the marketer to be more on target with establishing and correlating prices with overall organizational objectives. Previously, pricing studies and scientific anlaysis for pricing decisions took a secondary role within the corporate community. Today, economic and competitive conditions have elevated pricing research to a higher status. Top managers now frequently demand it.

▶ Intracompany Coordination Is a Must Among Marketing, Accounting, Finance, Production, Engineering, Physical Distribution, and Marketing Research People

Marketing people need pertinent information and feedback from other departments. For better pricing decisions, further declassification may

Figure 13.1. *Symptoms of problems with pricing structure*

Rigid target pricing that guarantees certain profits but appears to be out of line with industry norms.

Excessive number of complaints, from both customers and salespeople, about prices higher than those of competition.

Above-average inventory writeoffs because merchandise is not moving.

Constant brand switching of consumers to other companies' products.

Failure of the company to win a fair share of bidding contracts.

Constant feeling of having lost in the negotiating of final prices.

Inability to pinpoint costs and profit contributions for individual products or business units.

Constant price cuts and price wars.

Repeated *reaction* to price moves of the competition.

Competition on price alone.

High number of markdowns.

Consumer confusion over actual quoted prices.

Too many pricing points that alienate or confuse buyers.

Lack of customer loyalty; constant badgering by customers for the lowest prices.

Failure to do a management audit within a reasonable time period.

---

be needed: complex cost data, profit-related issues and measurements, credit and collection procedures, cash flow analysis, logistical support, and so on. All these variables have a direct impact on final prices. The marketer doesn't always have control over, or direct access to, these types of data. Therefore, effective coordination and communication with these other departments are needed to effectuate pricing decisions. (MIS will be the "bridge" over these sometimes troubled, but opportunistic, waters.)

As more firms progress into a full marketing era perspective (or become more market based as opposed to having a mere cost-plus reference), their marketing people will have greater say in pricing decisions. There is already a solid trend for top management to expect marketing people to assume greater leadership in the pricing function.

During the gathering of pertinent price-related information and interaction with other executives, a few situations symptomatic of a real pricing problem may come to light. Figure 13.1 identifies some of these. If any of these situations seem to exist in an organization, a systematic audit and analysis of the pricing function may be needed. Immediate action may also be necessary, since it is difficult to get back customers or gain market share lost due to higher competitive prices.

▶ To Determine Prices for Individual Products, Certain Steps Must Be Followed

First, a number of questions have to be asked:

1. Who is the market target?
2. How sensitive is the target to prices?
3. Who is the competition? How financially strong are they?
4. What are the relevant costs of marketing and producing this product? What are the potential breakeven points and return on investment or profit margins? What are competitors' financial variables and goals that could influence prices?
5. Are there any legal, political, or other government constraints in price setting?
6. What impact does the prevailing economic cycle (such as inflation or deflation) have on setting price?
7. What role does price play in consumer behavior?
8. How important is price in the marketing strategy of the product?
9. How often are review and modification of pricing strategies needed?
10. Does the company follow through with pricing studies to see if it has developed effective pricing strategies?

The following steps should be followed in setting individual prices:

Step 1. Identify the organization's long- and short-range financial and qualitative objectives. The strategic objectives will help give guidance to the specific pricing objectives that must be formulated. In general terms, an organization may be concerned with such matters as achieving a specific return on investment, increasing earnings per share, growth, survival, and maintaining status quo or good corporate citizenship in the community. Pricing decisions serve as a tool for accomplishing the strategic and tactical objectives of top management. Everyone in the company must be made to understand the overall corporate mission/goals and how the pricing function relates to attaining strategic expectations. This function can have immediate impact on sales revenue. As noted, this impact is one reason why chief executives have become much more interested in pricing strategy.

Step 2. Spell out realistic marketing objectives. The typical marketing objectives may be stated in such terms and figures as sales volume, market share profit margins, return on investment or return on assets, new accounts or products, and image preferences.

Step 3. Determine which groups of consumers are viable market targets. This ongoing systematic process—including market research and analysis—helps to crystallize the most effective prices for products.

Step 4. Formulate and evaluate pricing objectives. The objectives may deal with costs, competition, consumer demand, and image categories. These categories are interdependent and interrelated with the marketing objectives and the specific pricing tools that must be selected. A few examples of pricing objectives may illustrate:

- Offer new trade discounts 5 percent on current prices in order to penetrate distributors.
- Retain current customers by matching any competitive price changes.
- Aggressively comply with all government regulations that pertain to pricing practices; to be safe, have legal counsel review pricing practices.
- Attract an affluent market by upgrading product quality while instituting a 40 percent price increase.
- Increase purchase size and frequency among current and future customers with a new 10 percent quantity discount.
- Build traffic volume by offering five weekly loss leaders in the store.
- Discourage new competition by slightly lowering the average profit margin by 15 percent.
- Explore new transportation alternatives to lower costs by 2 percent.
- Increase inventory turnover to decrease carrying costs by 1 percent.
- Study ways to decrease raw material costs and pass on all savings to customers.
- Explore more subcontracting opportunities to achieve better pricing efficiency in the government bidding process.
- Offer a new 3 year leasing program for high-tech accounts for the purpose of penetrating the robotic market.

These pricing objectives show the relationship between pricing tools and the areas of competition, cost behavior, profit expectations, consumer behavior, channel members, government and legal constraints, and other marketing variables. All of them are interdependent and will affect the pricing objectives and practices that are finally adopted.

Step 5. Analyze, forecast, and monitor the numerous variables that influence pricing decisions. A team of managers can evaluate the strengths and weaknesses of the company's pricing practices. With the help of in-house marketing researchers and/or other sources of pricing-related information, the team can integrate pricing decisions with the other components of both marketing and business strategies. The fact-finding team must try to estimate a number of variables—such as cost and competition—that will affect future prices. With these various forecasts, personnel in pricing must follow through and study the successes and failures of the price structures that were formulated. The criteria for the report card will be tied into the measurable objectives developed in steps 1 and 2. Of course, with the dynamic environment the review process must be timely and expeditious; otherwise the pricing strategy will become obsolete.

Step 6. Implement and sell the pricing decisions to internal and external groups. There must be conviction and commitment among personnel, for example, salespeople and brand managers, that the price structure is sound and effective. It will then be easier for them to convince consumers and justify prices in the marketplace. This step should also encourage ongoing feedback from various parties. It will serve as significant input in beginning the entire pricing process all over again.

▶ Pricing Strategy Must Take into Account the Expectations and Preferences of Other Channel Members

Although all channel participants try to maximize their own situation and negotiate the best deal, all must appreciate the impact of pricing decisions on the entire channel. Airline executives learned that with deregulation travel agents were becoming quite powerful, because passengers needed help in obtaining information on the best fares and routes. To their dismay, airline managers found that pricing decisions—including commissions for travel agents—had to reflect some of the desires of the agents. The airlines could not offend the agents, because

they were rapidly selling more and more of the air passenger business. In fact, for many airlines well over half of their passenger business was being booked through travel agencies.

There are cases when a company has to leave a channel because the pricing practices in it are inconsistent with the firm's strategies, because business attitudes have changed and the company must look for new avenues in which to market the product.

The basic premise is that companies must make sure that other channel members are in agreement with their pricing philosophy and approach, so that they can develop a cohesive channel pricing strategy.

Admittedly, in numerous cases products are distributed in a number of ways, especially in the aftermarkets. Marketers could then lose track of how prices are set. A price may even contradict the way the company wants to position the product in the marketplace. Despite these exceptions, marketers must still be influenced by how all channel members might react to a pricing decision. Hence, such decisions should partly anticipate how the members might respond. The best methods to determine this response are surveys, the sales force, and trade associations that serve a particular group of channel members or industries.

▶ Pricing Strategy Must Take into Account Probable Cash Flow Problems

Many cyclical industries and small businesses experience episodes of feast and famine. The upside with its potential for high prices is enviable, but the downside with its excessive capacities and supplies can be a humbling experience.

In a recession, we often hear the cliche, "Cash is king." Sometimes a pricing strategy must follow this basic rule. Many commodity marketers or small-business owners are saddled with huge fixed costs and thus conclude that it is too burdensome and costly to completely shut down operations (e.g., mines) or even temporarily slow down operations. Instead, prices are drastically lowered merely to enhance cash flow and maintain operations.

▶ Careful Breakdown and Examination of Cost Data Are Parts of the Pricing Process

Costs are only one factor to consider in determining prices. Nevertheless, by keeping costs lower than those of the competition and being

aware of the costs of doing business in different segments of the organization, management is more likely to make intelligent discretionary pricing decisions. Profit margins can be more flexible, loss leaders more frequent, and perseverance against the competition more prolonged. Chapter 6 has already discussed costs at length, so the subject is not belabored here. Perhaps the following statement is the best way to conclude: *Beware* of the little expenses, for even a minute leak in the dam will soon cause a major break and create a catastrophic flood. Poor planning and controls on costs have indeed flooded many executives with pricing problems.

▶ Unplanned Markdowns Are Sometimes Necessary to Correct Poor Buying Decisions or a Bad Inventory Mix

In many industries the practice of marking down is a way of life. But some marketers are reluctant or stubborn to admit mistakes. Everyone in business, at one time or another, has been overly optimistic or misjudged the marketplace. The first inclination (and the natural tendency) is to try to recoup the loss. In many cases this compounds the problem with additional frustrations and expenses. These may include higher inventory carrying costs, obsolete merchandise, damaged goods, employee theft and pilferage, or higher opportunity costs.

In my own observations, the most successful retailers and wholesalers are often those that are not afraid to take markdowns and turn over goods that are not moving. One president of a large automotive dealership dramatized the point: "I still must turn over the wheat and corn even if they are bad. How else would I be able to work the soil and plant new crops?" Markdowns can separate the chaff from the wheat.

▶ Numerous Markdowns, Price Deals, Rebates, Bonus Offers, and Discounts May Confuse or Alienate Consumers

A company must be wary of excessive price promotions, which could make consumers overly price conscious. If a company does not want to be associated with low prices or is attempting to compete on other variables, such as service or product quality, numerous price deals could backfire. Some buyers may resent patronizing a place where only price is promoted. Others might constantly postpone purchases because the price keeps coming down. Hence the number, timing, and amount of price cuts must be coordinated with the other parts of the marketing strategy.

In fact, many pricing theorists would argue that excessive need for markdowns may dictate new strategy. The seller must learn how to develop a new competitive advantage. The firm may have to create uniqueness to survive and prosper: a certain market, location, product, service, technology, or efficiency in serving consumers.

▶ A Change in Base Price May Force a Modification in a Product or Service or in the Quantity Offered

In many markets and industries, consumer buying habits and tradition can prompt product rather than price adjustments. For instance, vending machines require a round-number or an even amount of money. Since raising the price of an inexpensive vending machine item 50 to 100 percent would alienate consumers, the marketer needs to alter the quantity sold. Even products sold over the counter, like coughdrops, candy, and gum, may dictate an even or round-number price to avoid customer resentment over having to wait for change or uneasiness with a nontraditional odd-number price.

In short, when a company considers making a price change, it should investigate whether its engineers, product managers, or production people can "work backward" and fit the product's physical properties or quantity to a base price.

▶ Marketers Must Learn to Determine How Sensitive the Marketplace is to a Price Increase or Decrease

In academic terms, what is the price elasticity of demand for a product? Through secondary research, price experimentation, computer simulation models that measure price-related variables versus quantities sold, regression analysis, test marketing, and surveys, it is feasible to get a feeling for how consumers might react to future price changes. Marketers must know the relationship between price and sales because its effect on the bottom line is so dramatic. From past experiences, marketers do know that price elasticity is influenced by such factors as:

- Market targets
- Type of product and level of consumer-perceived quality
- Available product substitutes
- Competition's reaction

- Level of consumer confidence in the economy
- Availability of credit and financing charges
- Warranty policies
- Degree of consumer urgency for the product

When I served as a consultant to a mass transit system, the directors had one nagging question for me: Should they raise prices to offset their losses, or should they lower prices in hopes of getting more bus riders? Since my experience in this industry was limited at the time, I took three different approaches in trying to answer this question: (1) secondary data research on the industry, (2) statistical analysis of historical price changes and previous sales patterns of this firm, and (3) pilot survey studies with bus drivers and current/noncurrent riders. I concluded that price elasticity would work in only one direction. Lowering fares would not necessarily increase the number of riders and would actually hurt total revenues. Alternatively, an increase in fares would cause some riders to look for other means of transportation, and the additional revenue from the more captive market would not offset the loss of those riders. Due to political pressures, potential bad press, and the urgent need to get more of the general public to use the buses, the directors decided *not* to raise fares, since the local community was subsidizing the transit system. They did, however, convince a number of different groups that it would not be prudent to lower the fares; the city would then have to support mass transit even more heavily.

Textbooks do not always emphasize the important point that elasticity of demand may work in one direction with a price increase or decline, but not in the other direction.

▶ Marketers Must Communicate the Reasons and Logic for a Price Change

There often is a valid and logical reason for raising prices. Marketers must first convince their sales force of this necessity, since salespeople are on the firing line with customers. If salespeople are unsure or unhappy about the increase, prospective consumers will be even more so. An expedient approach might be to just tell consumers that the increased price is the result of increased costs, but they may respond with, "that's your problem, not ours." They may be disgruntled, especially if the competition does not follow suit or if they are concerned with an economic problem at the time, such as high inflation. Conse-

quently, a decision to raise prices may require more thoughtful action in justifying and convincing the marketplace of the merits and logic of the decision. For instance, a marketer might modify other marketing strategies, such as a more convenient location, additional services, or increased customer service, or might change the packaging of the product, which would justify a higher price in the minds of potential buyers.

▶ Is There a Positive Correlation Between Higher Prices and Consumer Perceptions of Better Quality?

Does the market target equate a higher price with better quality? Sometimes a group of consumers will assume that higher prices automatically indicate greater product value. Pricing strategy must therefore reflect consumers' own psychological perceptions of product quality and price. Ego-sensitive merchandise (e.g., certain brand-name clothes, prestigious product lines (e.g., exclusive country club membership), and exclusive brands or model classifications (such as Mercedes-Benz, Rolls-Royce, and BMW cars) often enable marketers to set premium prices.

Marketers seek premium markets because the profit margins are quite attractive. Sometimes they even reposition the company or product line by modifying other parts of the marketing program to go after the premium end. Whatever an organization's preferences, it must know how current and potential consumers define quality in terms of actual prices and how this definition fits into the strategic objectives of the firm. Lowering prices may not always be necessary to increase the bottom line.

▶ Selective Pricing Strategy Is Sometimes Desirable to Enhance Accountability and Controls

A firm often finds it must start charging for what were previously free services. In some cases it can allow one group of customers to support other market segments: The more profitable accounts pay extra to help the firm provide services to marginal accounts. However, if the marginal accounts do not grow and become more lucrative, the firm may eventually have to charge them also for services so as not to lose the more profitable customers. "Garbage" accounts may force an unbundling of free services in order to reflect the cost of doing business with them.

Selective pricing enables some retailers to more accurately reflect the costs versus benefits of doing business with each retail market. Airlines and hotels, for example, have learned to make a distinction between business and pleasure travelers. The business community may not be as price sensitive toward paying for extra services. At the same time, however, these travelers may have very high expectations for the quality of the services.

▶ Loss Leaders Should Reinforce a Company's Desired Image and Lead to Sales of Other Products

Loss leaders—services or products sold below cost—are a popular tool among marketing executives. Many banks offer discount brokerage service to affluent customers, even though such service may be unprofitable or take time away from more lucrative banking services. These banks want to serve as many of the customers' financial needs as possible; they are afraid of losing customers to securities brokers, thrifts, insurance firms, and mass retailers who now offer more traditional financial banking services. Other banks believe that this loss-leader strategy will hurt their credibility due to the volatility of the stock market, and that this new service will not necessarily bring in additional business. Some managers of discount stores and supermarkets sometimes wonder if loss leaders don't merely attract customers who only buy the products that are priced below cost. If so, this marketing technique is an expensive proposition. Obviously, then, loss leaders must be constantly monitored to see if they really do increase sales of other profitable products. Some retailers even follow loss-leader customers around the store to see if they buy other products, especially impulse items.

In conclusion, when a company is having financial difficulties, loss leaders can be quite effective for turning over inventory or improving cash flow problems.

▶ Marketers Must Carefully Analyze All Pricing Allowances, Trade Allowances, and Special Deals to Channel Members

These short-term pricing promotions should coincide with a firm's long-term goals. In many industries, price discounts to middlemen have become common practice. They are used to:

- Obtain or maintain shelf space
- Push new products

- Defend the business from competitive onslaughts
- Generate channel and consumer loyalty
- Provide initial sales increases—a shot in the arm approach
- Penetrate new markets
- Increase the level of consumption among current consumers

Although promotional pricing allowances are a multibillion-dollar practice, marketers must ascertain the true value of this approach to their own situation. They can hope that part of the discounts are passed on to final consumers and that the discounts do not just increase profit margins for wholesalers or retailers. They can also hope that final consumers and middlemen do not stockpile their inventory at the time of the pricing discounts. This can cannibalize future sales of the product.

If a company maintains a steady diet of price allowances, channel members and consumers will take these discounts for granted and frown when the company decides to lessen the frequency of price cuts. Also, a price allowance policy may make a strong consumer following harder to develop in the long run; buyers become more loyal to prices than to particular brands.

Once companies within an industry start trade-pricing promotions, however, stopping them is difficult. The competitors are afraid of each other and therefore perpetuate this practice even though they dislike it. In fact, the marketplace—including channel members—quickly learns to aggressively seek or demand discounts. Consequently, marketers must learn when and how frequently to offer discounts that are the most profitable in the long run.

▶ Marketers Must Know the Conditions and Factors that Dictate Either a Penetration or Skimming Pricing Strategy

One of the most common pricing issues is whether the company should set a low (penetration) or high ("skim the cream") price. This question is particularly relevant for new products or markets. Figure 13.2 highlights the conditions when skimming or penetration strategy is most appropriate.

In most situations, a decision on a low pricing strategy coincides with aggressive growth objectives or is used to fend off competition. A firm that decides to adopt penetration pricing must be careful to pinpoint sales estimates, break-even options at different levels, and cost breakdowns and to calculate profit and return on investment projec-

Figure 13.2. *When to use skimming or penetration pricing strategy*

Skimming		Penetration
Large number of buyers; inelastic demand Unique product Consumers unable to compare value Economies of scale not possible Product under patent protection Advanced technology niche High development costs for competition Elite/prestige market target that equates high price with high quality	OR	Large market share desired as soon as possible Product very price sensitive Economies of scale feasible Need to improve cash flow Immediate and wide exposure desired Desire to discourage competition (low margin markets) Product easily copied

tions. Inadequate analysis of these areas may weaken its marketplace position while merely strengthening competitors who have been more exacting in analysis. A simple rule is: Don't get into a price war if you (1) lack the competitive financial strength or financial wherewithal to "get out" or (2) have few advantages with the cost side of doing business. Of course, sometimes those who penetrate first—everything else being equal—capture the lion's share of the market due to market inertia among consumers. Consumers sometimes become used to patronizing a particular business or buying a specific brand. Some may argue, however, that consumer loyalty to the marketer who was first in with the lowest price has become less common in industries involving a highly competitive environment.

As noted in Figure 13.2, a skimming policy is feasible when there is a high degree of differentiation in marketing strategy. Positive differences from the competition often permit higher prices. Also, higher pricing strategies are possible by going after smaller markets or market segments that have been untapped. The company that decides on higher prices must make sure it has a niche that justifies these prices in the eyes of consumers. It is feasible to charge more when product identification is strong or the company has a solid reputation in the marketplace.

A good example is the strategy adopted by AT&T after deregulation. To offset lower long-distance rates by the competition, AT&T decided to emphasize its own quality and excellent service with long-distance calls. Time will tell if this upbeat strategy works in the new competitive long-distance phone market.

If a skimming pricing strategy is selected, the company may eventually have to lower its prices. The need for lower prices may be dictated

by new technology, increased competition, more private brands, a patent or license expiration, market saturation, or a product life-cycle change from growth to maturity. A shrewd marketer will recognize the need to make necessary, quick adjustments. A common if understandable mistake is to stubbornly insist on higher profit margins and to maintain high prices even when the business climate has drastically changed.

In summary, a company must first identify the conditions that help it decide when to skim or penetrate with pricing strategy. After making the decision, it must carefully and constantly review the situation to see if pricing must be adjusted to reflect a changing environment.

▶ With Many High-Priced Items or Industrial Capital Goods, the Marketer May Have to Price According to the Economic Orientation of Consumers

Sellers sometimes need to determine price by analyzing customer's rate of return for utilizing a product. How will the customer save and make a profit by purchasing this item? What is the customer's cost of capital? What might be the financial payback time for consuming the product? How favorable is the ROI for the buyer? What are the buyer's direct and indirect costs? When setting prices for many items, the seller needs to determine the buyer's economic benefits and project these to its quoted prices. Many salespeople, account representatives, and other marketers have to interact with the industrial/commercial customer's own finance, accounting, engineering, and purchasing executives. Various interested prospective customers, including household consumers of high-ticket items, will want to evaluate the economic value of a specific purchase at a proposed price. In developing pricing strategies, a good marketer must make fairly good financial projections of the economic impact that might occur for customers. Bleak economic projections for prospective customers may indicate that the prices are too high for the market in question.

▶ If Competitive Bidding Is a Pricing Option, the Firm Must Learn the Art

Estimating a price for a job is frequently a tedious, costly, and time-consuming process. The company has to anticipate what the competition might submit. Marketers who are novices in the competitive bidding process quickly become frustrated because they either fail to

obtain enough contracts or end up losing money on their accepted bid. The following do's and don'ts give food for thought in evaluating approaches to this tricky area.

Do's and Don'ts in the Bidding Process

Do's	Don'ts
Allow adequate time in planning and preparing the specifics of the bidding function.	Allow any group or department to dominate the preparation of the bidding proposal. A good proposal should integrate realistic technical, marketing, financial, and cost data. If the proposal is biased toward one corporate function, the bid may fail (see the subsequent section on why many firms fail to get government contracts) or management may become disillusioned with the business contracts actually won.
Develop a set of criteria and standard questions that help in the bid/no-bid decision process; sometimes the wisest choice is to forgo bidding. Questions include:	
Do we have the necessary expertise, experience, and financial capabilities to submit a bid?	
At what level of capacity are we currently operating? Do we need this business to take up some operating slack?	
Can we meet the quantity and delivery requirements that might be required?	Forget the prospective customer's problems, needs, requirements, and expectations. Both technical and economic wishes must be recognized.
Consider making up a standardized policy and procedure manual to facilitate the bidding function (which could include the criteria and questions just noted)	Ignore your company's strategic objectives and capabilities; this exercise will give direction on the type of business to consider, and how large a commitment should be made in seeking bidding business, including government-related contracts.
Consider a formal audit and control procedure that examines previous successes and failures; the historical data will enlighten the bidding team and enhance future bidding proposals.	Raise management's hopes on winning a bidding contract, no matter how good the chances may appear; last-minute "politics" or long-term in-house team debates by the buyer may upset earlier optimistic statements.
Make someone—project director or department head—responsible for the bidding function.	
Consider these pertinent questions when preparing a bidding proposal:	
What are the realistic costs of fulfilling our obligations?	

Do's and Don'ts in the Bidding Process (*continued*)

Do's	Don'ts
Should we include price escalator clauses? Will the prospective buyer accept these clauses?	
Who will our competition be and what might be their costs and estimated pricing bids?	
Is there a good chance for follow-up bid opportunities or repeat business? Will a low first-round contractual winning bid give us preferential treatment on future bidding business from the buyer?	
What are our estimated chances of succeeding with the bid proposal?	
What impact will this business have on other markets and product offerings?	
Are the forecasted profits from the bid proposal realistic and favorable?	

These do's and don'ts may reinforce worries about the complexities of initiating competitive bidding proposals. Some firms do decide that the amount of work and effort is not worth the payback. This belief is quite prevalent when it comes to government buying. The Department of the Navy has published an excellent pamphlet entitled *Guidelines for Preparing More Effective Technical Proposals for the Navy Department*. This pamphlet highlights many reasons why the Navy Department rejects various bidding proposals. The reasons and comments are quite generic and appropriate for bidding firms going after both private and government business. They are outlined in Figure 13.3.

▶ Pricing Through the Negotiation Process Often Requires a Special Person and Tremendous Support from the Many Departments of the Selling Organization

In many business situations a seller and buyer must spend a great deal of time bargaining for a fair price. Negotiation can cover a wide spec-

DEVELOPING SOUND PRICING STRATEGIES

Figure 13.3. Common reasons for bid rejection

Oversimplification of the technical requirement or problem
Misinterpretation of or failure to comply with specifications
Failure to demonstrate an understanding of the technical requirement
Proposed solution not feasible within existing time or cost constraints
Overoptimism in estimating performance or impact of proposed solution
Failure to include detailed and realistic cost and pricing information
Lack of realism regarding how the proposed solution will be integrated with existing operations
Technical requirement dealt with in vague terms or in sweeping statements; not clear that offeror knows how to achieve promised solution
Personnel, program management, or facilities to be used in accomplishing the task not adequately detailed
Failure to respond to requirements of the solicitation

Source: *Guidelines for Preparing More Effective Technical Proposals for the Navy Department,* Washington, D.C., U.S. Department of the Navy. (No date given for Pamphlet).

trum of complex topics, and the negotiating person or team may need supportive help from the home office. The process may entail close examination of technical and cost data as well as definition of the technical product specifications that might be developed for the buyer. Sometimes legal advice will be needed to ensure compliance with existing laws. The negotiator may have to check frequently with top management to see how much latitude is available in reaching a compromise.

Negotiation thus requires patience, feedback, communication, and an understanding and supportive staff. The seller should have plenty of knowledgeable assistance, because the buyer may have a team of experts. This point is extremely important in highly technical markets or in large transactions with foreign governments, who may have cultural or legal biases/restrictions for completing the negotiation process. Ideally, the agreed-on price should be perceived as a fair one by both the buyer and seller. Other benefits (such as delivery schedules, credit, discounts, and service support) should be clearly defined and mutually beneficial to all parties.

▶ Leasing May Be a Feasible Pricing Option

A lease arrangement can give impetus to sale of a new product or to new exploratory markets. The customer has the opportunity to try the product or service on a limited basis. This is especially useful with

complex products or concepts that are hard to visualize in terms of customer benefits. Leasing arrangements can be a cash draining proposition for the seller, and cash flow might be a problem for companies in a weak financial condition. Hence, each company must weigh the benefits and the detriments of adopting a leasing strategy.

Pricing and leasing decisions cannot be separated. The company may decide to push leases by charging higher prices for outright sales, or it might take the opposite tactic—lowering cash sale prices to discourage leasing sales. The decision must harmonize with the preferences/opportunities in the marketplace and the capabilities of the firm.

In conclusion, I must stress that the competition can easily copy any company's pricing strategy. Also, consumer attitudes and preferences about prices change drastically from time to time. A modern progressive marketer must therefore be very systematic and logical in developing a pricing strategy. The pricing function cannot be left to chance or allowed to be a mechanical or glib part of the marketing program. It is now a significant aspect of marketing management. Pricing decisions may even have become Darwinian in nature—survival of the fittest may be determined by who has the most efficient and best pricing program!

14

Getting Big Results from Advertising Strategy

Advertising is usually a significant aspect of a marketing strategy. Yet this promotional tool is often the one most misunderstood by management, especially nonmarketers. There are a multitude of misconceptions about managing the advertising function. Confusion may abound over (1) the actual planning or developing stages and (2) formulating the most effective advertising strategies.

This chapter explores the types of advertising decisions and analyses that executives must make. Giving all of the production mechanics of creating and designing specific advertising campaigns is beyond its scope, but it does include useful guidelines. These are appropriate for the advertiser, advertising supplier, or executive who must directly or indirectly influence advertising decisions within an organization.

Everyone is bombarded with advertisements every day. Advertising is a constant presence. At times it may seem like an unwelcome intrusion on basic rights. Nevertheless, its absence for even one day would probably be felt. Indeed, the constant advertising barrage makes executives concerned with finding the optimum advertising strategy. It is a tedious task to convince or persuade consumers in the marketplace. They often expect both entertaining and useful advertisements. And management, which pays the bills, has extremely high expectations for what advertising should accomplish. Succeeding in this field is an immense challenge, from every point of view.

▶ Management Must Know the Advantages of Advertising

Advertising is a tool that can help the organization achieve strategic objectives and goals. It can help to increase profits, sales, market share, or frequency of buyer purchases. It can also help to generate positive feelings and thoughts about the organization and its products, services, or societal contributions.

If used properly, mass selling can be a beneficial medium for demonstrating products or services. It can also educate consumers and other groups about various concepts or issues. Advertising can create awareness and influence attitudes. In essence, it is a communication medium that helps an organization relate to the market.

The advertising function offers worthwhile opportunities. It is especially useful for marketing highly standardized products and for reaching a mass market that is widely dispersed. Advertising, if used properly can be quite economical compared with other promotional devices. In fact, it may be the least expensive method for reaching a large number of prospects. In addition, advertising might be recommended when selling price per unit is small and a great deal of preselling is needed (e.g., with impulse items).

Whenever a product goes through a long channel of distribution and the marketer seems to lack control over other channel members, advertising may be the best vehicle for pulling the product through the pipeline. Furthermore, a high gross margin or contribution margin per sales dollar allows discretionary budgeting for advertising. The margins are so attractive that the company does not mind investing additional ad dollars to increase dollar sales. Advertising may even give a higher and faster return on investment.

Advertising strategy has been emphasized for unused production or marketing capacity. A company may want to cover some costly overhead. Or it may need to deal with the nagging problem of a cyclical or seasonal business. Constant advertising may help to even out the peaks and valleys of a business.

A product with a very short life requires more ad dollars. Repeat purchases become critical to the bottom line. New variables or objectives might also dictate more advertising dollars. For example, new competition, products, markets, channels, services, or operational problems will require advertising that is informative. In these cases an educational process is needed to create awareness while eventually obtaining the desired action from the advertising audiences.

Not only may advertising motivate marketing personnel—including the sales force—but it may also help to produce an excellent list of pros-

pects, such as in a direct mail campaign. Mass selling may also help to supplement the scattered and dissimilar efforts of manufacturers representatives, sales agents, and other groups who may not be actual employees of the organization but are selling arms of the firm.

▶ Certain Misconceptions Plague Advertising

Marketers must know, quite simply, what advertising can and cannot accomplish before they can create or manage effective advertising strategies.

The following are myths:

1. *Advertising is a quick fix and panacea to all of an organization's immediate problems.* Too often executives falsely believe that enlarging their advertising budget and emphasizing this tool will resolve all their marketing problems. More advertising, however, will not necessarily turn around declining profits, lost sales, lower market share, and decreasing morale. Advertising is only *one* aspect of marketing strategy. Corrective action to any problem may first entail modifications of *other* marketing techniques. Hence, an automatic increase in advertising could merely throw good money after bad.

2. *The more advertising dollars spent, the bigger the splash and impact in the marketplace.* Success does not depend on how much is spent but on how well advertising dollars are used.

3. *An advertising program can overcome immediate image problems.* It is spurious to think that an advertiser can buy a better image or easily generate positive attitudes to correct negative consumer opinions. The products or services themselves must earn respect and consumer confidence. It could take years for an image to improve, and image cannot be purchased. The oil industry, for example, learned that no matter how much they spent on advocacy advertising and public relations, the public was still critical of higher prices and energy shortages. Oil executives were perplexed when they were unable to overturn this negative public perception with advertising.

4. *Entertaining, clever, humorous, or artistic advertisements are always effective.* Consumers may remember an enjoyable commercial but be unable to recall the product or concept that was actually being promoted. An ad can be too clever or humorous.

5. *Larger or longer (broadcasting) advertisements are the most effective.* One of the most common questions business people have is whether

they should pay for one big ad (a "splash") or for a series of smaller ads. Ideally they would prefer both size and repetition, but perhaps the budget does not allow this luxury. Since distractions for the reader or listener are numerous and forgetfulness is common, repeat advertisements may be the wisest strategy for a positive response. If the choice must be made, I recommend repetition over size.

6. *Advertising dollars would be better spent for personal selling.* There are times when salespeople feel that the firm's advertising is weak and ineffective. But they should appreciate the contributions of advertising to their own sales presentation. They know, for instance, that good advertising helps in the preselling stage, to develop prospect lists and create consumer awareness and interest. Advertising can also help salespeople communicate the features of new products, improvements, and company policies as well as answer postselling questions to the actual buyers.

7. *Strong advertising can sell or correct a marginal or weak product.* Executives should not expect advertising to sell a product that is unable to stand on its own merits. Consumers become quickly disenchanted when product quality fails to meet their preferences or expectations.

8. *Advertising can stand alone, apart from other promotional techniques.* Even though mass selling can be a powerful tool, it is only one part of the promotional process and the marketing program. Advertising strategy cannot be developed in a vacuum. Its interdependence and interrelationship with other promotional techniques and groups of people, such as channel members and sales personnel, must be recognized and appreciated.

9. *Advertising is only for big business and corporate giants.* Although advertising can be costly, small businesses cannot afford to ignore this valuable tool. It generates business opportunities for all types of organizations.

10. *Advertising leads to immediate results.* Mass selling should be viewed as an investment that takes time. Its benefits may be slow in coming. In fact, just when management loses patience is often the time a campaign begins to show results or promise.

11. *A successful advertisement or campaign should not be changed.* Admittedly, finding a winning advertising strategy is an arduous task, but the environment of the marketplace is dynamic and volatile. Thus it is foolish to think that adjustments are unnecessary even with a strong campaign. Naturally, a successful advertising strategy should not be

tampered with just to effectuate a change. Instead, constant monitoring and consumer feedback are required to pinpoint the correct time to implement a change in a mass selling strategy.

12. *Advertising creates demand.* This belief was especially popular in the late 1950s and in the 1960s. It is naive to think that an advertising campaign is the *sole* ingredient in or stimulus to a purchase in the marketplace. Household and business consumers are complex entities motivated by a host of unexplained and unforeseen forces.

The foregoing myths may be debated by scholars of advertising. So many individuals dissect advertising in our society that positive and negative opinions clash on nearly every issue. But this list provides a basis for realistic thinking about the contributions of advertising to a business strategy. Overnight miracles cannot be expected for business problems that have lingered for months or years.

▶ Marketers Should Be Aware of Common Long-Range Advertising Blunders

Long-range errors are those that affect a firm for a long time, as opposed to tactical mistakes whose effects last, say, only a year or less (e.g., a poor ad campaign that is used for three months). Long-range errors include the following:

1. *Aiming advertising only toward the actual buyer and ignoring the real decision makers or strong influencers.* Sometimes the purchaser is a "mere clerk" while individuals behind the scene make the important buying decisions. For example, a purchasing executive of a firm may seek promotional literature and information about plant machinery. All of this information is passed on to engineers, production managers, and financial executives. These individuals actually select the particular supplier and equipment. Consequently marketers must define the audience for their advertising. These groups frequently change over the years, so comprehensive market analysis is essential.

2. *Cutting the advertising budget whenever there is a recession or times are bad.* Some marketers formulate their advertising budget as a percentage of previous or forecasted sales. If there is a business downturn or the future looks dismal, the amount decreases. It may be argued that when times are rough, lowering the advertising expenditure is one way to save money. In reality, however, the bad times may make it imperative to advertise *more.* I once heard an astute executive say, "We

take the approach that when times are good we should advertise, but when times are bad, we *must* advertise." Usually, marketers who hang in with their advertising dollars are the ones who minimize the effects of the economic downturns, increase their market share, or come out of the recession much quicker than the competition. Thus, marketers should logically and systematically formulate the amount to be allocated yearly to the advertising function. In fact, a 5- or even 10-year plan may encompass an advertising amount and strategy that ignores cyclical fluctuations.

3. *Failing to assign responsibility and authority for the advertising function within the organization.* In the past, many managers would conveniently blame their advertising agency for the disappointing results of a campaign. An advertising agency is, of course, partly to blame for failures, yet the liaison person within the firm who works with the agency is also responsible. This individual is in fact crucial in seeing that the agency meets the firm's specific advertising objectives. The person chosen for this job should have the aptitude, interest, resources, and conviction to help the campaign succeed.

4. *Failing to create a total media plan.* An inadequate media plan or the absence of such a plan can produce a number of strategic and tactical mistakes. Instead of anticipating possible problems and opportunities, the company may end up reacting to situations at the last minute, resorting to more expensive advertising space or time for commercials. A poor media plan often results in selecting the wrong medium (such as a particular magazine) at the worst time, choosing the wrong audience, having an inferior message, and paying the highest prices. (The mechanics of developing a media plan are discussed later in this chapter.)

5. *Ignoring the advantages and purposes of the different types of media employed for advertising strategies.* For example, television is an outstanding medium to demonstrate the virtues of a product. A general rule is that the visual part of a TV ad accounts for about 85 percent of the ad's impact on viewers, while the talking part has an impact of only about 15 percent. Yet many merely talk about the product or service without utilizing the powerful visual effects of television. Everything else being equal, maybe this "talking" commercial would be just as effective and less expensive in a print medium, such as newspapers or magazines. The marketer thus should use the unique advantages of each type of media and allow each to complement the other in a multimedia approach. Strategic advertising requires that specific criteria be set up for making media selections.

6. *Trying to cover too much in the advertising campaign.* An advertiser sometimes tries to broadcast too many benefits at once. There is confusing "noise" in such a campaign. The competitive advantages of the product's niche escape the consumers' grasp. In the long run, consumers become unsure of what the organization is supposed to represent and what kinds of products it sells.

7. *Forgetting to perform an in-depth management audit to determine the advertising campaign's impact on the organization's strategic objectives.* Advertising can be a good communicative and persuasive weapon in the corporate arsenal. Periodically this weapon must be examined by several means, including marketing research studies, to measure its level of performance. Since there are many intangibles to observe and evaluate, a formal, scientific approach must be adopted.

▶ A Logical and Systematic Process Is Needed to Set the Advertising Budget

There are no magic formulas for building an advertising budget. Budgeting is not an absolute science; usually a number of factors determine the amount of money to be assigned for advertising.

The most popular ways to set a budget are:

1. *Past or predicted sales approach.* Advertising dollars are calculated as a percentage of sales. This method is probably the most popular. It views advertising as a cost of doing business, and the budgeted expenditure is a reflection of how the company is doing. Although this method is simple to use, it can cause problems when business is declining. Managers may decrease the amount of their advertising dollars when this may actually be the best time to *increase* the budget.

2. *Market share approach.* One school of thought holds that there is a positive correlation between profitability or return on investment and market share. Consequently, many marketing managers are judged on market share figures. This criterion has led some firms to base their advertising budget on achieving a certain market share objective. Is market share a valid benchmark for setting the budget? Pinpointing the exact amount needed to capture a certain market share is difficult. And as mentioned in Chapter 11, a positive correlation between profit-related figures and market share does not always exist.

3. *Competitive parity approach.* This method encourages matching the competition's advertising budget either dollar for dollar or by some

ratio, say, 90 percent. The dollar amount thus will fluctuate as the leading advertiser's ad budget changes. This approach by itself is too reactive: It merely responds to what the competition is doing.

4. *Objective task approach.* In this approach specific advertising objectives are defined and then the tasks and associated costs required to accomplish the objectives are determined. In theory, this method makes sense. It involves analysis and study of desirable objectives and then writing of an appropriate media plan to meet expectations. In reality, clear delineation of what is needed to achieve goals is not always easy. The environment is fluid and the necessary tasks may change, so that adjustments will be needed. The required adaptations can be difficult to implement during actual execution of a media plan. Further, the firm may not have the resources to follow through on all the tasks. On the other hand, this method does encourage systematic study and identification of objectives, establishment of priorities, and analysis of alternatives in making strategic decisions. Over the years this exercise can be extremely informative.

5. *Affordability method.* Some managers first earmark money for bills and then use what is left for advertising. They view advertising as a luxury, as if it had little relationship to sales. Ironically, organizations that follow this approach may be the ones that need to advertise the most. The situation becomes a "Catch-22." Without the proper level of effective advertising, their vitality decreases and they can "afford" less and less.

The age of accountability is also influencing the budgeting process for advertising. Management is trying to review past events, including sales, and analyze what impact the advertising strategy had on these trends. There is an outcry for more advertising and media research to measure the effectiveness of specific advertising campaigns. Various sales incentives have been poured into ads that not only help in closing a sale but also provide feedback on the advertisement. For example, coupons and contests placed in ads have given valuable data for deciding on future budgets. More surveys are being done to test brand awareness and advertising recall. Furthermore, a better understanding of consumer behavior and how advertising relates to such behavior is enhancing the question of accountability.

In summary, in formulating a budget, marketers should consider these salient variables: past advertising-sales patterns, the competition's advertising (both amount and quality), the company objectives for marketing and advertising, economic forces, the research methods for judging advertising successes or failures, and the other steps in the

CREATING BIG RESULTS FROM ADVERTISING STRATEGY   173

Figure 14.1. Fifteen practical suggestions for getting the most out of the advertising dollar

1. Let the media offer suggestions; they often give free valuable help on advertising strategy, especially for smaller firms.
2. Explore opportunities to place ads during off hours or in unusual print locations; the less expensive rates allow economical testing of new ideas.
3. Put toll-free numbers in ads to get immediate responses and feedback.
4. Periodically experiment with cheaper classified advertisments to see if their drawing power is as great as that of display ads in the editorial part of the magazine or newspaper.
5. Investigate whether last-minute discounts are available from media sellers for unused time or magazine spots. Discounts can be up to 60 percent.
6. Avoid the one-time, expensive splash—for example, a sporting event—that depletes limited funds.
7. Develop tight controls to minimize the need to reject finished advertisements.
8. Stuff "piggyback" advertising material in mailings regularly sent to customers. Credit card billings, bank statements, special announcements, and so on offers an inexpensive way to send direct mail advertising.
9. Consider bartering opportunities for the product or service in exchange for the production of ads (such as artwork, printing, and copywriting) or for media time or space.
10. Explore the feasibility of cooperative advertising with other channel members. Most manufacturers are receptive to cooperative advertising with their middlemen.
11. Consider advertising in the geographic editions of national publications. Advertising rates may be cheaper and the core market will probably be in these locations anyway.
12. Take advantage of discount terms, if offered, by paying cash.
13. Share ad costs with neighboring businesses or firms offering a complementary product (make sure these partners have good reputations).
14. Periodically try reducing the physical size of the ad. A full-page ad does not get twice as much attention as a half-page ad.
15. Carefully aim the advertising at the prospects or consumers who give the greatest returns.

media plan. These other steps are interrelated and will often affect the budget, tasks, and strategies that are formulated. For instance, a certain advertising message or type of media will influence how many dollars might be spent for advertising. If management wanted to increase the number of television commercials while maintaining advertising levels for other media, a significant increase in ad dollars would be needed.

Advertising budgeting is a complicated process, and several staff meetings and discussions with in-house executives and the advertising agency may be needed before a budget is arrived at that is right for the company. Figure 14.1 shows pragmatic ways for making the advertising dollar go further.

▶ A Good Media Plan Should Be Prepared Well Ahead of the Time Required to Place Specific Campaign Messages

The media plan might be considered the core of the advertising campaign. It provides a disciplined approach for strategy formulation. A good media plan helps to prevent the common mistakes made in developing advertising strategy.

The media plan should be prepared well before a campaign is to start. This preparation time is called "lead time." Depending on the magnitude of the advertising campaign, lead time could be anywhere from a couple of months to a year or longer. During the lead time, the work of budgeting, formalizing media objectives, selecting media and preparing the ads is undertaken. Some media offer reduced rates for early commitments to buy time or space. Even if the company uses an advertising agency, enough time must be allowed for strategy mapping.

▶ A Good Media Plan Should Contain Clear Statements of Advertising Objectives

The media plan should clearly state what the advertising is to accomplish. Objectives could include:

1. *Reach.* The number of individuals, groups, households, or organizations that are exposed to either an ad or a group of advertisements, as in an advertising campaign.
2. *Frequency or Intensity.* The number of times the advertising message is to be given within a certain period of time.
3. *Target Audience.* Where the media plan should be targeted and the amount of geographic coverage desired. Is local, regional, or national coverage preferred?
4. *Continuity and Scheduling.* Whether to have constant advertising exposure or to give greater weight to a particular season or the end of the budgeted year (the seasonal nature of the business will partly determine the pattern of scheduling).
5. *Creative Preferences and Copy Requirements.* A preference for certain colors; visual, sound, or message effects; product demonstrations; or complex messages limits the type of media that can be used.

Defining these five objectives helps to formulate where the advertising should carry the company. Actual media selection determines how

these objectives are to be achieved.

The following are examples of specific advertising objectives.

- In the New England states, reach 70 percent of persons aged 55 and over with four impressions within four months.
- Aim national recreational/camping advertisements at 50 percent of boat buyers of the last two years for the upcoming spring season, ensuring that they will be exposed to at least three advertising messages via three direct mailings.
- Make 60 percent of our Southwest target market of adults aged 18 to 40 years aware of our new soft drink with five advertising messages within the next year.
- Reach 15 of our biggest industrial accounts with five advertising impressions to ensure reinforcement and lower postsale problems.
- Demonstrate the new consumer high-tech electronic product over national television and increase product knowledge among young urban professionals with incomes over $30,000.
- Increase and direct newspaper coupon advertising incentives at 20 secondary markets in the Northwest with exposure to four advertising messages.
- Increase frequency of purchase by targeting 10 percent of the advertising budget to last year's consumers who completed warranty cards.
- With five advertising impressions, increase product awareness at our weakest Southeast market of women between the ages of 18 and 34.
- Improve brand association with the parent company by directing four advertising impressions at automotive dealership owners in our 10 biggest Midwest markets within a six-month period.

The key rules are that objectives should be specific, clear, and free of general cliches or platitudes. It is meaningless for marketers to say, for instance, that the advertising will increase sales (really a marketing objective) by changing consumer habits (a general and difficult task). Furthermore, the objectives should be stated in a communicative context, with use of such communication terms as "goodwill," "awareness," "knowledge," "preference," "attitude," "recall," "conviction," and "liking." Most sophisticated marketers try to measure the current situation (pretest) and then, through the advertising campaign, to improve the levels of awareness, preference, attitudes, social concern, and the like.

The function of marketing research and testing of advertisements

serves as a control to see how well desired advertising objectives are being met. Lastly, advertising objectives serve as a starting point for selecting media and deciding which ones to emphasize in the media plan. Without these objectives, the marketer may wander aimlessly and end up using media with little logic, poor continuity, or a lack of overall marketing mission or purpose.

▶ A Good Advertiser Must Develop and Evaluate In-House Criteria for the Variables that Aid Advertising Decisions on Optimal Media Mix

The overall strategy in media selection is to deliver an effective message to the greatest number of target market people or organizations at the minimum or most reasonable cost. To facilitate media choice, it is prudent for marketers to develop a checklist or control system that allows objective evaluation of alternatives. Some of the criteria might include:

- Cost per contact of the medium's audience members, often stated as costs per 1000 viewers or readers
- Total costs for placing the advertisement
- Availability of special discounts
- Trading area and exposure of medium
- Degree of market and geographic selectivity
- Credibility of source (for example, trade magazines may have a higher credibility than billboard ads for business customers)
- Visual and/or sound quality
- Life span of the ad
- Passalong rate to other people
- Lead time for placing the ad
- Flexibility for making last-minute changes
- Medium availability
- Media mix decisions of competitors
- Noise level of medium (built-in distractions such as traffic flow for outdoor billboards)
- Amount of assistance medium provides in preparing ad (for example, newspapers often set type and do basic artwork)
- Media combinations (different media should complement each other and have a positive synergistic impact in the marketplace)
- Previous performance level (a tracking procedure to tell which media seemed to do the best in the past)

It would be difficult to consider all these points in making media decisions. The nature of the business, the products offered, and the marketplace will determine which media characteristics should carry more weight than others.

▶ The Advantages and Disadvantages of Different Types of Media Must Be Understood

Since all media have weaknesses, a marketer must take a multimedia approach in formulating advertising strategy. Each medium has some benefits that can be used to meet objectives. Also, the lifestyles of consumers and the scope of the media vehicles are constantly changing. It is therefore wise to modify the media mix to reflect the dynamic marketplace and organizational objectives. Figure 14.2 highlights the most important advantages and disadvantages of each type of media.

It is also necessary to select outlets within a specific type of medium. There are countless numbers of broadcast stations, television networks, newspapers, magazines, billboard locations, and so on. The criteria for selecting media mentioned earlier will also help in making outlet choices within the classes of one type of medium.

▶ Good Advertising Copy Must Be Appropriate to the Marketplace, the Chosen Media, and the Expectations of the Managers Who Are Paying Advertising Costs

A copywriter often goes through a number of revisions and possibly even tests the proposed copy on a sample of the prospective audience. Experienced advertisers admit that it is hard to be absolutely positive about the exact wording. Management may feel that the advertising copy is inappropriate, and may have uncertainties about even the choice of words and the writing style. Nebulous criticism by management is understandable, even though copywriters believe that little guidance is being offered.

Writing is a creative and artistic process with no set rules for success. Consequently, managers should not feel uneasy if they have major or even minor suspicions about the wording of advertising copy. Their degree of doubt will determine if more revisions are necessary or if a test period for running the advertising is required.

The company must make sure that the copywriter understands its product and knows how it is to be positioned in the marketplace. Copy-

Figure 14.2. Advantages and disadvantages of different media

	Advantages	Disadvantages
Television	Reaches large/specific audience Combines sight, sound, and motion Gives opportunities for creative demonstration Is geographically selective Program may be national	Has only partial audience selectivity Has high cost Commercial production requirements are high Message has short life Ad must compete with others in short time period Frequent repeat is necessary
Radio	Reaches large/selective audience Is personal and intimate Is immediate and flexible Has low cost (per unit of time) Is usually local Has mass use Uses music	Is less attention getting than TV Appeals to only one sense Message has short life Background sound competes Ad must compete with others in short time period Frequent repeat is necessary
Newspaper	Has low cost Advertiser can make short-term commitment Is flexible and timely Printed word has high believability Is geographically selective Reaches large/selective audience	Offers limited color Lacks secondary readership Has short life Has poor-quality reproduction Is read hastily
Magazine	Provides market segmentation Allows good color Has prestige Has long life Has secondary readership Offers quality reproduction	Audience build-up is slow Lacks flexibility Has long closing dates Is more expensive than newspaper Has waste circulation Offers no guarantee of ad position unless premium paid in advance
Direct Mail	Offers audience selectivity Is personal Is flexible No other ads compete Is speedy Is likely to be kept/posted Has special uses Variety of formats is available	Has high cost per reader Gets little atltention Throw-away factor is high Mailing lists may not be up to date
Billboard	Is flexible Has impact Competing ads relatively absent Has low cost Has large size Offers repeat exposure	Is open to public attack (ecological implications) Offers no audience selectivity Must be seen quickly Has creative limitations/brief message Viewer has many distractions

writers have a tedious time writing crisp, powerful copy if they cannot first explain the product's attributes in their own words. This is especially important with high-tech and industrial businesses; marketers must make clear the technical aspects of their product.

Copy must be written from the reader's or hearer's viewpoint. The advertisement should be personalized and written with the needs, interests, and concerns of readers in mind. The ad must capture the interest and fancy of each reader, even if there are over 30 million; each should feel that this ad is personally appealing. Also, if the biggest concern of readers is seller reliability or delivery time, the copy should address this point. Other benefits, such as cost or safety features, that are not as critical should not be overemphasized.

Copy should be clear and concise and should convey a convincing story. It should have a major theme or idea that makes the audience remember the commercial in a positive manner. A wordy message evokes negative or apathetic behavior.

Interestingly, a few copywriters have become successful novelists because they learned how to be brief but lucid. Every word counts and has a meaningful purpose. Brevity is required to capture people's attention, keep their interest, and save costs of time or space.

Consumers are, however, willing to read long copy when they have a high degree of interest, the product is complex, an educational process is needed, or the length meets specific advertising objectives. People read long copy that has a purpose. The key is that every word must mean something.

Although advertising does not always entail a total selling job, ad copy does explicitly or implicitly ask for the order. It should encourage or persuade its audience to do something—even if this is merely to ponder a point or idea in the ad's message. The copy should contain a motivating "hook."

The following questions help in evaluating copy and deciding on its contribution to the overall advertising strategy:

Clarity. Is the message clear? Will readers or listeners understand the meaning? Are words or phrases ambiguous? Does the message fit within the audience's cultural context?

Appealing and Action-filled Words. Are there sparkling and vivid words? Are the words active rather than passive? Are there mundane superlatives, cliches, or idle puffery? Are the unique benefits and appeals spelled out? Do the claims come alive, making readers or viewers become excited? Are the words and phrases written for the reader? Will the consumer benefits be clear to the audience?

Purpose. Does the copy offer a clear benefit and emotional appeal?

Does it emphasize the organization instead of the consumer? Has the desired story been told or just parts of it? Does the writer understand and know how viewers feel? Are the product and image positioned correctly? Do the factual message and intent clearly come across? Does the copy ask for the order or meet other related advertising objectives?

Feedback. Has the message been formally tested to evaluate its impact on the audience? How do consumers perceive the ad? The product? The organization?

At one time people defined copy in a narrow sense. It was considered only the verbal part of a message: the written material or spoken dialogue. Today the term "copy" also encompasses such visual elements as headlines, logos, illustrations, photographs, artwork, borders, color, layout, graphic material, and even sound factors (such as music and special effects). All these elements are essential in transmitting an effective and memorable message.

The tips that follow describe elements that can affect consumer perception of copy, and how they can be instrumental in advertising strategy.

▶ Musical Jingles and Lyrics Can Be an Effective Advertising Technique to Generate Attention and Constant Recall

As one advertising executive once noted, music is an emotional shorthand. Catchy lyrics, upbeat music, and fine tuning can give the listener a positive feeling. Consumers pay more attention when there is upbeat music with a powerful "hook line." Ideally, listeners may either sing or whistle the lyrics or melody to themselves. The advertisement then becomes a compelling force when the consumer is ready to make a purchasing decision. Basically, entertaining music should enable the advertisement to stand out from other advertisements that also seek the audience's attention.

This capability is quite significant when the product being marketed is undifferentiated or mundane. It could move the product beyond the mass competition by creating positive feelings about it.

It should be noted that the advertiser is trying to entertain the audience. However, the effects of the ad must be monitored to make sure that consumers remember not only the lyrics or melody but also the advertiser and the offerings being marketed. Irritating voices, flat or corny lyrics, obnoxious syntax, and amateurish music are to be avoided. Repetition is critical in advertising, but the music cannot be overdone, because people become tired of an ad that is repeated too often.

The creation of a musical ad is an artistic endeavor. A poor musical arrangement will do far more harm than good. The services of a music studio with experienced personnel will probably be needed.

▶ Humorous Copy Is Often an Effective Technique for Making a Selling Point, Being Persuasive, or Instilling a High Recall Level in Consumers

Humorous copy can be very effective, but it carries the high risk that the humor will be perceived as corny or fall flat or that it will be so entertaining that the advertiser's message is ignored. Furthermore, a humorous ad may be considered in bad taste if the target market is in a somber mood (if the subject at hand is, for instance, taxes, bills, health, financial planning, or death). Some consumers do not appreciate levity with certain product categories. Despite the risks, however, a humorous ad campaign could hatch interest that pays off in the marketplace.

Sometimes an advertiser cannot afford to match competitors' advertising budgets. The humorous approach can be an effective antidote for a smaller ad budget. Consumers notice an ad that makes them smile or laugh, and they remember that advertiser's products.

It is sometimes prudent to pretest humorous commercials to ensure positive feedback and to see if consumers are indeed amused. In addition, follow-up research on responses shows how the humor is being received.

In general, a humorous advertising campaign can be an effective force and should be seriously considered on a periodic basis. Some marketing research studies show that viewers like humorous commercials best.

Will a humorous approach put life in an advertising strategy? The company can consult its advertising specialists about opportunities for employing a funny message. However, the skill of a microscopic surgeon (copywriter) may be needed to cut a sharp, humorous, and profitable advertisement.

▶ A Good Headline Is Informative, Gets the Audience's Attention, and Encourages Viewers to Look at the Rest of the Advertisement

The headline must function as the motivating force to the intended audience, so it should mention a reward or benefit that appeals to the target markets. Sometimes a brand or company name appears in the headline to get maximum mileage for the name.

Although there are no rules for the exact wording, length, or form for headlines, the headline must be carefully worded. People read headlines more often than text. Hence this part of the copy must not be an afterthought to the advertisement. Some samples of good headlines are:

- Tailor Made Just for You (men's clothing store)
- Tide's In—Dirt's Out (Proctor & Gamble)
- It Lets Me Be Me (Clairol's Nice 'n Easy Shampoo)
- The Digest Reads America (Reader's Digest)
- How to Take Out Stains (Rinso, Lever Brothers)
- They Laughed When I Sat Down at the Piano—But When I Started to Play! (U.S. School of Music, direct mail campaign)

▶ **A Well-Designed Slogan—the Major Selling Theme—Enables Consumers to Remember a Key Selling Feature**

A slogan is repeated and used constantly during an advertising campaign. An advertiser's dream is for a slogan to become so popular that everyone is aware of it and repeats it in the context of everyday life. This is an unusual situation, considering how many ads appear daily. However, sometimes the slogan is so powerful, catchy, and different that an advertiser can use it over a period of years, for example, "You're in good hands with Allstate," "Where's the beef?," and "Ford has a better idea." If the theme is well received and consumers are not tired of it, it should continue to be used.

A common company error is to change a slogan because *management* is weary of it. Managers thus seek a new creative theme. Yet the audience may still find the slogan catchy and different. After a number of exposures, the audience favorably remembers the advertiser's basic message. Why not stick with a good thing?

▶ **The Visual Elements—Photos, Layout, Illustrations, Artwork, Color, Typesetting, and Printing—Should All Be Coordinated with the Objectives of the Message**

These supportive elements help convey benefits, arouse emotions, provide conviction, and give a forceful persuasive tone. Without these visual aspects the message may not come alive or generate excitement in the audience. Sometimes, in fact, the appearance of the ad is more important than the exact meaning of the words. People remember a look that is both upbeat and pleasing.

It is impossible to delineate absolute rules for creating the visual aspects of an advertisement. Certain guidelines, however, are helpful for evaluating visual elements:

- Photos and realistic art are usually seen and remembered more than drawings or other illustrations.
- Elements should be in proportion to each other and to objects in the background. All elements should be balanced, to avoid a cluttered appearance.
- The visual parts should take advantage of the special features of the types of media selected: color in magazines, live animation on television, silhouetting in newspapers.
- On a single page, one dominant illustration is ordinarily more effective than many.
- The visual arrangement should be such that the most important elements in the advertisement are noticed by the reader.
- Rectangular photographs are usually more effective than photos of other shapes, especially irregular shapes.
- The visual elements should reinforce benefits and rewards.
- Black-and-white photographs should have good contrast, with very little gray.
- The use of contrasts between various elements, such as print, color, photos, and layout, should attract attention while highlighting key selling points.
- The visual elements should achieve balance, unity, completeness, excitement, and reality.

Feedback should be sought from the audience, especially core markets, to see if the visual elements have a positive, negative, or neutral impact.

▶ A Company's Name, Logo, and Brands Should Reflect Contemporary and Acceptable Norms

This may entail periodic updating of the company's image. Copywriters and marketing people should work together to make appropriate changes.

Sambo's, the restaurant company mentioned earlier, is an example of a firm that was slow to respond to changing cultural attitudes. Minorities were particularly indignant about the racial slur implied in

this restaurant's name. Management, however, remained steadfast and reluctant to change it. The company eventually declared bankruptcy. This is a lesson that marketing people must be responsible for: identifying and anticipating any strategic company symbols that might be perceived as offensive or antiquated.

▶ Advertising Messages that Espouse Product Quality May Not Be Readily Accepted by the Marketplace or Even the Target Audience

Many consumers are skeptical about advertising as a reliable source for product quality information. Instead they are more likely to rely on the recommendations of relatives, friends, and fellow workers; on brand reputation; on previous experiences with the advertised product; on objective consumer reports; and on editorial material in the popular press (this last source is what makes news releases so useful as a communicative and persuasive force). This high level of skepticism forces marketers to be sensitive in finding techniques that make their advertising more believable.

Periodically, particular attention can be paid to employing:

- Informative and factual messages that dramatize positive statistics or facts about superior product performance
- Positive testimonials from satisfied users
- Produce endorsements from independent testing firms
- Supportive statements from respected celebrities or opinion leaders
- Facts about the longevity of the product's applications or the organization itself
- Satisfaction guarantees with some type of liberal compensation or return policy if the consumer is unhappy
- Favorable warranties to ensure product performance
- Actual demonstrations of the product's good quality

▶ Well-Known Celebrities Can Be Used to Strengthen Advertising Copy, but Only with Extreme Care

For decades, advertisers have used famous spokespeople for endorsements. A popular cliche was that when a copywriter was unable to cre-

ate good copy, he or she found someone famous to compensate for the mediocre script. Yet progressive marketers realize that the famous individual becomes an integral part of the overall marketing strategy. Consumers identify the celebrity with the organization. If either develops an image problem, both parties suffer.

Some reasons for using celebrities in ads are the following:

- To attract attention
- To improve the organization's national image
- To better differentiate products that are hard to set apart competitively
- To motivate the advertisers' own employees, who are impressed with meeting the stars
- To enhance awareness and recall level of the advertisements
- To use people who are not camera shy and are at ease communicating to millions of viewers
- To create additional excitement by having personal appearances with the public or channel members, such as distributors
- To take advantage of stars' authoritative force

The use of celebrities nevertheless caused headaches for some advertisers. A few actual illustrations:

- An Olympic star was accused of taking and selling drugs.
- A well-known actor was caught with narcotics at a major airport.
- A singer was critical of the homosexual movement.
- An actress became involved with embarrassing political issues.
- One athlete's career took a nosedive and he became a goat instead of a national hero.

If, despite the risks, a company wishes to use celebrities, it should do so only with good reason. There should be a logical connection between the celebrities and the products they promote. Consumers desire credibility and prefer sincerity in testimonials. The use of athletes, for example, is a natural way to create a masculine quality or winning image. Many actors give a wholesome or dependable picture that is hard to beat.

The selection process of a certain celebrity must be comprehensive. Surveying the target market is a useful method to determine if the star under consideration is acceptable. Sometimes companies ask consumers about various alternative celebrities or allow respondents to make

suggestions. In this case consumers come up with the initial list of possibilities.

The celebrity chosen must believe in the product. A mass audience has a knack for spotting phonies. In addition, the spokesperson must have valid experiences and a creditable consumer image that coincides with the type of product. Otherwise the company may have problems with federal government agencies, especially with the Federal Trade Commission. Egotistical celebrities are to be avoided. Their image with the public may detract from the advertised products. A few celebrities (not many, since the endorsement game pays so well) either refuse to endorse products or feel that they are doing an advertiser a huge favor by lending their name. Therefore the attitudes of stars should be gauged before they are signed to advertising contracts. Although charisma sounds like an abstract trait, celebrities who have it can help products that seem mundane or are difficult to differentiate from those of the competition.

If unforeseen negative factors do arise with the celebrity spokesperson, a quick divorce is the most prudent decision. Once in a while this action requires some payment to the celebrity while the contract is in force, even though the person is no longer being used. Far better to make this payment than to reap further the adverse publicity.

▶ Comparative Advertising Should Be Used Judiciously

Research results are still tentative on the benefits and merits of employing comparative advertising. Consumers and regulatory agencies appear to welcome comparisons of competing brands. They believe that additional factual information allows better purchasing decisions. Of course, a distinction must be made between factual advertising and sales puffery. An identifiable fact—if it is a consumer advantage over the competition—provides impetus to comparative advertising. But the "fact" must indeed be reality.

A few suggestions may help a company decide if comparative advertising is suitable for it, and what should be avoided. First, if the company is small or if the competition can greatly outspend it in advertising dollars, the company should avoid a head-on clash. Eventually the competition's copywriters will find a more creative twist and consumers will be inundated with ads. These comparative ads may have higher recall levels, given the greater frequency rate. A frontal attack may only wake up the sleeping giant. The small firm may instead want to make a "flank" or "guerrilla" attack.

Second, it is fruitless to make comparisons if the marketplace is indifferent to the benefits being compared. This rule may seem obvious, yet many advertisers do not first ascertain their target market's preferences, so their messages are ignored.

Third, cliche copy, such as "We're number one," "finest," "best," "top quality," "best-seller," is to be avoided. The audience expects factual comparisons, not trite statements. Comparisons must be worthwhile, or the audience will be disappointed and insulted.

Fourth, competitors or their products should not be disparaged. The company who does so can be sued for damages if libelous statements are communicated to the audience. The company may also have to prove its claims with reliable research data.

The use of comparative advertising is growing because many advertisers and consumers seem to like it. Some advertisers have found it useful in capturing market share, while consumers find it informative. My feeling is that comparative advertising, especially in print media where there is ample room to state product advantages, may be very useful in business-to-business advertising markets. Business readers like specific comparisons that highlight competitive differences and support their purchasing decisions.

The key issue, however, is whether this advertising strategy is best for a particular company. Does the company have the resources and necessary product differentiation to have an advantage using comparative advertising? Is it on safe legal grounds in implementing this strategic copy approach?

▶ Cooperative Advertising Must Be Carefully Orchestrated, Since It Is a Potentially Strong Partnership Between Manufacturers and Middlemen

The usual purpose of cooperative advertising is to stimulate immediate consumer reaction to a joint promotional effort by both the middleman and the manufacturer. The two parties typically share the costs and are both identified in the ads. For instance, furniture and appliance manufacturers might contribute advertising dollars to dealers and retailers who mention their brands in local advertising markets.

Cooperative advertising is often encouraged by the manufacturer to get the retailer involved with the advertising effort and push the product through the channel. However, the supplier cannot expect the retailer to be always excited about joint efforts. Middlemen will sometimes feel that manufacturers have an obligation to promote their own

products and "pull" them through the channel. Many retailers are bombarded with cooperative offers. They want assurances that the products are marketable. Cooperative advertising is not a good tool for them if the product is new, slow-moving, low profit and marginal, or in a tailspin.

Cooperative advertising allowances are sometimes given to middlemen. These are much like price discounts (a common practice with soft drinks, food, and household cleaning items). Middlemen are not necessarily expected to spend this money for advertising the particular product. Instead, the technique is used to encourage them to carry the product; it is an indirect price discount. Industry tradition has in some cases made this practice a requirement, because of the highly competitive nature of the businesses involved. Some brave manufacturers have tried to discontinue the practice, but retailers merely shift their loyalties to another supplier.

Basically, cooperative advertising offers a partnership and working relationship that usually benefits both parties. Smaller dealers obtain advertising help for building traffic volume. The manufacturer may provide artwork, setup, newspaper print, and the like. The production costs are then lessened without lowering porduction quality.

Alternatively, the manufacturer may obtain a more loyal dealer who is willing to push the product. Cooperative advertising and added loyalty are often observed with specialty or shopping goods (those products where consumers make comparisons with competing products or brands) such as appliances, televisions, and stereos. Furthermore, with cooperative advertising the national manufacturer gets more for its advertising dollars because local dealers use local media with lower advertising rates.

A couple of disadvantages of cooperative advertising should be mentioned. This advertising does entail extra costs and time for keeping records and administering the program. Also controls must be established to enforce the program. The dealer must often present proof of advertising and submit receipted invoices. This practice puts some strain on relations with dealers. Furthermore, there may be disagreement on how the products should be promoted. The message strategy is not always agreeable to all concerned parties.

Do's and Don'ts of Cooperative Advertising

Do's	Don'ts
Develop the dealer co-op program flyer to read like a promotional piece.	Complicate the program by writing in legalese language when developing the forms and rules.

Do's and Don'ts of Cooperative Advertising

Do's	Don'ts
Get the sales force behind the program to promote it to middlemen.	Ignore follow-up to gauge dealer reactions.
Spell out the media that can be used, the time period, copy alternatives, and other requirements.	Forget to partly determine dealer preferences and ideas before planning and implementing the co-op program.
Plan inventory to ensure adequate supplies during the co-op campaign.	Stop other promotional events, since they will often complement and supplement the co-op program.
Give reimbursements quickly.	
Examine the competition's co-op programs to spot your own strengths and weaknesses.	Expect one sponsor to dominate while the other one is being slighted; equal billing is a reasonable expectation.
Consider how the co-op campaign can fit into the total marketing program. What type of strategic fit is needed?	Slight dealers by ignoring what they expect in the product positioning of messages.
Get media people involved to see how the co-op program might be improved.	Only use co-op advertising money for product "dogs." Dealers resent this subtle pressure.
Make sure that products are being advertised in a way that meets advertising objectives.	Offer price allowances via the co-op program to certain dealers. The discrimination could be illegal.
Give the co-op tool a chance; a few years may be needed to realize positive results.	Forget some type of control procedure to minimize abuses, for example, ads not being run, or being billed more than actual costs.
	Use cooperative advertising as a negative tool whereby certain dealers get it; all dealers should have an opportunity to get involved.

▶ In Selecting an Advertising Agency, Marketers Must Develop Procedures to Measure Objectively How Well Each Candidate Might Represent Their Company

An agency could be the positive force that starts and moves the advertising function. Depending on the type of agency and contractual agreement, the advertising agency might:

- Analyze the company's overall marketing strengths and weaknesses
- Pinpoint present and potential markets for products and services
- Examine the competition's promotion
- Prepare a promotional and/or media plan
- Produce advertisements
- Contract for media space and time
- Perform research studies to measure advertising results
- Formulate strategic plans

An agency thus may be involved with (1) the production aspect of advertisements, (2) the creative process of offering innovative ideas for the promotional mix, and (3) marketing support services. Many smaller agencies lack the resources to perform activities such as consumer research and advertising studies. These service firms usually sell themselves on the creative aspect. Their forte is developing unique and catchy concepts that are attractive to both the client and the marketplace.

The type and size of the advertising agency selected is a function of the company's needs and resources. If the company is weak in marketing research, for example, it may want to select a full-service house. On the other hand, a large packaged goods marketer like General Foods has quite different supportive expectations/requirements in specialized marketing areas. Whatever the situation, a sound screening process is needed for choosing and working with an advertising agency. No company wants to pay for specialized services that are superfluous. Nor does it want an agency that is unable to understand either its products or the markets that it serves. Therefore, an agency cannot be selected just because its advertisements seem clever and cute. Hot creative agencies do rise quickly, but they fall just as fast. They may win all kinds of awards, but will they meet advertising objectives and help sell products?

Advertiser-advertising agency relationships require the proper chemistry. They require trust, communication, and respect. Both parties must give candid comments without being afraid of reprisals. The advertising function is a process that requires compromises, negotiations, and healthy exchanges under all types of situations. Personality conflicts can severely damage this alliance and the closeness that is obligatory. Since confidence and conviction are constructive ingredients in formulating good advertising strategy, the advertiser must have strong faith in the people of the agency, including any freelancers hired.

It is not unusual for an agency to replace an account executive simply because of a question of "chemistry" between certain individuals. Personality can also lead an advertiser to switch to a competing agency.

The following six steps may be useful in the search for an advertising agency:

Step 1. Determine the agency characteristics that are the most essential and desirable (do not refer to the subsequent list in doing this first step). First determine mentally the basic and salient traits needed, and then write them down. (You can easily add to the list after thinking more about this chapter's section on dealing with an agency.)

Step 2. Compare the list with the following questions:

Do the personnel have experience working with our markets?
Do they understand and have a good feeling for our products and organization?
Do they have expertise and capabilities in doing advertising for the different types of media we may wish to use?
Are there any potential conflicts of interest with other clients if this agency is selected?
What types of services are needed from the agency? Do personnel have the resources to provide them? Do they have the creativity, production, and marketing skills needed?
Will we allow them to subcontract their services to other advertising specialists? If so, how capable are these specialists, firms, or freelancers?
What has been their track record in advertising? Do they supply ample references from previous clients? What type of turnover rate do they have with their clients? Why? What type of awards and accolades have they received within the industry?
How important will our account be to the agency's business? Will enough time and energy be devoted to us? Who will actually handle our account?
What type of scorecard do they have for meeting deadlines?
Do the personnel have high morale? Are there any interpersonal relations problems among the employees or the professional personnel?
How do they plan to measure the results of our advertising?
How do they plan to interact with our marketing people?

Do they use call reports that highlight projects, progress, and individual responsibilities? (Not all agencies believe in call reports, feeling that personnel give ample personal contact; yet call reports do give clients a status report on the work progress with action taken or planned.)

What are their charges and billing procedures?

Is the agency financially sound? (There have been cases where an agency went bankrupt and advertisers had to pay bills for media space that the agency had already hired.)

What are the policies for fees, if any, if an agency is invited to make a presentation for our business?

Step 3. Contact and interview three to five agencies. Once the word is out that you are looking for an agency, you will have no problem getting prospects. But shun the shotgun approach of interviewing every agency that submits its name.

Step 4. Possibly request a formal presentation from the finalists, such as detailed proposal of the advertising plan. Since the time and cost of this to the agency may be high, be prepared to pay for formal presentations. Agree on the costs ahead of time.

Step 5. During the formal presentations, gauge each agency's marketing moxie. Be careful of the "dog and pony" shows. You want to be inspired but not overly impressed with the artistic and creative aspects.

Step 6. After selecting an agency, carefully explain to the agency why it was picked (a forgotten step sometimes). This will ensure continuity on what you expect in the future. Explain your expectations and desired performance levels. Provide the agency with the time, personnel, and information needed to get the advertising job done.

▶ A Consistent, Formal Procedure Is Needed to Determine and Measure the Effectiveness of Advertising

Although measuring the contributions of the advertising investment to the total marketing program is a toilsome task, an earnest attempt is mandatory. Otherwise the management team will not know which aspects of the advertising budget and strategy may require modifications. For instance, research data may help determine how well advertising objectives have been met; if the desired audience is being reached;

strengths in the media plan, such as media selection or copy-related aspects; and the impact of the advertising program on consumers and the rest of the marketing elements.

The bottom line is to make the advertising program accountable. It is a popular myth that the measurement of advertising performance is impossible and therefore should not be attempted. And it is sometimes hard to get managers to spend money on advertising research. They feel that the money is better spent on additional advertising. This attitude merely compounds the problem of wasted advertising dollars.

Various pretest studies are an excellent device to (1) predict how the target audience might respond to the advertising and (2) examine current consumer behavioral attitudes. In the second situation, the company can follow through with a posttest to see whether the advertising has altered consumer behavior. Pretest alternatives are:

1. *Consumer panel or jury.* Before a campaign is started, a group of targeted consumers is asked to individually rate various proposed ads. This rating could include their perceptions, attitudes, interests, and feelings toward buying the product. This technique gives a good opportunity to discard ads that receive the most negative ratings. Some companies have used this method successfully by having their own sales force, distributors, and other interested parties evaluate proposed ads. When one ad is finally selected, these partners tend to be more supportive.

2. *Portfolio tests.* Individuals are asked to look at a group of tests. After they have spent some time with all of them, they are asked unaided or aided questions to see how much they can recall about each of the ads. This approach may show which ads have the highest recall.

3. *Physiological tests.* These tests are based on the idea that an audience reacts to what gets its attention. With the use of various equipment (galvanic skin response meter, psychogalvanometer, tachistoscope, and computer hardware for voice pitch analysis, brain waves, and pupil dilation) a researcher looks for a biological response to particular ads. Although the test does not tell the meaning of the response, it gives a feeling for the intensity. Everything else being equal, the higher the response level, the more likely that the ad is generating attention.

4. *Focus group interviews.* In-depth interviews with small groups are used to get a range of ideas about various proposed ads. Unlike the consumer panel or jury, which gives a quantitative type of data, the small focus group gives qualitative results. The data may even help in creation of new concepts that could be embodied in the final ads. Or it may

amplify some deep association of ideas and words in the advertisements that may have gone undetected.

Pretesting is a powerful way to prevent problems with particular advertisements; it may even save the firm from a potentially embarrassing situation. Pretesting may give an indication of how the organization is currently perceived and recognized.

Advertising posttests can serve as (1) a method of seeing how well an advertisement or entire campaign has been remembered by the audience and (2) a means for detecting positive changes in audience thinking, behavior, or attitude. The overall research strategy in the posttest is to quickly survey consumers, often by telephone, as soon as advertisements have been placed. The researchers usually try to measure behavior by recall and/or comprehension. The study could deal, for instance, with measurements of awareness, likeability, believability, meaningfulness, or motivational impact. Some companies—especially those with huge advertising budgets—may even perform two studies, one qualitative and one quantitative. Management may be interested in the numbers to see if the ads are noticed, in order to select future media. It may also want an in-depth interview, to evaluate the psychological and sociological variables. This second study could aid in future decisions on message, product positioning, and the like.

Posttests are especially useful if the market is widely dispersed and hard to reach with the sales force. These studies usually give excellent feedback and provide direction for future advertising decisions.

▶ Certain Advertising Techniques Are Persuasive and Also Allow Direct Measurement of the Actions of Consumers

The advertisements of many small companies or direct marketers attempt to elicit an immediate course of action or to close the sale.

These advertisers can employ a number of techniques that ask for the order and also serve as measurements of advertising effectiveness. Such techniques provide verifiable numbers and documentation to top management. They are:

1. *Coupons.* These can serve as a sales incentive while identifying strengths/weaknesses of various elements in an advertising strategy. By coding different coupon runs, a company can evaluate the drawing power of various copy, media, pricing alternatives, and so on.

2. *Contests.* A contest can sometimes be implemented to generate consumer responses to certain advertisements. The response rate is

then measured to ascertain the strength of the advertisements in question.

3. *Toll-free numbers.* The firm may try different toll-free numbers in different advertisements and then tabulate the number of phone calls received from each advertising campaign.

4. *Specific communicative stimulus–response effect.* The advertisement may ask consumers to mention something about the ad when they visit the business. Some form of monetary discount may even be given, for example, a price discount or free gift if the consumer mentions the ad or a reference point that was requested in the ad. The number of responses can be counted or a "gut feeling" can be obtained about the success or failure of the advertisement.

5. *Loss leaders or treasure hunts.* Advertisers may try to build store traffic by advertising loss leaders. These items may be strategically placed so customer traffic flow and sales volume of other product lines can be observed. Some retailers, for example, make a game out of their advertising by offering clues that will give consumers monetary gains when they come to the store. This tactic may create excitement for the ads while giving feedback on the advertising. One industrial machinery marketer tried to generate excitement among an audience of purchasing executives. A series of promotional ads was mailed to them. One ad contained an 18-hole golf game and asked the executives to mail back their game strategy for playing the 18 holes. Winning players were allowed to go on their own treasure hunt in a national department store chain. The interactive responses to the campaign enabled the advertiser to examine advertising effectiveness.

Periodically a company should try to measure customer inquiries from its advertising. These hard numbers enable it to move beyond the more subjective or qualitative type of advertising research. Top executives or nonmarketers frequently seek concrete figures before approving a certain advertising budget. Counting the number of inquiries from a specific advertisement is one way to get these figures.

▶ Sooner or Later Someone in the Organization Will Assume or Seek a Correlation Between Sales Volume and Advertising Results

Ultimately, the criterion for judging advertising effectiveness in profit organizations is sales. Nevertheless, there may not always be a correlation, because numerous variables influence sales, some of which are not

Figure 14.3. Integrating advertising strategy with consumer behavior

Common Consumer Situations	Implications to Advertising Strategy	Illustrative Tactics
Noise and clutter. Consumers constantly bombarded with other advertisements and lead a busy life	Use ample attention-getting devices	Catchy Headlines Color Graphics Humor Music Endorsements Point of purchase
Social status or organizational positions. Household and business buyers rely on reference groups for making buying decisions	Identify opinion leaders and aim advertising at them	Testimonials Trade shows Free samples Specialty advertisements Direct mail
Preoccupation with many needs. Consumers have limited resources but many needs	Arouse interest and desire	Emphasize benefits in message Offer special incentives "Last chance" offers Comparative ads Demonstrations
Confusion and limited knowledge. Consumers seek product information for purchasing decisions	Produce factual and informative advertising	Descriptive copy Educational displays Long factual message Toll-free numbers for product information Promotional but informative packaging Comparative advertising
Absentmindedness. Advertising message quickly forgotten	Repeat advertising, maintain continuity, and provide repetitive exposures	Multimedia approach Teaser campaigns Image ads Repeat benefits Catchy jingles, slogans, & themes Tie-in promotions
A push. Consumers need conviction and must be motivated to act	Induce action	Coupons in copy Advertising giveaways Endorsements from satisfied customers Contests in advertisements Cooperative advertising with dealers
Dissonance. Consumers have doubt and want reinforcement after making a purchase	Continue to communicate with previous customers	Money-back guarantees Product warranties in message Direct mailing—thanking customer for purchase Image advertising Constant advertising campaign

controllable. In fact, sales may increase in spite of bad advertising or decrease in spite of good advertising.

To solve this dilemma, some companies run controlled field studies ("split tests") to examine how various changes in advertising impact sales. This is one viable method of advertising research, but implementing it is costly and controlling the environment in the real business world is difficult. Three other research methods may provide data on correlating advertising behavior with sales patterns: examination of past data, econometrics, and model building.

Although observing the sales effect of advertising is tedious, an earnest effort must be made to do so. Otherwise management will perceive advertising as a cost of doing business instead of as an investment, and it will become one of the first budget items to be reduced in difficult times.

Figure 14.3 illustrates the role and scope of advertising in various consumer situations in the marketplace. Consumers have indeed learned to rely on advertising for ideas and information. The key to effective advertising, however, is that it coincide with consumer behavior.

15
Developing and Managing a Sound Sales Force

Probably more material has been written about personal selling than about any other marketing topic. The subject is usually divided into the human/psychological aspects of selling, the process of selling, and the generic topics (such as motivation) related to sales management. Since so much descriptive material about personal selling is available, I will take a how-to approach and highlight procedures that can improve sales strategies and sales management practices. This chapter also covers common questions and problems that executives encounter in trying to improve overall selling performance.

▶ Marketers Must Sympathize with the Common Career-Related Complaints and Concerns of Sales Personnel

As in other professions, salespeople experience periodic problems and job dissatisfaction. In dealing with a sales force, the marketer should think about the particular challenges of selling. Although all of the following traits may not be typical of one organization, they illustrate the breadth of concerns in this area.

The selling process requires sales personnel to deal with management functions while still being effective in the sales presentation. To succeed, they must know how to plan, organize, coordinate, control, and follow through. This requires daily, weekly, monthly, and even yearly tactical decisions. They must make numerous choices in budget-

ing, managing time, interdepartmental networking, and so on. Decisions must sometimes be spontaneous. No matter how well they plan, uncontrollable circumstances abruptly surface, usually from the home office or customers.

In addition, salespeople must work with and through other people. They must interact with their peers and other departments in the company. Supportive backup help and committee selling are often mandatory. A cooperative intracompany network system is vital.

The sales force has to go through many people in an organization before finding skilled decision makers. This can be tedious.

Listing the steps in a sales presentation is easy. But the continuous successful application of these steps by sales personnel is difficult. Salespeople must orchestrate the various steps to each selling situation by meeting the specific needs, problems, and benefits of the prospect. Selling demands an uncanny knack of being able to flow with the situation while still meeting certain selling objectives. Most salespeople cannot control their environment. Instead they must learn to adapt to interruptions, various personalities, different physical surroundings, uneven group dynamics, changing policies, and the like. They must therefore modify and customize their sales presentations to fit the environment.

Salespeople must identify and address the prospect's unmet needs and problems. They must therefore be good listeners and highly sensitive to both obvious and subtle clues. They must sometimes exercise interpersonal *and* product technical skills.

A sales force may need a continuous diet of training and updating to stay abreast of the latest product innovations and specifications. It may also need schooling on particular complex topics relevant to the industry it serves. Some sales personnel get "burned out" because of the steady schooling requirements. They may feel they are on a treadmill with no end in sight.

The physical requirements of some selling careers can be stringent. Certain sales jobs require constant travel, lifting of supplies and equipment, and much standing, walking, waiting, and driving. Many salespeople are away from the office for relatively long periods of time, and some see this as a strong advantage. However, the exhaustion and isolation of traveling can cause problems with job expectations, moral support, and career growth. Salespeople may feel left out of office politics. Lack of communication or few home office visits may create self-doubt. They may believe that the periodic sales meetings and conferences are too infrequent.

It should be noted that many companies rely on their personal sales staff more than on any other marketing group. The marketing budget is often geared toward this group. Hence top executives may have high expectations or tight controls over the performance level of the sales force. They may desire specific numbers and accountability for achieving certain sales revenues. The sales staff will therefore have to balance the revenue side with the costs side of doing business. Sometimes the two can be contradictory. Furthermore, salespeople must deal with other intracompany peers who are evaluated with different criteria. Sometimes short-run conflict surfaces over buyers' needs and an intracompany departmental objective; for example, liberal credit terms desired by a buyer versus the seller's finance department's tight credit restrictions for improving cash flow. This short-run conflict creates additional in-house pressures on the sales force.

Following is a list of prime causes for career dissatisfaction among salespeople:

1. Inadequate or complete lack of information from the home office or management.
2. A laissez faire approach that keeps salespeople in the dark on their own career development.
3. Little opportunity to grow professionally.
4. Little responsibility and control over job content.
5. Few opportunities to offer suggestions or make recommendations about improving marketing strategy, especially within their own territory.
6. Lack of respect for personal selling within the organization.

▶ The Interests and Abilities Required from the Sales Staff Should Coincide with the Requirements of the Sale

Different types of sales positions and selling tasks are interrelated and interdependent. Sales positions include industrial, retail, door-to-door, wholesale, missionary, telephone, manufacturer representative/agent, and national account manager. Some of these positions call for order takers, while others need order getters.

An order taker mainly processes orders and helps complete the sale. This person might arrange the displays, stock items, fill out forms, respond to correspondence or phone calls, and answer simple questions.

Order takers may even merely serve to carry out sales that were already closed by order getters.

Order getters use professional selling approaches. They must be creative and analytical, carefully identifying customer problems, needs, and concerns. They assume an advisory approach in their relationship with prospects. The tasks of generating viable customer leads, making in-depth presentations, and closing the sale with proper postsale servicing are vital responsibilities. Instead of dealing with routine tasks, order getters must constantly make creative pitches to ever-changing markets. As a corollary, they often have to pursue additional training, possess a technical skill or certain aptitude, and/or work with all levels of executives. With the current complexities and challenges of the marketplace, more and more selling situations seem to require the order-getting approach.

To enhance its sales strategies, a company must identify the type of selling tasks and approaches that seem most appropriate for it. This clarification has far-reaching implications for decisions on staffing, training, compensation, motivation, and type and degree of support to give the sales force. The complexities of decisions are magnified if the salespeople are to be pure order getters. More time and investment are required to successfully sustain this group. They need the mental and physical tools to grow and prosper. They may also require all types of backup support to ensure powerful, creative, and fruitful sales.

The company must avoid the common mistake of putting order takers into a selling environment that really requires order getters. For example, a former client, an electrical distributor, decided to penetrate the industrial market by using retail/wholesale salesclerks who were mere order takers. These salespeople had problems dealing with purchasing executives who sought sophisticated answers for potentially large transactions. The experiment did not succeed, because the owner was afraid to invest in development of a new type of creative sales personnel. He was also reluctant to train the current staff or give them field support. His industrial market is still nonexistent.

▶ The Degree of Corporate Emphasis and Budgeting Bias for Personal Selling Should Depend on Specific Variables

These variables will dictate the relative thrust and type of personal selling strategies to be employed. Interestingly, in a small number of firms management has a bias for a certain type of personal selling, such as

door-to-door selling. It is preferred because the situation requires strong involvement by the sales force.

The sale of complex, customized, and expensive products often requires the personal touch of a sales person, who explains the products and closes the sale.

The type of goods sold sometimes dictates how much emphasis should be put on personal selling strategy. In intermediate markets, creative selling is critical for fixed assets, including raw or fabricated materials, installations, capital goods, and accessory equipment. Buyers for these goods want to negotiate and explore issues on capital budgeting, product applications, servicing, and trade-in valuations. In the consumer sector, specialty or shopping goods will frequently need sound sales strategies to prompt consumer actions. With some intermediate products, a number of technical questions on product performance, pricing, and servicing must be answered on a personal basis. In most cases, the sales personnel are the ones who then finalize the deal. Without them, these types of products could not be marketed.

An emphasis on personal selling may be more efficient when the geographic market is highly concentrated. Everything else being equal, the incremental travel-related expenditures are somewhat modest compared with the potential benefits of personal visits with good prospects. Also, in some cases promotional media are unavailable or inefficient, and personal selling is the best option for promotion.

Many marketers have a few key accounts that are critical to their bottom line. VIP treatment is required to keep these large customers satisfied. Personal selling and regular visits may be the absolute minimum. Many marketers have even organized in-house accounts or the national account management (NAM) concept. (The NAM structure will be explored later in this chapter.)

As a general rule, a sales force is needed to close the sale of a high-priced item. Buyers are reluctant to say yes until someone personally explains/shows the wisdom of making the purchase.

Short channels of distribution allow easier direct contact with purchasers. Eliminating most middlemen enables the marketer to pinpoint selling opportunities to various prospects while keeping track of the physical movement of goods. Alternatively, a powerful sales force may be needed to push the product through a channel.

Intense and strong competitive forces often motivate personal selling strategies. Top management focuses its attention on the sales force when competition increases. As one company expands, its sales force increases, and competing marketers usually decide to add to their own

sales force in turn. It then becomes a tough struggle to just maintain the status quo and counteract the competitor's efforts. As a matter of fact, for many small businesses the personal selling approach may be the only way to differentiate themselves from larger firms. For example, many small specialty retailers have found that personal selling is the one best way to offset the competition presented by large retail chains.

Last—and maybe most important of all—many purchasers in all types of segments and markets are becoming more sophisticated. And in certain economic sectors, consumers have learned to *expect* personalized explanations and service, and will not tolerate anything less.

In summary, when making allocation decisions on the amount to spend on personal selling versus other marketing activities, the company should appreciate the type of products, competition, and customers involved. Most companies use a combination of promotional tactics: a cup of advertising here, a cup of sales promotion there, and a huge bowl of personal selling for creating that tasty/profitable dish!

▶ Managers Must Identify Potential Problem Areas Where the Sales Force May Need a Push

Figure 15.1 shows major managerial challenges in motivating the sales force and suggested management tools for doing so.

▶ Since the Sales Force Requires a Great Amount of Self-Motivation, Management Must Find the Right Inspirational Blend of Compensation Incentives and Support

A company often has to carefully analyze and experiment with the monetary and nonmonetary aspects of its compensation structure, especially for sales personnel. Salespeople move in cycles, like the economy, preferring different approaches for combating economic and psychological fears. For instance, in the uncertain 1970s, many salespeople desired more security to protect them from depressed economic conditions. Hence many companies, such as Digital Equipment, decided to pay straight salaries. This practice gave management more control over the sales force, while the salespeople could feel more secure. Some executives believe that the 1990s will see a return to emphasis on commissions and systematic experiments with a combination of base salary and incentive bonuses.

A possible compensation package might include a base salary, which

Figure 15.1. Overcoming sales force apathy or dissatisfaction: Creating enthusiasm

Indifference or Complaints About:	Sales Management Tools
Too much paperwork	Administratively support, then give more selling time
Excessive goodwill/missionary work	
Handling unfounded complaints	Contests/sweepstakes
Gathering data for marketing research	Special one-time cash rewards
Unnecessary travel	Prizes; special status or recognition awards
Collecting dead credit accounts	Management by objectives
Slow payments on bonus or commission	Special bonus awards for hard selling situations (new account sales)
Many staff meetings	
Old/dead products	Participative product development by sales force
Long lead time between sales effort and sales	Involvement of sales force in planning meetings/workshops
Weak product mix to sell	
High-priced items	Clear policies and procedures on credits/collections
Poor territory design	Fair compensation structure that rewards harder selling tactics
Requirement to always push new products	
Cold canvassing new prospects	Reasonable time payment on commission
	Careful planning of travel itinerary
	Participative role of sales force in planning sales meetings
	Analysis of territorial design for fairness
	Offer promotional opportunities

covers the basic needs of housing, food, and transportation, and variable compensation, such as some type of commission, bonus, stock option, or the like. This part of the package may inspire top performance. The combination pay package is more prevalent than a straight salary or 100 percent commission.

At times either a straight salary or a commission structure alone may be wise. A straight salary is feasible if lead times from marketing effort to actual sales are long, tight control is required, order taking prevails, or security and a guaranteed standard of living are desired by salespeople. Straight commission may be advisable for small businesses that cannot afford salary costs without actual sales. In some industries the salespeople prefer straight commissions because they like the unlimited earnings potential and freedom from tight control. Many of these salespeople perceive themselves as entrepreneurs.

Numerous organizations have been successful with short-run bonuses or incentives. For example, sweepstakes, contests, redeemable bonus points with gifts, vacation trips, awards, prizes, and recognition

announcements (such as plaques) have been fruitful in giving immediate rewards or building morale. Even professional salespeople enjoy these carrots. Success is even more pronounced when winners of the temporary bonuses or incentives are made known throughout the organization. Publicity reinforces the need for high achievement and the ego satisfaction derived from it. Extra short-run incentives may be needed in down markets. The compensation program might even address potential areas of indifference by emphasizing incentives for fulfillment of less popular selling tasks.

The following questions serve as a handy checklist for planning and designing a motivating pay structure for sales personnel:

Does everyone understand the structure and know what is expected?
Do salespeople have continuous input into fine tuning of the pay structure?
Does the compensation program tie in with the desired strategic organizational and marketing objectives of top management?
What relationship does actual pay have to the sales quotas?
How well are talented sales personnel rewarded? Is there a good positive correlation between pay and performance?
Is the plan understandable and fair to both management and salespeople?
Does the plan penalize sales personnel for things beyond their control?
How do the pay levels compare with those of the competition? Are they adequate to keep good people, including entry-level people, oldtimers, and high achievers?
What type of supporting efforts are needed, such as automotive, expense accounts, fringe benefits, stock options, professional association dues, club memberships, and travel amenities?
Does the system offer financial security and enough incentive?
Does actual pay coincide with the conclusions of the performance appraisal analysis?
When inflation is prevalent, do salespeople actually earn the extra income or do they merely ride the inflationary coattails?
Does the system offer rewards for doing the harder or less desirable tasks (opening new accounts, missionary work, or selling harder product lines)?
Does the plan adjust to the conditions of the marketplace?

Figure 15.1. Overcoming sales force apathy or dissatisfaction: Creating enthusiasm

Indifference or Complaints About:	Sales Management Tools
Too much paperwork	Administratively support, then give more selling time
Excessive goodwill/missionary work	
Handling unfounded complaints	Contests/sweepstakes
Gathering data for marketing research	Special one-time cash rewards
Unnecessary travel	Prizes; special status or recognition awards
Collecting dead credit accounts	Management by objectives
Slow payments on bonus or commission	Special bonus awards for hard selling situations (new account sales)
Many staff meetings	
Old/dead products	Participative product development by sales force
Long lead time between sales effort and sales	Involvement of sales force in planning meetings/workshops
Weak product mix to sell	
High-priced items	Clear policies and procedures on credits/collections
Poor territory design	
Requirement to always push new products	Fair compensation structure that rewards harder selling tactics
Cold canvassing new prospects	
	Reasonable time payment on commission
	Careful planning of travel itinerary
	Participative role of sales force in planning sales meetings
	Analysis of territorial design for fairness
	Offer promotional opportunities

covers the basic needs of housing, food, and transportation, and variable compensation, such as some type of commission, bonus, stock option, or the like. This part of the package may inspire top performance. The combination pay package is more prevalent than a straight salary or 100 percent commission.

At times either a straight salary or a commission structure alone may be wise. A straight salary is feasible if lead times from marketing effort to actual sales are long, tight control is required, order taking prevails, or security and a guaranteed standard of living are desired by salespeople. Straight commission may be advisable for small businesses that cannot afford salary costs without actual sales. In some industries the salespeople prefer straight commissions because they like the unlimited earnings potential and freedom from tight control. Many of these salespeople perceive themselves as entrepreneurs.

Numerous organizations have been successful with short-run bonuses or incentives. For example, sweepstakes, contests, redeemable bonus points with gifts, vacation trips, awards, prizes, and recognition

announcements (such as plaques) have been fruitful in giving immediate rewards or building morale. Even professional salespeople enjoy these carrots. Success is even more pronounced when winners of the temporary bonuses or incentives are made known throughout the organization. Publicity reinforces the need for high achievement and the ego satisfaction derived from it. Extra short-run incentives may be needed in down markets. The compensation program might even address potential areas of indifference by emphasizing incentives for fulfillment of less popular selling tasks.

The following questions serve as a handy checklist for planning and designing a motivating pay structure for sales personnel:

Does everyone understand the structure and know what is expected?

Do salespeople have continuous input into fine tuning of the pay structure?

Does the compensation program tie in with the desired strategic organizational and marketing objectives of top management?

What relationship does actual pay have to the sales quotas?

How well are talented sales personnel rewarded? Is there a good positive correlation between pay and performance?

Is the plan understandable and fair to both management and salespeople?

Does the plan penalize sales personnel for things beyond their control?

How do the pay levels compare with those of the competition? Are they adequate to keep good people, including entry-level people, oldtimers, and high achievers?

What type of supporting efforts are needed, such as automotive, expense accounts, fringe benefits, stock options, professional association dues, club memberships, and travel amenities?

Does the system offer financial security and enough incentive?

Does actual pay coincide with the conclusions of the performance appraisal analysis?

When inflation is prevalent, do salespeople actually earn the extra income or do they merely ride the inflationary coattails?

Does the system offer rewards for doing the harder or less desirable tasks (opening new accounts, missionary work, or selling harder product lines)?

Does the plan adjust to the conditions of the marketplace?

What are the overall advantages/disadvantages of the compensation program?

Are the incentives realistic enough so the sales force has a fair chance of achieving them?

Does the pay plan avoid high pressure or overloading of customers?

What type of vested retirement package is included to prevent good, experienced sales personnel from leaving and taking good accounts with them?

When was the last time the organization's sales compensation program was carefully studied?

In conclusion, nonmonetary motivators and rewards are needed for the sales force. As noted, discipline and self-motivation are required in a professional sales career. The firm can help its sales force by making sure that the selling job is enriched with positive attributes. The job environment should include opportunities for growth, social acceptance, more responsibility, challenge, recognition, and advancement. Pay levels should be an objective proof of these positive attributes. Yet the sales force also needs stimuli to achieve the positive nonmonetary rewards. Some popular tactical stimuli encompass more supportive office help, larger territories, new national accounts, larger offices, exclusive internal club memberships, more managerial duties, new titles, recognition at national meetings or conferences, and positive communication via company newsletters, house organs, and the like.

▶ Expense Account Policy for the Sales Force Must Be Clear and Fair

An expense plan could be:

- Nonreimbursement for expenses
- Unlimited coverage for selling-related costs with no maximum amount
- Flat allowances for certain selling expenses
- A range of allowable amounts for various categories

All of these have pros and cons while being applicable to different situations. The company must decide on the one that best fits its organizational structure and can help meet its objectives under the constraints of financial strengths and weaknesses. The expense plan must

also tie in well with the company compensation plan while motivating salespeople and giving the company managerial/operating controls.

Minimum guidelines to be considered when selecting a policy are:

- The reimbursed amount should reflect actual expenditures incurred.
- Expenses allowed should reflect the different geographic costs of doing business.
- Expenses should be reimbursed as soon as possible, if credit accounts are not available.
- The plan should be consistent and equitable for all sales personnel.
- The plan should be easily understood and easy to administer.
- Salespeople should not have to limit their efforts owing to inadequate reimbursement levels.
- The amounts should coincide with the type of customers and markets being served.
- The plan should be competitive with industry standards and what the competition is doing.
- Padding of expenses should be watched for and discouraged.

If company policy is to not reimburse the sales force's expenses (such as for manufacturer representatives), the compensation structure should reflect this. Otherwise the sales force will not be motivated to push the firm's goods or even work for it.

▶ A Logical and Organized Set of Standards Is Needed for Fair Judging of Sales Personnel Performance Levels

To enhance the decision-making process for motivating and compensating the sales force, solid objective measurements of performance are needed. The major goal of an evaluation program is to accurately and fairly determine each person's performance. Management can then identify the most outstanding salespeople and encourage their traits in other sales personnel. This systematic process may also provide major background material for recruitment and selection of new sales personnel. The criteria add vital input to counseling and training programs, too. Further, deserving salespeople appreciate attempts to objectively and fairly reward them. And last, new personnel feel more secure, since they can learn from this system what is expected of them and receive from it good guidance and motivation.

Every organization or selling situation has its own benchmarks for measuring sales person performance. Unfortunately, some companies rely mainly on dollar sales volume or gross margins. In this case salespeople are not fairly evaluated, because individual disadvantages may be created by territory potential, missionary work, postsale servicing, net profit contribution, and so on. Marketers cannot afford a glib or superficial evaluation scheme.

Some powerful and objective measurement variables for each salesperson that can be adopted or experimented with are:

1. *Sales per customer.* This criterion also shows who the most productive customers are and how salespeople should allocate part of their time.

2. *Number of calls.* The number will show if enough or too many calls are being made. In the case of too many calls, the salesperson may be making superficial presentations or merely order taking.

3. *Orders-to-calls ratio.* How well do the salespeople plan and close the deals? Are they just making calls or actually making sales?

4. *Sales per order.* This ratio may illustrate whether sales people can do some suggestion selling and increase their sales on each order (the incremental contribution can be dramatic, since the marginal travel-related costs are almost negligible).

5. *Costs per order.* Are the expenditures reasonable, given each sale? Is it too expensive to consummate the deal?

6. *Sales-to-potential ratio.* It is difficult for management to accurately or completely determine the sales potential of each defined territory. Nevertheless, a close approximation of territorial potential enables executives to see how well salespeople penetrate their territory. Are they merely skimming the cream?

7. *Sales-to-sales quota.* This factor indicates how well sales personnel are meeting the expectations of management and of themselves.

8. *Number of new accounts.* This variable highlights efforts to build new business.

9. *Number of accounts lost.* Is there a negative or disturbing trend? Are salespeople losing accounts that will hurt future company sales?

10. *Gross margin percent.* When subtracting the cost of goods sold, management can observe the best product mix being sold by each salesperson.

11. *Net profit contribution margin.* This figure shows sales revenue minus various cost data. Exact expenditures depend on whether a distinction is made between direct and indirect costs and fixed versus variable costs. The profit contribution margin allows exact determination of how each salesperson contributes to the bottom line.

12. *Total sales.* Historically this has been the most popular tool for measuring performance. It is still effective as long as some of the other variables listed are also utilized.

In the evaluation process, qualitative judgments can also be made. Salespeople must possess a pleasing and congenial personality. They have to work with a variety of people. A cooperative, positive attitude with a desire to learn and grow are additional assets. They should be team players who are proud of the firm they represent. All of these traits, however, do not prevent salespeople from rocking the boat once in a while. In fact, their questions or the search for improvements may overturn a lethargic or complacent organization.

After both statistical and qualitative standards have been set, the company can study their impact and fine tune them to reflect the ever-changing environment. The standards preferably should be based on prior research and analysis of the factors that influence the sales force and how well the standards fulfill management's objectives and expectations. Proper evaluation schemes also help in setting quotas, in recruiting or selecting new salespeople, and, perhaps most importantly, in rewarding salespeople for jobs well done. For example, developing new accounts may be a major objective for the firm. Hence, a compensation package could be designed for those who help reach this objective.

▶ A Counterpart to Evaluating the Sales Force Is the Setting of Sales Quotas

Sales quotas are performance goals that should serve both management and the sales force. They are usually based on any of these categories:

1. Sales volume
   a. Dollar amount
   b. Unit amount
   c. Customers/accounts
   d. Product lines
   e. Geographic areas

2. Expenses
    a. Travel
    b. Entertainment
    c. Food
    d. Lodging
    e. Home office support
    f. Miscellaneous
3. Efficiency
    a. Gross margin
    b. Net profit
    c. Contribution (margin) to overhead
    d. Market share in territory
    e. Expenses to sales
    f. Ratios, such as costs/call, calls/day, and sales/call
4. Activity
    a. Number of calls
    b. Number of new accounts
    c. Educational courses completed
    d. Complaints received
    e. Returns and allowances
    f. Service calls
5. Behavior
    a. Product/industry knowledge
    b. Cooperative tasks
    c. Loyalty attributes
    d. Time management
    e. Personality
    f. Sincerity
    g. Attitude/interest
6. A combination of the foregoing (probably the most traditional approach)

In setting specific sales quotas, management should interact with the sales force. It must find out if there is consensus on the expected levels of performance. The overall economy, territory potential, actual market estimates, and unique characteristics of each sales person's circumstances must be taken into account. A good beginning is to study the successes or failures of the sales force in reaching previous goals. A hu-

mane, empathetic approach is used with each group, so none feels threatened by the discussion. Setting of sales quotas should be a supportive team effort.

▶ When Using Sales Quotas, Management Must Make Salespeople Feel Like Winners Instead of Losers

This rule is essential to the productivity and morale of the sales staff.

In their book, *In Search of Excellence,* Thomas Peters and Robert Waterman clearly dramatized the importance of this winning perception among salespeople. To paraphrase: Excellent companies design systems that make people feel like winners, because targets, quotas, and goals are set (often by people like themselves) to allow this to happen. For instance, IBM ensures that 70 to 80 percent of its salespeople meet yearly quotas, while in a competing company only 40 percent of the sales force meet them. Thus at least 60 percent of the salespeople in this company think of themselves as losers.

Sales quotas can indeed be a winning tool. Here are some successful tips:

- Make sure they are realistic.
- Make sure they are equitably and objectively determined.
- Allow for modifications whenever profound changes occur either in a certain territory or within the total industry.
- Avoid complicated quotas that no one understands.
- Consider a quarterly or semi-annual review to observe progress.
- Make sure there is acceptance and agreement between the sales force and management.
- Utilize systematic research and analysis to help formulate quotas.
- Ensure that the sales quotas match company and marketing objectives.
- Give support to help salespeople meet quotas.
- Tie in the sales quotas to actual results to evaluate and reward the sales force.

The last suggestion must be adopted. Otherwise the sales quotas will seem meaningless and a wasted administrative exercise. Sales quotas, if used properly, can be a worthwhile communicative and motivational technique in sales management.

▶ To Achieve Optimal Sales Strategies, Management Must Carefully Construct Sales Territories

It is the executives' responsibility to ensure proper territorial design for maximum sales force efficiency. Otherwise territories may lack adequate sales coverage or have too much. The time spent by salespeople in their territory must be well worth the dollar sales return.

How can the allocation of sales force personnel enhance the territory design and improve company strategies? What factors should be considered when deploying sales personnel? How will the proposed structure help meet bottom line objectives? These questions do not have easy answers. But a search for answers may improve a company's territory management.

The following methods help in finding answers.

1. *Market account analysis.* An attempt must be made to measure the market potential of and previous sales levels in each territory. The special expertise of salespeople and their unique relationships with accounts are considerations, as is the length of cooperative relationships with accounts. An essential factor is that the territory design serve the customer and achieve satisfaction. The company especially wants to give ample time and resources to major customers. A common mistake is to design a territory that is too big for adequate follow-up or repeat calls on key accounts and time for calls on new prospects or promotion of new products. The first consideration of territorial design, just like the other parts of the marketing strategy, is customers and how well they might be served.

2. *Cost factors.* The cost of serving different territories must be studied. Will the distribution and logistical costs of supporting the sales force be justified in terms of profit contributions to the organization? The *Survey of Selling Costs* (published annually in *Sales and Marketing Management* magazine) is a good starting source in attempting to estimate initial costs for new territories or to set control procedures.

3. *Workload.* The size of the territory must be analyzed to explore the amount of work needed to handle the accounts. Travel time, call plans, calling frequencies, and amount of time spent in actual selling should be quantified. Geographic areas must be reasonable so that the sales force can handle its accounts without being on the road constantly or having too few planning or selling opportunities.

4. *Territory potential.* Sales personnel must believe that the size of their territory offers them a decent sales performance level. Realis-

tically, territories are seldom designed so that everyone has equal potential. Too many variables, such as geographic uniqueness and idiosyncrasies, make equality impractical. The best territories are often used as a carrot and given to the best performers or assigned to those who have "paid their dues." The central objective, however, is to ensure that the firm obtains good coverage and adequate market potential.

5. *Competitive forces.* Often new or tougher competition forces the company to rethink its territories. The competition may be quite aggressive and seek the company's accounts in certain markets. This threat may necessitate modifications, more support, realignment, or smaller territories. The firm should not go overboard in reacting to the competition, but should alter its strategies for better territorial management. This situation becomes more demanding in no-growth markets, where the company has to fight to keep the same market share. Alternatively, the company has the opportunity to change a territory in order to benefit from weak competition in certain markets.

6. *Product mix.* The products may be complex and heterogeneous. To truly serve customers, individual salespeople may have to specialize in the applications, specifications, and attributes of only one product line. This requirement will result in the sales force crossing over into each other's territories.

7. *Capabilities of salespeople.* Some salespeople may have an uncanny ability and aptitude to take on additional accounts or territories. Sometimes a firm finds advantages through consolidation of territories. Not only does it enhance productivity in these cases, but it may motivate professionals to raise their own career goals.

8. *Overall selling/administrative time.* Most salespeople probably spend more time on paperwork, travel, tracking orders, waiting, indirect sales activity, and administrative tasks than on actual selling. And most sales require a number of repeat calls—some estimate four to six—before the deal is clinched. Management must see that the sales force devotes as much time as possible to actual selling. Time management becomes an integral aspect of territory planning. Travel time, routing, call reports, warehousing/distribution, and field support systems with adequate numbers of sales branches are elements that should influence both time and territorial decisions.

More companies are using computers and/or in-house models to compose their territories. Computer programs can provide quantitative answers to the traveling/territorial sales problem. Also, some models have started to surface that manipulate data and prescribe action (the more

popular ones are GEOLINE, CALLPLAN, TOURPLAN, ALLOCATE, and DETAILER*).

▶ An Organized and Formal Sales Training Program Helps to Convert Both New and Established Salespeople into a Productive Force

A well-planned and well-executed training program gives a company a number of benefits in the personal selling field. First, it can minimize turnover problems by giving salespeople the confidence and proper tools to succeed. It instills a winning/successful approach. More knowledge and support can build better morale. Salespeople know that the company cares about them, if simply from the money and time spent in the training sessions.

Second, old dogs can be taught new tricks. Bad habits may be eliminated if salespeople are presented with new selling techniques, concepts, or additional product features to be highlighted during the sales presentation. Third, the sales force learns to recognize what is considered important by management. Training sessions can serve as a communicative and control mechanism by simply bringing the sales force together within a centralized location at a particular time. Fourth, the whole gambit of sales quotas can be discussed, analyzed, and solved. The sessions may offer concrete ideas on how salespeople can beat their quotas.

Fifth, sales training can prevent some administrative headaches or problems. Although salespeople may detest forms and the accompanying paperwork requirements, they do appreciate clarification on how to best complete their responsibilities. Training modules can show the sales staff how it can efficiently and painlessly follow through with required administrative tasks.

In general, good sales training provides a company with a competitive advantage. The sessions can motivate, stretch, and challenge the sales force as they communicate tactical procedures for highlighting the competitive strengths of the firm. Given all of these advantages, most companies are probably remiss if they do *not* have a sales training program or if they treat it as a necessary evil. Sound sales training programs usually have pervasive and positive influences on serving customers and improving business relationships in the marketplace.

*For more information on these models, see two excellent articles: James Comer, "The computer: Personal Selling and Sales Management" (*Journal of Marketing*, July 1975, pp. 27–33;) and David Hughes, "Computerized Sales Management" (*Harvard Business Review*, March–April 1983, pp. 102–112).

Do's and Don'ts for Preparing a Sales Training Program (*continued*)

Step 1. *Assess training needs.*

Do's	Don'ts
Encourage sales force input and ideas on what should be covered and how it might be taught.	Ignore the importance of putting priorities on the order of addressing sales problems.
Carry out formal research, such as a survey and secondary research comparison of other industry programs, to ascertain the best types of training programs.	Dwell only on previous issues and needs; anticipate trends and future challenges.
Evaluate previous training sessions—what went right or wrong?	
Identify problem areas in sales and look for training solutions.	
Seek management input on what training sessions are expected to accomplish. Is there a discrepancy between what management and the sales force desire from the sessions?	

Step 2. *Formulate the educational and behavioral objectives of the training sessions.*

Do's	Don'ts
Decide on a taxonomy of educational objectives, such as knowledge, comprehension, application, analysis, attitude modification, and synthesis.	Try to cover too many training objectives within the budget/time constraints.
Consider an evaluation method for seeing if the objectives have actually been met.	
Communicate the educational objectives to participants at the beginning of the program.	

Do's and Don'ts for Preparing a Sales Training Program

Step 3. *Decide who should do the training.*

Do's	Don'ts
Make sure that the trainer has the respect of the sales force.	Pick a trainer who might be considered a mere spokesperson or "spy" for management.
Find someone who can integrate knowledge of the organization, products, and market place with the art of selling.	Select a trainer as an afterthought to the whole process.
Allow the trainer to have candid exchanges with salespeople without either being afraid of rebuffs from top management.	Be afraid to use successful salespeople as instructors. They usually relate very well to participants.

Step 4. *Select the appropriate facilities and location.*

Do's	Don'ts
Pick an environment free from business interruptions or distractions.	Choose as a location a "pure" tourist spot, which gives a vacation atmosphere.
Choose a convenient spot that will reduce travel time for as many participants as possible.	Skimp on the amenities that should accompany the training session; a pleasant and attractive surrounding facilitates learning.
Find surroundings that will allow use of training aids, such as audio and visual aids, interactive video disks, interactive computer instruction, videocassette recorders, and typing/production events.	

Step 5. *Decide what should be covered.*

Do's	Don'ts
Introduce and/or review essential sales skills, for example, overcoming objections, closing the sale, improving negotiating techniques.	Ignore the need to update the staff on organizational policies and procedures.

Do's and Don'ts for Preparing a Sales Training Program

Step 5. *Decide what should be covered.*

Do's	Don'ts
Include successful sales skills and practices of the sales force that might be emulated by others.	
Consider discussing communicative skills—speaking, writing, listening, and group dynamics.	
Include product knowledge training.	
Offer insight into customers' needs, concerns, problems, and future outlook (this topic is usually given little attention; hence there is too much emphasis on selling concepts instead of a true marketing orientation within the sessions).	

Step 6. *Decide on the best pedagogical mix.*

Do's	Don'ts
Use techniques that call for active participation by the sales force.	Tax participants by making individual sessions too long.
Provide learning experiences that will be transferable from the learning sessions to the job.	Rely on only one teaching technique, especially the inefficient "lecture" method.
Use a variety of teaching techniques by interspersing them throughout the training sessions, for example, role playing, video taping, question/answer format, guest speakers, films, programmed learning, case reports, minilectures, and the like.	Be afraid to change tack during the session if something seems irrelevant or out of touch with the audience.
Give feedback during the sessions on how well participants are doing.	Use a canned presentation style that applies to almost any type of general sales situation and is not specifically geared to the industry.
Allow for practice, repetition, and reinforcement during the training program.	
Have contingency methods and subjects for adjusting to the particu-	

Do's and Don'ts for Preparing a Sales Training Program

Step 6. *Decide on the best pedagogical mix.*

Do's	Don'ts
lar needs or group dynamics of the participants. Allow for feedback *during* the training so the need for adjustments can be noted.	

Step 7. *Follow up to judge the impact.*

Do's	Don'ts
Design an instrument that helps all parties evaluate the program at the end of the last session. See how well salespeople have met the training objectives after they get back in the field, ideally four to six months later. Integrate participants' suggestions into future training programs. Follow up with communication such as a newsletter that will remind participants of what they learned in the training sessions. Make training continuous so that participants can come back for reviews, retraining, or to explore new fertile areas.	Make training sessions an isolated experience that seems to end after the sales force leaves the "unrealistic" training environment. Be afraid to seek criticisms about negative aspects of the training program.

Experienced salespeople are likely to move through various career cycles. With these cycles they go through different moods, ranging from strong self-confidence to deep depression. Some will even face tremendous self-doubt and midcareer crisis. An effective and continuous training program should deal with this common challenge. The company should offer constructive opportunities for these loyal salespeople to grow and develop. They often need recharging and motivational incentives to prevent declining productivity and bad habits. Older, experienced salespeople are a vital asset, and the company must let them know it. Management should get them immersed in the training program, including the planning phase, and listen to their suggestions. Their experience and wisdom can be worth a hundred textbooks on

sales training, especially as it applies to unique practices within the industry.

▶ An Objective, Comprehensive Procedure Is Needed for Finding and Hiring Good Salespeople

The old cliche that you can't win the race without the horse is clearly applicable to the staffing of a sales department. Salespeople are company ambassadors, perhaps the only contact customers ever have with the organization. Thus the successes or failures of the sales force are magnified in the marketplace to reflect the firm as a whole. It's easy to see why many organizations make a huge investment in selecting, developing, training, and managing the sales department. A constant high turnover of sales personnel can create a murky relationship with customers while costing the company a lot of money.

It is a tedious task to judge applicants for available sales positions. No organization is immune from making mistakes in selection. Every company has experienced salespeople who failed to fulfill expectations, others who exceeded its hopes, and still others who were rejected only to go elsewhere and become leading salespeople in the industry. Despite this unpredictability, however, some steps can be followed to improve the odds of finding the very best people.

Step 1. Develop realistic and specific job descriptions, outlining duties and responsibilities. To arrive at these descriptions, make a thorough analysis of previous and current selling situations with successful salespeople. Do not state minimum duties, which encourages mediocrity. Make sure current salespeople, personnel who interact with new salespeople, and the executive have a chance to respond to the proposed job descriptions. After the descriptions have been finalized, communicate them to applicants, recruiting sources, and company personnel.

Step 2. Decide on the desirable qualifications. Every organization should establish its own set of specifications. A good sales audit (covered briefly later) helps to pinpoint the employee traits that seem to work best for the firm. Although it may not be feasible to create generalized precepts about successful/unsuccessful salesperson traits, the analysis will usually better crystalize the minimum requirements and will be an excellent starting point in developing *higher* standards and job specifications.

Step 3. Pick the best personnel sources. An employer must consider a variety of sources: present employees; current employee referrals; former employees; educational institutions; professional contact with bankers, civic groups, accountants, and so on; sales personnel from competitors or noncompetitors; customers' employees; industry association referrals; want ads; unsolicited applications; and corporate headhunters or employment agencies. The company must be careful to not tap too many of these sources; it doesn't want to be overwhelmed with applicants, many of them unqualified. Over time, and with a formal hiring procedure, it will find that certain sources seem to stand out for finding applicants who eventually become successful salespeople. In my experience, word-of-mouth channels about openings can be extremely effective. Many firms also benefit from the informal method of looking for high achievers among the salespeople or other professional workers in other organizations. Often it is a simple matter of approaching them to see if they are interested in a move. Outstanding salespeople are widely known and easy to identify. A company should make it a standard practice to have its own sales force, channel members, associations, and business contacts make referrals. This list of names for future reference and recruiting is a gold mine. It can save a lot of time and expense while significantly increasing the chances of finding the best-qualified candidates to become part of the team. Above all, qualified current employees should know about any anticipated opening and be given fair and ample consideration if they wish to apply.

Step 4. Decide who should actually be hired. A number of aids are available for making crucial hiring decisions: application forms; psychological, aptitude, interest, and intelligence tests; role playing; videotaping of final applicants; and the long interviewing process itself. All of these methods have their strengths, but choose only the ones that are applicable to the situation.

1. Develop an application form that highlights the desired information spelled out in the job description and qualifications. How well do they match?
2. Be sure that the screening tools actually show how well the candidates can sell themselves and the products. (Personally, I am not very excited about a battery of tests, since their validity and reliability in predicting sales success are questionable, and tighter federal restrictions have made them more difficult to use.)
3. Make sure candidates are compared with company expectations,

not with each other. This may even mean renewing the search and delaying the actual time frame for hiring.
4. Have a few respected individuals interview the final candidates. They may offer insight into subtleties that are easily overlooked when just one or two people interview the candidates.
5. Make interviews long enough to counter superficial impressions, physical appearance, and glib charismatic personality traits. In other words, go beyond the compatibility or "warm" feeling stage during interviews.
6. Examine the candidates' social intelligence level to see if they have the ability to adapt to various situations.
7. Seriously consider second or third interviews with the final applicants. For some hard-to-explain reason, follow-up interviews at a later date and a different time often result in rethinking of perceptions and opinions on some of the final interviewees.
8. In the preinterview and postinterview stages with serious candidates, communicate with business and social contacts who know and work with the candidates. A quick and careless approach can be devastating. Far too many people "look good on paper" but have major deficiencies that are hidden. Thus, consider contacting a number of people from a variety of sources who have dealt with the individual in question.

Step 5. Follow through with recently hired salespeople. Also contact those who have been hired to get their suggestions on ways to enhance the hiring process. They may give you insight into which future applicants might be the best salespeople.

Step 6. Interview sales personnel who are resigning. Their feedback may shed light on creating better job descriptions and specifications and on selecting tomorrow's top sales personnel.

▶ For Wider Market Coverage and Penetration at Reasonable Costs, Possible Use of an Outside Sales Force Should Be Explored

Not all firms can afford a big in-house sales force. In fact, many small businesses rely exclusively on an external sales force, which allows them to reduce final costs and save on cash flow. Hence, outside salespeople (usually called manufacturer representatives, sales agents, or

Figure 15.2. Advantages and disadvantages of using an outside sales force

Pros	Cons
Reduces fixed costs and administrative demands	Divides loyalty among different principals
Makes costs more predictable: no sale, no expenses	Agent carries many items
Helps overcome cash flow problems	Agent may sell competing goods
Gives immediate market access and penetration	Agent could be mere order taker
Allows sharing of advertising and promotional costs	Harder to train, monitor, motivate, and control agents
Provides experienced sales force	Agent may lack in-depth product knowledge
Lowers cost of training	
Offers wide variety of markets	Customer may not be sure if deal should be made with reps or principals
May increase frequency of calls per customer	Potential communication problem
Offers industry market intelligence	

sales representatives) are an alternative to an in-house sales department. Approximately 50 percent of U.S. firms today are involved with some form of outside selling.

Marketing experts admit that an outside sales force offers advantages and disadvantages. Figure 15.2 lists the most common pros and cons. I believe that sales agents play a useful and profitable role for many firms. But as with anything else, management must work to make sure this group is a valuable asset rather than a liability. As one manufacturer told me, "We have to sell our sales agents on selling our products." These agents must be convinced that it is worthwhile not only to carry a company's products but to professionally push them. Too many agents will carry lines but neglect them, leaving the company with dormant service and few profits.

Company survival, however, may clearly depend on sales agents, so they must be selected carefully. Selection criteria should be based on the agent's market coverage, reputation, sales results, financial strength, products handled, management abilities, knowledge of the company industry and customers, product expertise, and a willingness to creatively sell the organization's products.

Management must establish a close working relationship with those who serve as the outside sales force. It can begin by implementing planned programs and effective communication channels to build

a worthwhile and profitable relationship. For example, it can offer training sessions, product literature, inventory data, advertising/promotional support, backup technical assistance, and cooperative advertising. It may even go out in the field to help close the sale. This last task is sometimes overlooked. In many selling situations, an agent may require personal customer visits by the principals. Sometimes this personal visit is requested by a prospect for extra assurance. A few principals have balked at this requirement. "Why have sales agents if I still have to visit the prospects?" Yet this particular visit is the best way of showing support to agents while selling through them. Naturally, the quality and number of visitations must be reasonable. Principals should not do the complete selling job for agents.

One issue that surfaces periodically is whether to use sales agents who carry competing product lines. There are all kinds of pros and cons on the wisdom of this decision. To be candid, the answer really depends on how strong the sales representative's business is in the principal's market target area. Often good agents like to carry a whole line of products from different and even competing principals. This wide representation gets the agent into the prospect's office for a fair hearing. The principal may frown on this situation, but sometimes accepting it may be easier and more profitable than finding or developing new agents or using an in-house sales force. However, the company must then find creative ways to motivate the sales representatives so they push its products more than competitors' products. Some companies have even created a new position, that of manufacturer representative specialist. This person is responsible for maintaining a positive relationship with selling agents.

The Manufacturers' Agents National Association (MANA), with national headquarters in Irvine, California, provides outstanding insight on efficient methods of operation between agents and principals. MANA publishes a monthly magazine called *Agency Sales*, which gives ideas and tips for both the manufacturers' agents and principals. This magazine also contains sections in which agents can advertise product lines they would like to represent and in which principals can advertise for manufacturers' agents. It is a nice clearinghouse for both groups to locate professional marketing/manufacturing support. MANA publishes codes of ethics for agents and manufacturers. In short, MANA is an excellent starting point for a company considering a principal–agent relationship. This relationship may be an inexpensive way for both producers and sales representatives to start out. The principals can obtain national exposure while the sales agents get a large source of merchandise without manufacturing investments.

▶ The National Account Management Structure Is a Consideration if Key Customers Require Extra Care and Service

Some organizations, such as Westinghouse, White Trucks, Olin, and Digital Equipment, have established a national account management (NAM) arrangement. Its purpose is to give extra attention and service to large customers by assigning sales executives to these accounts. With these customers the company is often involved in complex transactions that need careful coordination of product specifications, applications, inventory requirements, and logistical support. Consequently, top executives want experienced and well-trained salespeople. Inexperienced sales personnel could cause considerable damage.

All marketers have their own criteria for grouping customers as national accounts. The most common requirements, however, are the following:

- Orders exceed some minimum sales volume (most popular criterion)
- Purchasing operation is centralized
- Operations are dispersed geographically
- Many departments and levels of management are involved in making purchasing decisions
- Individual transactions are substantial

A company that wants to start this organizational structure or to improve its current NAM program should recognize and apply these essential tactics:

1. Develop a good policy and procedure manual for planning and implementing the NAM program.
2. Carefully decide on the criteria that make customers eligible for this special relationship.
3. Create comprehensive job descriptions and qualifications to help in recruiting, selecting, and training national account managers.
4. Make sure other professional personnel respect these managers and give their support.
5. Use the NAM position as a favorable career move with good opportunities for growth and financial rewards.
6. Let the customer know its business is so valued that a special high-level person has been assigned to the account and a long-term happy relationship will be a major objective.

7. Decide who should have authority over national account managers.
8. Provide continuous training and support to national account managers, including teaching essential skills in negotiating, selling, product/technological applications, relationship building, and the like.
9. Make sure that top executives are committed to and supportive of the NAM structure (the best way is to monitor the cost/benefits to illustrate results).

In conclusion, the NAM arrangement is a good method of building solid and profitable customer relationships over a long period of time. Key customers quickly learn that the seller is serious about their business and really cares.

▶ Periodic Audits of Personal Selling Strategies Are Beneficial

For most organizations, the selling function is the heart of keeping the organization alive and prosperous. The need to audit this function is obvious, considering the wide dispersion of the sales force in the field, the variety of circumstances and selling situations, and the fact that changes usually hit the sales field staff first. The audit offers opportunities for making improvements in personal selling strategies.

The audit is begun by examining certain information sources. The most productive sources include sales reports, call reports, sales invoices, internal market research reports, expense reports, routing schedules, account analysis forms, and time logs. This examination should provide answers to questions that could positively influence the sales strategy. For instance:

> What is the relationship between incremental selling expenses and increased revenues?
> Who are the most productive salespeople?
> How much time is actually spent on selling?
> Which geographic areas need to be better served?
> Is there a better way to organize the sales force?
> How many calls are required on the average to make a sale?
> Would a prescribed routing pattern help ensure better coverage?
> What are the positive and negative trends in relation to profits? Sales? Expenses? Sales penetration?

A sales audit helps in making decisions about some of the issues, such as territory design, covered earlier in this chapter. In my experience, personal selling strategies are a good place to start when trying to enhance marketing strategies. Unlike audits in other marketing areas, sales audits yield contributions that are quickly realized and often tangible to top management.

16

Encouraging Better Results Through Sales Promotion Techniques

You can always do much more through push than you can do through pull
—*Unknown*

Through the years, sales promotion has been an afterthought to the planning and development of marketing strategy. It often consists of a concoction of techniques aimed at increasing sales. Some are successful; others are dismal failures.

Today a spontaneous, random approach is not suitable in this exceptionally competitive milieu. Firms that succeed are those that create professional and sophisticated promotion techniques. Considering that sales promotion for U.S. companies grows about 12 percent a year in expenditures and is currently a $48 billion undertaking, executives cannot afford a capricious approach to this strategy.

Sales promotion can be described as nonpersonal presentations that supplement and complement personal selling and advertising. By its nature, it is nonrecurring and used only for a limited time. Management often expects the promotion to induce immediate action in the form of consumer sales or encouragement of channel members to respond to this extra sales push.

The most common types of sales promotion include contests or sweepstakes; coupons; samples; rebates; bonus packs; deals (merchandise, service, price); stamps; in-packs, on-packs, and near-packs; trade coupons; trade allowances; premiums (gifts or surprises with purchased product); games; fixtures; trade shows or fairs; and refund of-

fers. Marketers have learned that many of these techniques can be combined or altered to give a host of strategic alternatives. The key is deciding on the best combinations for achieving the organization's objectives while appealing to members of the targeted marketplace.

Three examples give a splendid representation of the creative opportunities in the sales promotion area:

1. A manufacturer of snowblowers promised to refund the entire purchase price of its machines if the winter's snowfall amounted to less than 20 percent of the average snowfall for the area in which the machine was bought. The only stipulation was that the snowblowers be bought before December 10. The sales promotion scheme significantly increased sales.

2. An airline company offered customers their money back if rain was above average during the traveler's vacation time at certain sunny resort areas. In postinterviews, management seemed very pleased with the response.

3. A local Pepsi-Cola bottler promised a new Cadillac to five spectators of collegiate basketball—chosen in a drawing during half time—who could make a basket from half court.

Unfortunately, many sales promotion programs fail. They are either out of touch with the times or poorly planned and executed. The following precepts are helpful in formulating favorable strategies.

▶ Certain Types of Sales Promotion Are Appropriate in Certain Circumstances

The essential role of sales promotion tools is to (1) induce an immediate sale, (2) create a sense of consumer or trade urgency to do something, such as responding to an ad or offer (they have even been used as door openers to reach inaccessible purchasing executives), and (3) produce temporary excitement in the marketplace.

These three points are of tremendous interest to marketing executives and brand managers who often need something extra to reach *short*-term sales projections or other related marketing objectives. Sales promotion sometimes provides a quick solution to a temporary problem.

Naturally, a company does not want to inundate the marketplace constantly with spontaneous sales promotion programs. Such programs should rather be an occasional component of the total planned

marketing program. A sales promotion strategy must therefore be managed like any other marketing function. A plan, with a specific sales promotion budget, must be carefully established. Money budgeted for discretionary sales promotion can be set aside to handle periodic "quick-fix" problems, while the rest of the sales promotion budget can be allocated to regularly planned activities.

Types of sales promotions and circumstances in which they are effective are as follows:

1. Many consumers who have never tried certain products might be motivated to do so with sales promotion tactics. For example, a free sample, a bonus pack, or a money-off incentive induces prospects to test the product at little financial risk. Such techniques may be even more effective than advertising or personal selling promises. These sometimes appear to the consumer as empty and glib puffery. Getting consumers to try products—especially new products—is one of the biggest strategic applications of sales promotion.

2. A promotion that includes such tools as coupons, rebates, stamps, contests, and refund offers is well remembered by the marketplace. These added incentives create extra interest and excitement among the promotional audience. Consumer awareness and recall level for advertising is enhanced when various sales promotion techniques are incorporated in the message. These may serve to distinguish the ad from all the other competing advertisements.

3. A carefully designed program can sometimes counteract an adverse economy. Coupons, rebates, bonus packs, refund offers, and trade allowances furnish strong monetary incentives to consumers during a recession. In good economic times, premiums, contests, trading stamps, fashion shows, and fairs are popular. Consumers are in a more lighthearted mood and are attracted to the excitement generated by these promotional techniques.

4. Vigorous trade incentives are sometimes needed to motivate middlemen to do extra work on existing or new products or to adhere to practices that are ingrained within the industry. (Special price allowances, display allowances, extra samples, and attractive fixtures are examples of trade sales promotion techniques.) In the drug industry, for example, doctors are given free drug samples, and druggists are provided one free case when they order a certain minimum quantity. Ideally, to really motivate middlemen a sales promotion program should be periodic rather than continuous. Otherwise the motivation incentive is lost. In some industries this is easier said than done.

5. Periodically a sales promotion method is adopted by one company because the competition has done something similar. The company may find that sales or market share is decreasing due to a new competitive sales promotion program. It then starts a similar or better program to combat the differential advantage. Since sales promotion is a short-run tool, competitive retaliation is common. Such retaliation is likely if perishable goods, high market share, excessive capacity, or large fixed costs are at stake. Trading stamps, rebates, games, and contests are prime techniques in searching for an advantage over rivals.

6. Greater flexibility in pricing strategy may be feasible with sales promotion tools that emphasize money-off benefits. Once a price itself is lowered, consumers are reluctant to accept a price increase when a change must be made. Price-cutting promotionals, however, are usually perceived by consumers as a short-term opportunity. They understand that the lower price is only for a limited time. Consumers have learned that they must either take immediate advantage of the price break or pay the normal price at a later date. Price-off allowances—especially rebates—give marketers greater control over pricing. If the government ever springs another wage/price freeze, the marketers will not be locked into the lower price.

7. Certain sales promotion devices, such as coupons, can be used to measure advertising or personal selling effectiveness. Through formal control procedures, the company observes the rate of response to some type of advertising or personal selling stimulus. Coded coupons have been extremely popular to evaluate advertising media decisions.

▶ Management Should Not Expect or Rely Only on Its Sales Promotion Program to Build Long-Term Consumer Loyalty

No firm should expect a sales promotion method to procure extended allegiance. It is a short-term marketing tool and should not be seen as a solution to deep-rooted sales problems.

▶ Managers Must Understand Trends Now Prevalent in Sales Promotion

Knowing these trends may encourage managers to think philosophically about how they might get more mileage out of their own sales promotion strategies.

1. Management's attitude toward sales promotion has become more positive; sales promotion is now considered more than a weak stepchild to advertising.
2. Support for sales promotion is receiving increased emphasis in modern marketing strategy.
3. To overcome clutter and "me-tooism," more firms are using a combination of methods within the same sales promotional effort. For example, a sweepstake may be added to a coupon offer to improve the redemption rate.
4. Middlemen in the channel have become more sophisticated and are demanding better sales promotion offers.
5. Advanced technology and electronic equipment have given rise to better monitoring systems for evaluating the impact of specific sales promotion techniques.
6. Top management desires systematic procedures for quantifying the actual return on a sales promotion effort; closer examination of incremental revenue versus incremental sales promotion cost is expected.
7. More specialists and organizations have surfaced to provide help and advice for performing the sales promotion function. Many advertising agencies have organized special departments to provide a host of services in sales promotion.
8. The creativity and variety of merchandise and premiums have expanded to cultivate the interests and fancy of dealers and consumers.
9. The attitude of sales personnel toward sales promotion programs has become more positive. They perceive sales promotion as a competitive weapon for securing a more favorable customer or dealer reaction to their sales presentation.

▶ When Designing a Sales Promotion Strategy, Marketing Managers Should Be Particularly Sensitive to Common Problems

Major problems encountered with sales promotions are as follows:

1. Underestimation of consumer response rates—especially with money-off promotions—and thus exceeding budget expectations.
2. Fraud, misredemption, and questions on the purchase or use of the products and their accompanying sales promotion incentives.

3. Methods of distribution of the sales promotion package to consumers, middlemen, or other interested parties (electronic distribution may soon become as popular as newspapers, magazines, and direct mail for placing the offering in the hands of consumers).
4. Too low a face-value money-off incentive, which generates few incremental trials or a low redemption rate.
5. Apathy to or negative attitudes about the sales promotion idea from intraorganization marketing personnel or middlemen.
6. Retaliation by competition, which induces an expensive sales promotion war in the marketplace.
7. Creation of evolutionary conditioning, so that the trade and consumers expect and demand sales promotion incentives.
8. Administrative work connected with proof of purchase.
9. Postsales promotion rebound, in which the trade and consumers must work down their inventory (are future sales sacrificed at additional sales promotion costs?).
10. Cheapening of the image of the product or service if it is associated with sales promotion-price reduction techniques or if the techniques are overused.
11. Special sales promotion incentives that detract from the promotion efforts of advertising and personal selling.

With so many potential problems, good sales promotion program takes time and systematic planning. A last-hour defensive program in reaction to a competitor's action can be costly.

▶ Sales Promotion Strategy Must Be Carefully Interwoven with the Other Parts of the Marketing Strategy

Sales promotion techniques are very effective in obtaining extra productivity from other promotional efforts or cooperation from the sales force and firms in the trade industry. Research has shown that when managers use a sales promotion method in combination with another marketing tool, such as advertising, that tool is much more successful. In fact, sales promotion can be a conduit for getting action. It is sometimes considered a tie breaker for that positive competitive niche. Many brand managers, in fact, believe that it just might provide impetus for increasing market share percentages or consumer loyalties.

▶ One Person Should Have Authority and Responsibility Over the Sales Promotion Function

The merchandising manager, promotion manager, vice president of marketing, product manager, sales manager, or similar type of marketing manager may be the right person to take on the sales promotion responsibility. Since the career image and status of sales promotion have improved, setting up a sales promotion program is an opportune moment for attracting quality people and convincing them that the sales promotion avenue offers a fine chance to advance within the organization. An effective manager in sales promotion who is given adequate financial support and recognized status is a critical prerequisite for a sound sales promotion program.

▶ Sales Promotion Objectives Are Usually Defined as Specific and Measurable Goals

The following are examples of goals:

1. Between September and the end of December, increase trial use of our new cosmetic product line by the Northeast teenage market by 20 percent.
2. Reduce distributor inventory stock of the electronic motors by 10 percent within the next fiscal year.
3. Increase market penetration (dealer inventory building) by 5 percent with new appliance retailers within the next six months.
4. Motivate independent manufacturer representatives to increase sales by 7 percent in their own territories.
5. With the next direct mailing advertising, increase the number of consumer inquiries by 25 percent.
6. Increase the repurchase rate of 5 percent for our national senior citizen market.
7. Maintain current market share of 40 percent for our leading brand by matching all competitive sales promotion allowances.
8. During the Christmas season, build retail traffic by 10 percent with special events.

As previously noted, the sales promotion program is usually short term in nature and can encompass areas dealing with consumers, trade people, and/or the company's own marketing people. The selected sales

Figure 16.1. Integrating sales promotion objectives with alternative tactics

Sample Objectives	Various Tools
Increase trial use	Free samples; coupons; contests; free mail-in premiums; bonus packs; on-pack, near-pack, or in-pack premiums; cents-off specials
Induce customer inquiries	Trade shows; sweepstakes; refunds; free mail-in coupons; free seminars and workshops; product demonstrations; catalog offers; toll-free numbers on catalogs
Build dealer inventory	Merchandise/return allowances; multipacks; money-offs; point-of-purchase material; trade deals; dating (billing for goods shipped at a later date)
Reduce trade inventory	Consumer coupons; cash rebate for consumers; increase display allowances; bonus packs; two-for packs; contests
Increase consumer repurchase rate	Mail-in coupons for rebates; on-pack coupons; refund packs; multiple proof free premiums; self-liquidating items
Build traffic	Special sales events; contests; entertainment events; stamps; cash rebates; store display theme ideas; refunds
Get displays in stores	Theme material on displays; retail contests with displays; reusable displays for other merchandise; take-one racks; dealer allowances for using displays
Get new distribution	Plan-O-Grams; MIS services; dating; premiums; new trade incentives; catalogs

promotion strategy should have an impact on preventing or solving short-run problems in the marketplace. Creative juices often get started in the stage of pinpointing concrete but realistic sales promotion objectives.

▶ The Sales Promotion Strategy and Specific Programs Should Directly Match the Objectives Formulated

Management may like to pinpoint an objective and then decide which sales promotion tactics will achieve it. Often more than one tactic may be adopted to achieve one objective. Figure 16.1 highlights sample programs that might meet the objective categories normally used in sales promotion.

▶ An Ongoing, Thorough Audit and Research Process for Sales Promotion Is a Prerequisite to Creating Meaningful Sales Promotion Strategies

To avoid operating in the dark, the company should develop standard operating procedures that provide input on the best promotional alternatives. It might develop tracking procedures that help to analyze the strengths or weaknesses of a specific sales promotion concept. System-

atic primary and secondary data could be compiled and evaluated. Both quantitative and qualitative results could be sent to a centralized location for analysis. A feedback system could also be devised for tracking the competitions' sales promotion programs. Since there are numerous dynamic variations and combinations, this suggestion is tedious in practice.

Nevertheless, the company sales force, middlemen, the advertising agency, and a specialized tracking service for sales promotions are good places to start. These provide a wealth of valuable input on the potential enthusiasm and measurable results of different sales promotion options. Formal sales promotion research studies may also be beneficial. Considering that some firms spend 30 to 40 percent of their total promotional budget on sales promotion, the research expenditures may be a wise investment to maximize future sales promotion opportunities.

A solid and continuous sales promotion audit is basic to developing a total integrative sales promotion strategy. Scattered, piecemeal programs offer few strategic contributions. Without a formal method for judging previous and current promotional programs, the company must usually reinvent the wheel every time it wants to create a new sales promotion offering. It has no historical data on which to make intelligent decisions, and the process of selecting a new program becomes a burden.

Admittedly, creation of sales promotion strategy does require innovative showmanship and selling acumen. The audit will enhance brainstorming sessions during staff meetings while giving an objective picture of what can be done successfully in the marketplace.

▶ Sometimes a Sales Promotion Program Must Be Pretested to See How Well It Will Be Received by the Trade or Consumers

A poorly designed program can be costly and can also alienate the trade or consumers. A random survey or experiment could be undertaken to predict the impact of a proposed concept, especially if the concept is a national program or a major expenditure. One warning, however: Pretesting must be done quickly but objectively, lest the competition find out and enter the marketplace first with a similar program.

▶ The Sales Promotion Program Must Gain the Support of the Various Parties Who Are Either Involved with It or Influenced by It

In-house marketing personnel and middlemen can make or break sales promotion programs. They may have to give their own support in sell-

ing, logistics, facilities, time, finances, and so on. It is therefore vital for management to work with them as partners instead of perceiving them as slaves. Surprisingly, some marketers become presumptuous and demand that dealers or retailers redeem coupons, stock displays, set up exhibits, give special money-off incentives, and the like. The middlemen and even the company sales force may want some latitude on how the program will be implemented.

One way to achieve better cooperation is to encourage suggestions from these groups when creating specific sales promotion concepts. An open line of communication can be cultivated. The systematic audit, suggested earlier, also helps to overcome potential problems and conflict between the various interested parties who have a stake in successful sales promotion ideas.

A point to keep in mind: It is embarrassing to salespeople when customers or dealers find out about a sales promotion program before they do. The problem is compounded when those customers or dealers start asking the salespeople about the specifics. It makes the sales force look incompetent and creates the impression that the organization is poorly managed.

▶ The Logistics, Timing, and Duration of the Sales Promotion Program Must Be Coordinated

Frequently these variables are judged secondary. A beautiful idea fails because a firm may have been either too early or too late with the project. Adequate lead time is needed to produce and distribute the materials necessary for the program. Furthermore, transportation and warehousing bottlenecks create problems in getting the right sales promotion materials to the best locations. At times, physical distribution personnel and field salespeople must provide major supportive efforts in getting the sales promotion program started successfully. Their reactions are most beneficial in scheduling the time parameters of the promotion program.

Finally, *timing and* the *length* of various sales promotion programs should be evaluated. The optimal times for running different programs within the sales promotion strategy must be determined. It may be a grave mistake, for example, to run two different programs back to back. The second program could have negligible results if consumers or dealers still have a large inventory of the product. The duration of various programs should be timed to take advantage of—or compensate for—the company's media plan. The two could complement each other, or a certain program could be run during slack advertising periods.

Personal selling activities may also influence the timing and duration of different sales promotion programs. For example, a concept may be initiated that will increase customer inquiries, which would then give the sales force a solid prospect list. This tactic could be planned for a slow sales period. Sales personnel may appreciate having this list rather than having to canvas cold in the field.

In summary, given the basic types of sales promotion techniques, there are over 823 million sales promotion combinations and variations that can be offered in the marketplace. Companies thus have ample opportunities to be creative and aggressive in formulating their own unique strategy.

17
Avoiding the Common, Nasty Trade Show Blues: Boondoggles, Bathing Beauties, and Managerial Blunders

Marketers must recognize and study essential strategic and tactical procedures when participating in trade shows. At one time trade shows were perceived as a necessary evil or as an opportunity to have a good time at the company's expense. Managers were more concerned with the music, neon lights, computerized graphics, robotic tricks, human models, bunnies, or other superficial props than sound management preparation. There were a lot of noise and slick external cosmetics, but few sound marketing efforts. Now we are beginning to appreciate and understand the tremendous advantages that sales exhibits offer to the marketing program. Some of these benefits are:

- Customers can touch, see, and try the products on display.
- The shows offer face-to-face contact.
- They provide marketing intelligence data on what is happening in the industry, especially with the competition and key market targets.
- Consumers give vital input on ideas for product development.

Some of the ideas in this chapter came from my previous research and writing efforts. Part of the discussion has been adapted from my earlier article entitled "Marketing Management's Utilization of Trade Shows: Confronting the Opportunities, Mistakes, and Challenges."

I am grateful to Terri Langley, a manager with the Chevrolet Division of General Motors, who collaborated with me earlier on developing thoughts about trade show management.

The address of the National Association of Exposition Managers, referred to in this chapter, is 334 East Garfield Road, P.O. Box 377, Aurora, Ohio 44202.

- New products and services can be introduced and evaluated.
- The exhibits allow immediate reaction and evaluation of product concepts.
- Companies can use the shows to make valuable contacts with channel members and strike new agreements or business relationships.
- A show can be used to train the sales force or reward performance for top producing marketing personnel.
- Trade shows are sometimes the only cost-effective or acceptable way to enter new foreign markets.
- Exhibits give wide market/geographic exposure for a specific market segment.
- The cost per contact at a show may be no more than two to three times the cost of one sales call.
- Trade shows, if done properly, give a firm credibility while building company image (this is extremely important for a small firm that must develop a new relationship with a large business).

▶ Although Marketers Invest Billions of Dollars Annually in Trade Shows, They Often Make Common Mistakes

An understanding of these blunders is of paramount importance. Top managers often fail to recognize the potential benefits of a sales exhibit. They may falsely feel that the trade show is a feeble excuse for marketing people and technical personnel to indulge themselves in a merry time. A junior executive is given the quick superficial challenge of dealing with the daily demands of exhibiting the firm's products and money is allocated to the show because everyone else seems to be doing it. But budget and strategy are neglected. For obvious reasons, it is a mistake to not have a detailed budget for a specific show. Basic costs can be more than anticipated, and money may be spent on nonessentials while worthy show-related items are ignored because the expenses seem to be getting out of line. This situation leads to a weak advertising display with few effective selling efforts or other marketing endeavors.

Another common error is to staff the booth with marginal personnel. The booth should not be manned by people who are unable to attract and properly inform visitors. It may even be critical to send top executives to a trade show, especially if it is in a foreign market. Foreign prospects often like to deal with the top executives. It gives them a perception of higher status while saving their own precious time in the long negotiating process. It is a mistake to think that top executives can tie up the loose ends later and wrap up the deal.

Little or poor preshow promotion and lack of communication with prospects are two other major blunders. These mistakes waste a great deal of time at the show. The personnel may end up dealing with casual lookers, giving out vital proprietary data to the competition without realizing it, or sitting at the booth with nothing to do but watch the traffic flow by.

Even after the show is over mistakes can be made. Marketing people may fail to contact leads immediately afterward, which results in loss of possible sales and future customers and nullifies one purpose of attending the show. Failure to measure the value of the show is another common mistake. Neglecting to evaluate results will create problems in deciding the advisability of future participation in trade shows. This oversight will also compound ignorance on whether or not marketing goals have been met. Without an evaluation or control system, good money may be wasted on some shows while outstanding marketing opportunities may be bypassed at others.

▶ Preparation for a Show Should Proceed in Organized Steps

Many of the principles that follow have been recommended by the National Association of Exposition Managers. (I urge anyone who would like detailed information and advice about improving performance at trade shows to contact this excellent association; it has been very helpful to me in my own endeavors and research.) The address is listed in the acknowledgment section of this chapter.

The basic steps are:

Step 1. Get top management's support and commitment. If necessary, spell out for them all the benefits of sales exhibits. This endorsement will make it easier to concentrate on vital decisions.

Step 2. Set concrete and measurable objectives. A number of staff meetings with marketing personnel, managers from other departments, and external sources, such as the company's advertising agency or distributors, may be needed to set objectives. Leave plenty of time for these meetings. The time will be well spent, since the objectives will serve as a guideline for selecting specific exhibits and help later in evaluating how successful the organization has been with each show. Your specific trade show objectives may be similar to any of the following:

- Introduce one new product and evaluate consumer reaction with a pretested administered questionnaire.

- Identify 200 qualified new prospects and contacts from the projected 4,000 registered visitors.
- Write $200,000 worth of orders.
- Identify and attract five new potential distributors for our industrial chemical-related products.
- Hand out 3,000 pieces of promotional literature to attendees.
- Service five key national accounts with technical problems while demonstrating our product.
- Train and observe five new sales representatives on demonstrating our product.
- Improve overall company image by meeting the press, industry leaders, government officials, and key customers.
- Send three engineers to observe the technical product specifications and design of five competitors who will also be at the show.
- Enhance our marketing intelligence system by surveying as many of the attendees as feasible with a marketing research questionnaire.
- Evaluate specific proposed marketing strategy, such as pricing, credit terms, or discounting.
- As an incentive, reward our top four sales personnel and two engineers by sending them to the important Paris Air Show.

The number and type of goals you set will vary according to such factors as budget, size of the show, the industry and your products to be displayed, and economic conditions. However, avoid the common error of trying to accomplish too much at one show with inadequate resources and manpower. A few basic and well-thought-out objectives will go far in maximizing the value of one show.

Step 3. Carefully select a trade show. There are countless trade shows with both good and bad exhibits. Some are poorly run; others attract marginal prospects. Sometimes regional shows give a firm more for its dollars than well-known national or international exhibits.

To evaluate the best alternatives, you may wish to contact some of the reputable show management associations, including the National Association of Exposition Managers, Exhibit Designers and Producers Associations, Exposition Service Contractors Association, and National Trade Show Exhibitions Association.

Find out if the organizers of a prospective trade show can provide an audit (to verify the number of attendees) or a survey (audience profile) from previous shows. Some organizers may even supply data on those

who preregister for an upcoming show. Or you might like to develop your own audits or surveys from previous audits. Your sales force and channel members may be able to provide insight into which shows seem to provide the best opportunities.

By carefully selecting the show, you can make better decisions on

- The right mix of attendants and visitors
- The market segmentations
- Which products to show
- Budgeting the resources
- Staffing the booth
- Designing and building the exhibit
- Planning the promotion strategy

The basic premise is to pick the shows that best meet marketing objectives at the lowest reasonable cost.

Step 4. Provide enough money for the exhibit. How the budget is determined varies among trade show participants. Money for exhibits may be allocated as a percentage of (1) sales, (2) advertising appropriations, (3) publicity budget, (4) sales promotion amount, (5) personal sales cost, (6) product/brand expenditures, (7) territorial appropriations, or (8) total marketing expenditures.

It is critical to avoid the idea that the trade show expenditure is coming out of funds for a marketing unit or function. Marketing personnel may then feel that the exhibit is taking limited resources away from their own efforts. The sales staff, for example, may feel that they are being penalized with unnecessary trade show costs. Their lack of enthusiasm will cause morale problems and poor performance levels at an exhibit.

The ideal budget approach is the task approach. You first define your trade show objectives and then determine what is needed—including space, layout, and equipment—to carry out the exhibition. What often happens is that the amount projected for the necessary tasks will exceed the available finances. You must then cut back on your expectations, goals, and related tasks. Nevertheless, with this approach your perceptions and aspirations will be more realistic while expenditures will still be controlled. This budget technique requires detailed planning and marketing evaluation, but it is far more effective then allocating some arbitrary percentage and then working backward on successfully selecting and managing the exhibit.

Figure 17.1. Sample form for a trade show budget

	Expense Items	Preliminary Estimate	Final Estimate	Actual Costs
Exhibits	Rental Furniture Carpeting Electrical Flowers Housekeeping			
Displays	Development Refurbishing Shipping Storage Handling			
Personnel	Salaries Travel Meals Lodging Entertainment Uniforms Professional Talent			
Equipment	Audio/visual Signs Lighting Mechanical Telephone Supplies/tools			
Promos	Display ads Mailers Brochures Samples			
Controls	Registration forms Action logs Supervision aids			

Reprinted with permission from *Sales & Marketing Management Magazine.* Copyright August 20, 1979.

A detailed classification of trade show costs may aid in developing a budget (see Figure 17.1). To keep costs reasonable, I recommend that you

- Enforce tight planning procedures to avoid last-minute surprises on major expenditures.
- Ship the display material and equipment early; avoid last-minute and expensive freight charges.

- Avoid overtime charges in assembly or dismantling of the equipment.
- Make a detailed budget and carefully study historical, standard, forecasted, and variance costs.
- See how your costs compare with those of other companies.
- Consider the possibility of pooling your show costs with other companies or a government agency sponsored-booth like that of the U.S. Department of Commerce, for selected foreign trade shows.
- Examine the feasibility of using a catalog display or video show as a substitute for direct participation.
- Eschew the temptation of padding the booth with nonessential personnel; this practice becomes expensive very quickly. Use preshow promotion and preliminary contacts.
- Study the usefulness of contracting services out to trade show specialists, such as a display house or a professional trade show management firm.
- Develop trade show mailers, brochures, newsletters, and display ads that might have application to other promotional campaigns.
- Make one person responsible for planning, examining, and controlling the budget line items of a trade show.

Step 5. Formulate preshow promotion campaigns. You must effectively communicate that your firm will be participating in a particular trade show. Attendants and visitors must be attracted to the booth ahead of time. This preshow promotion enables everyone to take care of preshow preliminaries with prospects and thus allows more in-depth selling or servicing during the show itself. Preshow planning also allows meetings to be set up and helps in deciding how many people and who will be needed to staff a booth. In some cases you may decide to include higher levels of managers because of preshow appointments with major national accounts or leading government officials in foreign markets. Mailers and selected telephone calls may serve as formal invitations for key customers and prospects to visit your booth.

Popular preshow promotional techniques include stuffer mail; a drop-line in regular ads; a special ad about the show; news releases in the trade press; sales promotion gimmicks that tell of upcoming trade show participation; announcements of booth giveaways, contests, special events, or a preshow brunch; and a special appeal to the sales force or channel members to have prospects attend your booth at an upcoming trade show. To enhance preshow promotional efforts, get feedback from prospects on the degree of interest in visiting your display. I have

seen too many preshow promotional campaigns fall by the wayside. There was no follow-through. It is not enough to tell people that you will be displaying at a certain sales exhibition. You must convince them that it is to their benefit to look you up and seriously explore a business relationship.

Step 6. Initiate a sound staffing and training program. Trade shows are becoming quite competitive and professional. Visitors expect knowledgeable, professional people to staff the booth. Prospects want complex questions answered; if necessary, they want to be able to negotiate possible terms of business transactions. They too are seeing costs increase for attending exhibitions, so they expect a good return on their investment and time. High expectations by attendants and visitors will quickly exclude the inexperienced exhibitors and booth personnel.

Preshow training will help the booth staff. Give them ample chances to practice and respond to the trade show environment. Confidence must be established.

Make sure the booth has the right number of technical people. Sometimes booth visitors are technicians who like the "opposite number" approach, to talk with their counterparts in the seller's organization.

Prominently display the company name, product literature, and promotional materials. All subsidiaries could also be identified. Often the booth staff forgets about opportunities for cross-selling. New video display and electronic animation devices offer plenty of possibilities to support the personnel in the booth. Such displays can attract positive attention while answering repetitive simple questions. This video approach allows the staff to deal with unique questions, the sales pitch, and product demonstrations for individuals. I have seen small firms with a limited show budget do a commendable job of attracting interest and sales because of an impressive and informative video or animated show at the booth. In short, give the staff enough props and ammunition to support them and make them proud of being associated with the firm.

Exhibit personnel must be trained to size up the prospects who visit the display. They must not waste their time or efforts on idle curiosity seekers or the competition's personnel. In fact, staff must be forewarned about the type of proprietary information that the competition may try to wheedle out of them. School personnel on what detailed information to give out, especially to strangers. The training session must also remind them to fulfill the trade show objectives.

If appropriate, the staff may have to support the marketing intelligence apparatus. They may have to get visitors to complete surveys, or write a management report about the show itself and the marketing-related opportunities. The staff might also need to visit other booths and keep the home office abreast of the salient trends and future outlook. They can even spot strengths and weaknesses in your own organization. The trade show scene gives everyone a good feeling of what is happening in the industry.

Step 7. Start and require a formalized postshow follow-up. The staff is tired after working a sales exhibit and traveling across the country, and this problem is compounded by work and tasks that have piled up back at the office. You may need to prod returning personnel to follow through on trade show contacts. A formalized system will help them act on visitors' questions and qualified leads within a few days after the close of the show. Without follow-up procedures, the business will experience a loss of sales and customers while portraying a disorganized image. To help the staff, establish follow-up forms, sample letters, convenient mailers, and home office assistance. You might also set up debriefing sessions with key marketing and technical people.

Step 8. Evaluate individual sales exhibits. This last step is crucial to having an effective strategic sales exhibition program. The evaluation will help with future decisions on trade show strategy and how it will complement the total corporate marketing function. The success of show participation has to be determined.
First attempt to see how well the predetermined sales exhibit's objectives have been fulfilled. As previously noted, the more specific the goals, the easier it is to quantify success. Assessment of a completed show may measure such things as

- Number of leads
- New prospects
- Actual dollar sales
- New middlemen or suppliers signed
- Amount of promotional literature given to attendants
- Cost per lead
- Number of respondents who participated in a marketing research survey
- Amount and type of competitive data gathered from a show

Part of the evaluation scheme could be an in-depth study of the show's costs versus benefits. Good managerial accounting concepts may be needed. Costs data will have to be carefully gathered, interpreted, and analyzed. There may be tough questions and decisions about the sales exhibit's cost allocation decisions with (1) fixed, semifixed, and variable costing and (2) direct versus indirect costs. One alternative might be the contribution margin. This accounting method assumes that actual revenue derived from individual shows can be pinpointed and incremental costs/revenues scenarios can be spotted.

The gathering of primary data may be included in the evaluation process. A survey, an experiment, or an observation technique, such as one using electronic devices that give marketing information, may be decided on. The most popular is the survey approach. This method may include surveying the defined universe before, during, or after a show. If carefully designed, the survey may give both quantitative and qualitative data. It then becomes additional input into decisions for future trade show participation and strategy. The size of the trade show budget can dictate how much formal marketing research will be done for the trade show medium.

Figure 17.2 gives a handy checklist for evaluating participation in trade shows. If the company plans to make trade shows a major marketing tool in the future, it can modify and add to the questions on the list, thus customizing the process to its own situation.

The last major component of the evaluation is to determine how well the trade show fits with the total marketing program. Given the challenge of limited marketing resources, allocation decisions must constantly be made on the total marketing budget. At times marketing personnel may resist expenditures for trade shows as a waste of precious marketing dollars. It is therefore essential to document the contributions of each show to the overall communications and marketing strategy. Otherwise management may cut the budget for future trade show participation.

▶ Special Demands and Different Rules Can Apply to Foreign Sales Exhibitions

Trade shows are a major marketing tool in international business. Interestingly, they are often given a higher status by foreign firms than by those in the United States. Sometimes they provide the only avenue to tap new foreign markets. A formal invitation from the foreign or host government may be required to participate.

Figure 17.2. Checklist for evaluating trade show participation

Objectives	Yes	No
1. Were you successful in meeting the targeted number of prospects? 2. Did you successfully present the number of demonstrations you set as your goal? 3. Did you distribute the volume of literature you set as an objective? 4. Did you meet your goal in registering new names for the company promotion list? 5. Did you have positive feedback from visitors about your product. 6. Did you close the number of direct sales you planned? 7. Did you find the number of new sales representatives or suppliers you planned? 8. Did you receive the editorial coverage from the trade press you planned? 9. Did you learn all you planned to about competitors?		
Attendance 1. Was the total attendance what you expected? 2. Was the attendance what you expected in terms of job title, type and size of company? 3. Was the total number of visitors to the booth what you expected? 4. Was the cost-per-personnel demonstration or sales call what you budgeted? 5. Were the quality and quantity of exhibitors what you expected?		
Exhibit Media 1. Did the exhibit arrive on time and was it installed and dismantled according to schedule? 2. Was the traffic through the exhibit smooth and uncluttered? 3. Was the exhibit team professional and competent? 4. Did the exhibit attract the quality and type of prospects it was intended to? 5. Was the exhibit well lighted and did it provide ample space for sales personnel to talk with interested prospects? 6. Did the exhibit design adequately identify the company and fit it to the theme of the show? 7. Did the exhibit accurately reflect corporate colors and have adequate provisions for storing and distributing literature? 8. Were the exhibits of competitors more or less effective? 9. Were the overall design and appearance of the exhibit consistent with the standards of effective exhibit design?		

Source: "How to Evaluate Your Trade Show" (*Industrial Marketing,* October 1981). Reprinted with permission from Business Marketing; Copyright Crain Communications Inc.

The steps already discussed in this chapter also apply to foreign trade shows and can be used as a starting point. However, participants in international trade shows are very sophisticated and take a professional approach. Inexperience could be quite embarrassing for a company. The foreign idiosyncrasies, unique features, and different rules for each international trade show must be studied. For adherence to the special customs of foreign shows, here are some added suggestions:

1. Contact the nearest International Trade Administration of the U.S. Department of Commerce. It offers outstanding advice and publications on how to display products in foreign expositions.

2. See if a prospective foreign fair has received the Commerce Department's official "certification," a stamp of approval on its quality. Since such certification is relatively new, many good foreign expositions may still not have it; therefore, do not automatically eliminate a fair from consideration if official certification has not been awarded. Simply look into it yourself.

3. Seek information from state governments, trade associations, exposition management companies, and trade fair operators, all of which are becoming more active with foreign shows.

4. Give extra attention to the logistical and physical distribution functions. The extra distance and infrastructure problems may require additional time, costs, and manpower. There may be major concerns about foreign labor, customs, or transportation time in delivery of equipment.

5. Stay abreast of the political and international relations climate. In some parts of the world—especially the Middle East, Asia, and Latin America—foreign government approval for trade show participation can abruptly change either positively or negatively.

6. Determine if top managers are needed at the foreign show. A number of foreign attendants, customers, and government officials expect and demand to visit with the top executives in the booth. Having to deal with lower levels of personnel is sometimes considered a personal affront.

7. Try to staff the booth with multilingual people. Although English is a popular language throughout the world, local visitors appreciate the opportunity to talk in their native tongue. It may show how serious the company is about the trade fair.

8. Invite company foreign reps or distributors if they come from the country in which the show is held. They can be quite helpful in the booth and will be more loyal after the show is over.

9. If female personnel are to be sent, make sure this does not conflict with the local country's culture.

10. Determine local preferences on price quotations. Instead of F.O.B. (free-on-board)-quoted terms, many foreign buyers like prices quoted on a cost-insurance-freight (C.I.F.) basis. This includes duties, taxes, and other foreign charges.

11. Adapt products and equipment to local conditions. Modifications in the product's physical form or in the supportive equipment may be mandatory owing to the culture or to the facilities inside the building.

12. Design promotional materials and props to fit the flavor of the foreign market targets. A special advertising agency may be needed that knows how to attract the foreign market in question.

13. In some cases, make sure that the company is committed to participating in a particular foreign trade show for a few years. Some foreign governments and prospective customers become perturbed when the firm participates at their fair on a sporadic basis. They feel, perhaps unjustly, that the seller is not really committed or loyal to their country or markets.

My feeling is that we have only begun to capitalize on this efficient international marketing forum and that it will become an increasingly popular communication medium for international marketers.

Figure 17.3 on page 254 is a shorthand tool that reiterates the procedures covered in this chapter. It's a quick and handy checklist for planning a trouble-free trade show.

Figure 17.3. Checklist for trouble-free trade show planning

10 Months in Advance
___ Select space. Mail contracts and include a deposit to assure selection.
___ Make personal market analysis. Relate message to the show theme.
___ Plan display with all department heads. Put it on paper.
___ Consult with display builders.
___ Establish a realistic show budget.
___ Assign booth personnel.
___ Make hotel reservations.
___ Check show regulations.

5 to 6 Months in Advance
___ Finalize booth design and submit plans to show management for approval.
___ Make sure advertising department or agency is fully aware of the project and order publicity for advising customers of the exhibit.
___ Order all necessary products, equipment, and supplies.

3 Months in Advance
___ Review show management information materials.
___ Present the list of personnel for advance registration.
___ Check the exhibitor's service kit and forward necessary forms for rental, etc.
___ Organize a preshow promotion.
___ Prepare appropriate news releases for trade publication.

1 Month in Advance
___ Have display contractor erect display to be certain all is well.
___ Insure exhibit.
___ Recheck hotel reservations.
___ Finalize booth personnel schedules.
___ Check availability of all supplies required at the display.
___ Provide written schedules, exhibit plans, and objectives to booth personnel.
___ Make a final check on shipping arrangements, supplies, literature, products, etc.
___ Confirm exhibitor's service kit instructions on shipping date so that material will arrive on first day space is available.
___ Install exhibit on first day space is available to assure that all planned features are properly covered.

Reprinted with permission from *Sales & Marketing Management* Magazine. Copyright August 20, 1979.

18

Exploring and Improving Opportunities for Direct Marketing

You may be on the right track, but you'll get run over if you just stand there.
—*Unknown*

In geometric terms, the shortest distance between two points is a straight line. This well-known axiom is now being applied to the field of marketing strategy. Many firms believe that it may be more efficient, economical, and profitable to reach consumers directly instead of through marketing intermediaries.

All types of industries are using this direct approach. Such diverse products as cosmetics, children's toys, banking services, brokerage services, industrial robotics, machine and tool design, fund raising, and social causes are being marketed through direct distribution. Direct marketing has become one of the fastest growing tools, if not the fastest, in business.

The popularity of direct marketing is due to increased competition, higher costs for other promotional alternatives, poor or ineffective intermediaries, the urgency and need for communicating directly with consumers, and limited consumer time for shopping or purchasing goods. Also improvements in advanced technology and communication equipment have provided additional impetus to direct marketing.

According to *Direct Marketing* magazine, the purpose of direct marketing is to acquire and identify customers or prospects, then communicate directly with them. It is an interactive system that employs one or more persuasion media to effect a measurable response and/or trans-

action at any location. The medium could be mail-order selling, telephone selling, or another vehicle that encourages an actual transaction or a measurable response, such as consumers seeking more product information.

To avoid potential confusion, a distinction should be made between direct mail and mail order. Direct mail makes use of an advertising medium, such as newspaper, magazine, radio, television, or outdoor billboard. It may or may not try to solicit a direct response from the audience. Mail order seeks a measurable direct action from the intended audience. Mail order is thus analogous to a direct distribution channel. At one time, direct marketing used to be synonymous with mail order. Many of the procedures and successes were attributed to the mail-order approach. But today's methods are more diverse. Sellers, for example, might visit customers at home, use the telephone, or rely on an electronic or a mechanical device. They may also use television, radio, newspapers, or magazines, but with the goal of getting a direct, measurable response by offering encouragement to contact the advertiser.

This chapter offers general recipes and suggestions about direct marketing and guidelines for two major direct marketing approaches: mail order and telemarketing.

▶ Direct Marketing Should Fit the Customer's Lifestyle

Many household and business buyers are pressed for time. They often prefer the convenience and comfort of buying through a direct marketing medium. Household buyers may welcome the opportunity to buy on weekends or late at night when interruptions are fewer and they have more time to make decisions. This fact is especially true if both spouses work and need the extra services of direct marketing. Numerous business buyers also like the idea of dealing directly with the seller. Furthermore, some direct marketing approaches—for example, mail order, product catalogs, and hot-line phone numbers—allow busy purchasing executives to respond when it's most convenient. A company may conclude that it cannot afford to *not* try direct marketing.

In deciding on how much to use direct marketing, marketers must be sure that the market target can be pinpointed in recognizable, definable, and reachable characteristics. A successful and efficient direct marketing program is based on lists of viable prospects. A good list of names is a precious commodity in direct marketing. Thus, before launching a direct marketing program, marketers should contact list

brokers and see if they actually have lists that match company perceptions of the market segments. Otherwise, it may be cheaper and more profitable to do mass advertising or use intermediaries. Alternatively, the company can build its own list of names, which can then be used for a mail order or telephone sales pitch. This bottom-up approach is time consuming and expensive, but necessary if the company plans a serious direct marketing operation over a long period of time.

Interestingly, some consumers (identified later) *prefer* to buy or deal directly with the seller. In this case, the direct marketing method becomes an integral part of the total marketing program.

If no commercial list is available for a specific market target, direct marketing may not be as feasible as other marketing techniques or strategies. Today, however, there is a name list for almost any circumstance or need.

▶ The Product Should Lend Itself to Direct Marketing Techniques

Although the product may be difficult to ship by mail because it's heavy, hard to package, or has a low markup but high mailing cost, more and more companies are still finding opportunities to at least establish a dialogue with consumers via direct marketing. They use toll-free numbers, coupon advertising, sweepstakes, trade shows, warranty cards, service contracts on high-ticket items, credit card data, customer inquiries, and the like to build a valuable data base that allows direct access to their target markets. Personal selling or other activities may still be needed to close the sale. Yet in the current tough environment, it is hard to imagine any organization that could not use some type of direct marketing. The real problem is how much emphasis to place on direct marketing versus other techniques.

The following questions illustrate how the type of product may dictate the amount of emphasis:

Can the product be purchased in traditional channels with intermediaries?
Is it a shopping good for which in-depth personal selling explanations are needed for comparison purposes?
Does it need to be demonstrated for the customer?
Do consumers prefer to see, feel, smell, or touch it before they make a commitment? (Strong money-back guarantees help to offset this problem.)

Is it a high-price item for which a purchase decision requires multiple decision makers? (Business purchases of capital equipment or other fixed assets require the approval of many people.)

Does it appeal to mass markets? Would mass advertising be more efficient?

▶ Marketers Must Be Aware of How Competitors Use Direct Marketing

If no one in an industry is doing direct marketing, the method may have been found to be a failure. Competitors may have ascertained more efficient and appropriate methods. However, the business world changes, and new efforts could be commendable. To be candid, for almost all organizations (for-profit and nonprofit; small and large; reseller, industrial, and consumer firms; professional services and manufacturers) there is a growing urgency to consider some form of direct marketing. The competition is always searching for an advantage, and direct marketing could become their forte.

▶ The Efficiency and Cost Productivity of Direct Marketing Must Be Examined

There are always start-up costs for direct marketing programs, for example, for media advertising, management information system data base, telemarketing equipment, mail order supplies and equipment, personnel, and the like. The degree and sophistication of the program determine the amount of expenditures. A thorough cost/benefit analysis should be done. To avoid mere speculation or gross miscalculations, the company may wish to conduct an experiment or to test-market the direct marketing concept. This would give concrete figures to compare with those of alternative marketing strategies.

In many cases, direct selling costs may be between 30 and 40 percent of sales. Interestingly, by its nature and purpose, direct marketing gives ample opportunity to measure the actual response rate or number of sales. It is usually easier to evaluate performance level with direct marketing than with mass advertising, certain sales promotion techniques, or merchandising tactics.

Direct marketing can be expensive under certain conditions, such as a mass mailing of new product announcements in a full-color catalog. The cost per thousand reached in this case is more than with mass advertising media. Reaching the target must be done in the most cost-

efficient manner. Cost per thousand orders or inquiries may have to be a criterion.

Many direct marketers are willing to take a loss on the first sale to a customer. They hope that future sales to this customer will offset the promotion costs. In the mail order trade this is called "backend profit" business. Location of this consumer, who may buy other products or do repeat business, gives profitable follow-up business. This situation is why many experts argue that direct marketing should not be a one-shot occurrence. It is also why the product mix should contain multiple products, so that this newfound customer has many to choose from.

For direct marketing to household consumers, as compared with selling from a retail outlet, gross margin must be healthy. The promotion costs for obtaining each order can be high. Some direct marketers even state that the markup must be three to five times the wholesale figure if only one product is being sold. (Interestingly, in the mail order distribution of books, one common rule is that selling price must be seven times the production cost because of the high costs of direct marketing.)

Direct marketing is not an inexpensive strategy. But with patience, it may bring handsome rewards.

▶ How Would Intermediaries—Dealers, Distributors, Licensees, Retailers—Feel about the Company Going Into Direct Marketing?

Marketers should be sensitive to intermediaries' attitudes and feelings about a direct marketing program. Will the company complement, supplement, or detract from their business? Are their fears justifiable or unfounded? The company certainly must avert misunderstandings with its powerful allies, yet it still wants its fair share of business and profits. Often this is not an either/or dilemma. A direct marketing program could enhance the intermediaries' businesses. For instance, partners can be aided by such direct marketing techniques as qualifying prospects via direct mail, maintaining customer service hot lines, including package inserts referring business to intermediaries, or sending supplemental sales letters to their accounts. The results of the direct marketing program might later be shared with intermediaries.

▶ Marketers Must Have Adequate Control Over Product Mix

Patents, copyrights, licenses, advanced technology, exclusive territorial rights, customer lists, brand loyalty, trademarks, trade secrets, and other forms of protection are helpful when pursuing a direct marketing

strategy. Competitors, suppliers, and intermediaries are constantly looking at direct marketing approaches. They may seek the company's market if they acquire an advantage, such as buying or producing the product for less. The more control the company has over the product and its distribution, the harder it is for another company to take over.

One mail order entrepreneur told me he used to drop-ship merchandise from manufacturers directly to his customers. Even with his own labels, packages, and brands, he still had problems. Eventually, a few of the manufacturers contacted his customers directly and attempted to bypass him. After unpleasant experiences, he decided to keep control of the distribution system and carefully guarded his list of customers.

▶ The Reputation of the Company Is an Important Factor in Whether Prospective Customers Take Up an Offer

Prospective customers may be reluctant to accept an offer if the company is unknown or has a poor reputation. This problem is compounded if the company solicits via a display, classified ad, direct mail offer, or long-distance telephone ad. If trust and a positive image have already been established, however, direct marketing opportunities are enhanced. Many consumers have no fears or qualms about buying or giving their names to direct marketers who are well known. American Express, Neiman-Marcus, Lillian Vernon, Spiegel, Sears, JC Penney, Columbia House Record and Tape Club, L. L. Bean, Republican/Democratic national parties, Exxon, General Electric, and Chase Manhattan Bank are a few examples of successful direct marketers. They have built a solid reputation that strengthens their chances for success.

▶ The Prospect List Must Be Sufficient and Established Before a Direct Marketing System Is Initiated

As noted, opportunities are ample for purchasing lists of donors, householders, or business prospects. Depending on the type of list, the cost may be anywhere from $35 to several hundred dollars per thousand names. Usually the list broker will have a minimum order, such as 5,000 names. Since there are many mailing list catalogs, buying a list may be a good starting point for a direct marketing campaign. Yet marketing people are learning to develop their own market lists systematically. Some of my favorite sources and tactics for building valuable lists are the following:

- Credit application forms
- Warranty cards
- Service contracts
- Address label coupons
- Sign-up sheets for "customer preferred" lists, visitors, or complaints
- Address labels with contests, sweepstakes, or premium offers
- Offers of free material, informative booklets, or other information
- Incentives for customers who give the names of friends, neighbors, or relatives who are *viable* prospects
- Classified advertising/display ads seeking direct customer response
- Obtaining names from exhibits or trade shows
- Recording names from incoming toll-free calls
- Exchanging names with trade associations, suppliers, or intermediaries
- "Take-one" displays placed in strategic areas in the market target's locations (e.g., in mass transit buses)
- Package inserts from normal fliers that seek a response
- Networking with professional contacts who have access to people's names in the targeted market
- Sharing direct marketing costs by piggybacking with a noncompeting direct marketer
- Exchanging names with noncompeting businesses that have similar customer profiles
- Offering informative seminars, workshops, or entertainment and tabulating registrants
- Published directories in a certain industry or field
- Having the sales force forward names to a centralized place
- Customer inquiries from other promotional programs
- Individuals/businesses that have previously responded to direct marketing stimuli, especially to the company's

An established list of prospects is the heart of a sound direct marketing program. It can often save the company time and costs on repeat business or selling of other product lines. Future direct promotional material can be aimed at these consumers. (The best list is one of individuals who have already responded to direct marketing of similar products.) A strong data-based system is needed to compile worthwhile and numerous names. Many marketers have learned that their compiled lists are a major asset and they thus guard and use them carefully.

▶ The Message or Offer Must Hook the Audience

Direct marketing seeks a specific course of action from its audience. The urge to "act now" requires strong copy techniques. Consumer benefits, incentives, and offers must be spelled out clearly. Businesses and consumers are bombarded with direct marketing solicitations. A unique but winning approach is needed. The company might even test its creative ideas in the marketplace to see if it has a powerful technique.

▶ The Best Direct Market Medium for the Circumstances and Marketing Objectives Must Be Determined

To illustrate, telephone calling may be inappropriate for selling complex products for business-to-business markets. There are too many questions, issues, and product demonstrations to be handled with this method. But systematic telephone calling may still generate leads and be an excellent door opener, even with complicated products.

Direct marketing with free product-information booklets may be an excellent vehicle for markets that are normally hard to reach. Pharmaceutical companies have found this technique useful in contacting physicians who normally had little time for detail men or just preferred to avoid them. Another difficult group that can be reached in this way is top managers of major corporations. Careful medium selection may provide market targeting opportunities that have been ignored.

▶ Proper Coding, Tabulating, and Computerized Systems Are Needed

Since the objective of direct marketing is an immediate sale or some other type of response, positive or negative results from a specific effort should be easy to determine. Each direct marketing effort must therefore be coded, tabulated, and analyzed. This usually entails a huge volume, perhaps numbering in the thousands for one mail order offer, in the tens of thousands for a coded package insert, or in the hundreds for business-to-business telephone calls. As the direct marketing program grows, a computerized system is essential.

▶ Enough Production and Lead Time Must Be Allowed

A successful project requires the scheduling and coordination of creation, production, implementation, and response time. The marketer

must interact with the various people responsible for the components of the direct marketing campaign. Plenty of time must be allowed to deal with in-house and external specialists—artists, direct response agencies, list brokers, direct marketing consultants, and the like. The work load must be further harmonized to meet the schedule of the intended audience. It is a mistake to take the trial-and-error method with the production and distribution process of direct marketing.

Systematic procedures are needed to meet consumer responses or actual orders within a reasonable time. This follow-through process is known as *fulfillment*. Smooth in-house communication channels, logistical support, warehousing/distribution center, and quick action on each response are essential. Consumers become very impatient when organizations are slow to carry out their end of the bargain. This issue is especially crucial with mail order or telephone sales. Consumers put their faith and trust in a seller sight unseen, so they expect reasonable delivery time; otherwise their enthusiasm cools quickly.

▶ The Mail Order Approach Is Popular and Even Well Respected

Though it once had a very poor image, mail order is now used by a multitude of prominent industries, companies, and nonprofit organizations. It is used successfully for such worthy causes as public health, civic issues, education, philanthropy, social/community benefits, and political campaigns.

This particular direct marketing medium captures some positive trends occurring in the marketplace. More and more detailed market segmentation has been a bonanza for direct mailings. Direct mailing enables a company to be very selective and exacting in consumer and business markets. It can then also be very specific on content and distribution of the message. With the proper message, readers feel that the communication is meant for them alone and not for millions of other mass advertising viewers. They can study the material at their convenience. This may mean that the message is not competing with other distractions.

Contrary to a popular misconception, most people like to receive direct mail marketing. Certain market groups are particularly receptive, for instance, retirees, women, young urban professionals, and two-income families. Groups that are pressed for time (such as the last) may also be ideal targets for mail order.

Advanced technology and communication have made it easier for consumers to contact businesses with their questions, orders, and complaints. This is yet another beneficial to mail order marketing.

The Direct Marketing Association (DMA) has done an outstanding job of upgrading the mail order image while developing solid professional standards. The DMA's efforts combined with the rise in educational levels of society have led to greater willingness by consumers to respond to the new concepts and approaches typical of direct mailings. Rapid and expanding personal selling costs have also caused marketing people to explore these avenues to reach their target audiences. Mail order may help to increase sales revenues or at least make the sales force more efficient by helping in the preselling or postselling stages. Also, direct mail often allows the sales force to spend more time on actual selling, since it may save prospecting or qualifying time. It may also aid in cutting down administrative tasks.

▶ The Mail Order Medium Can Help a Company Move Beyond the Physical/Geographic Range of Its Business

A market is not limited to a number of square blocks or miles. I know a few retailers whose business became highly successful when they added mail order markets to their own "off-the-street" trade. In fact, in some cases this part of sales made the difference between being highly profitable and declaring bankruptcy. Perhaps for many retailers and other types of firms, their geographic markets are constrained only by their own imagination.

The following four tips give specific methods for being successful in mail order marketing.

1. Know how to keep costs down and maximize the budget.
    a. Although quality publications with direct response advertising offers may have higher-than-average inquiry costs, do consider them. They will often have better conversion rates than cheaper but inferior magazines.
    b. Develop tight quality control standards for the printing, paper, and other production variables. A cheap, shoddy appearance scares the intended audience.
    c. Spend enough money to enhance the perceived quality of the total mail order package; color, in some cases, may double or triple the selling power of the mailing.
    d. In some cases set enough money aside to follow for multiple follow-up mailings; some readers may not order until the second or third time.

EXPLORING AND IMPROVING OPPORTUNITIES FOR DIRECT MARKETING 265

- e. Do not skimp on the total mailing package even if it means one less run on a mailing; avoid a junk postcard image.
- f. Take advantage of special mail order rates.
- g. Develop tight credit and collection procedures to hold credit losses to a minimum.
- h. To save prospective costs, include self-addressed reply forms that allow the customer to refer names of friends. Getting referrals is a good way to build a mail order list inexpensively.
- i. Use pass-along literature and pass-along order forms that are reasonable in cost and effective in business-to-business mailings.
- j. Consider offering a discount or free gift if customers buy before the busy season. Specify a postmark date, for example. This could keep down future variable costs.
- k. When cold canvassing, provide a space that can be checked if consumers do not want to receive future mail order material. This might save future costs and minimize waste.

2. Know how to Convey the message.
    - a. Use illustrations when describing a product and its benefits.
    - b. Consider photographs; they are usually more powerful and credible than drawings.
    - c. Consider before-and-after photos to highlight product benefits.
    - d. Remember that well-written copy is usually more important than illustrations, photos, logo, and color, especially with business-to-business mailings.
    - e. Headlines should have a common reference point for readers while giving a strong promise-of-benefit approach.
    - f. Avoid exaggerated or hard to prove claims that could be questionable or even illegal.
    - g. With long copy, use several subheads to break and keep readers from being bored; write in short sentences or catchy phrases or clauses.
    - h. Put the strongest product benefits at the beginning and repeat the best ones at the end. Tell readers what major benefits they will miss if they do not buy the product or perform the action. Postscripts at the end of long sales letters have been popular and effective.

- i. Use direct address ("you") to personalize the material to the reader.
- j. Put a sense of urgency in the copy to encourage readers to act. Offer readers two or three chances to act.
- k. In the fulfillment stage, include a gracious thank-you message—it is deeply appreciated and provides repeat business.
- l. When fulfilling orders, write additional copy, such as a sales letter, circular, or sheet, that features other products.
- m. Whenever possible, tie product information and the message to current events; this gives a timely perspective to readers.

3. Know how to Enhance the response rate.
- a. Quickly reply to all orders or responses, since repeat business is the core of a successful mail order business; otherwise customers will think twice before ordering again.
- b. Make the order form big and easy to read. Spell out the terms clearly while explaining all handling, shipping, and credit charges.
- c. Make heavy use of testimonials from satisfied customers, since they are very credible and reassuring to the audience.
- d. Try using product endorsements from respected and knowledgeable spokespeople, including appropriate celebrities.
- e. Explore easy-to-use credit terms, so that customers can use credit cards to make convenient phone or mail orders.
- f. Consider heavier tear-out card inserts—particularly full page—in magazines or newspapers.
- g. Plan additional incentives to get more readers to respond to the offer or request. Some successful techniques have been
  Free trial offer
  Free merchandise to go along with purchase
  Sweepstakes with no obligation
  Extended payment schedules instead of one lump payment
  Special cash or quantity discounts
  Substantial money-off for acting within a short time
  Extra supply of the product offered for acting within a
  Certain time frame
  Mailed sample of the merchandise
  Low interest of low down-payment terms
  Free information, articles, booklets, catalogs, planning
  Kit, marketing survey results, and the like
  Free estimates

- h. Make strong guarantees to assure readers. The "satisfaction guaranteed" or "money back guaranteed" policy is one of the most important tactics for improving response rate.
- i. Use "teasers" on the outside envelope to entice readers to open and read the contents.
- j. Make the order form look official (with such devices as notary seals, money-paper format, or official club membership forms) while illustrating some type of value.
- k. Include a self-addressed prestamped envelope for convenience.
- l. Study the Western Union envelope and telegraph form, which gives a sense of immediacy.
- m. Test hand-addressed envelopes, inside addresses, or signatures.
- n. Whenever possible, avoid an impersonal label or address, such as "boxholder." Consumers do not like to be part of an anonymous crowd.
- o. Try having mailings and letters introduced by a top executive. Readers feel good about receiving material from top management. It gives them a positive feeling of being an important or preferred customer.
- p. Get readers involved by having them respond with a yes or no or having them place a stamp, token, or seal on a designated spot. To encourage participation, offer some type of monetary incentive or contest. A "forced" choice often gives a better response rate than a no-rejection choice.
- q. Try a high status or prestige approach. A "charter" or exclusive membership is appealing to certain audience members.
- r. Highlight toll-free numbers so customers can easily spot them.

4. Time mailings well.
   - a. Identify and select the best months for the mailing. For instance, arts and crafts mailings are very popular in February, March, September, and October, while books and record clubs mailings use December, January, and February. Direct mail marketers have found that during other months consumers are busy with activities such as gardening. vacations, moving, and changing jobs. Hence, the cost-per-message rate is higher in the summer months than in the winter.
   - b. Plan the mailing so consumers receive material in the middle of the week, ideally on Tuesday or Wednesday. On weekends,

household consumers are usually too busy with recreational activities. In the case of industrial buyers, the weekend time lag may cause them to forget. Also, many purchasing managers study their mail more thoroughly during the mid-week period.
   c. Periodically experiment during slow periods. Continuous testing may provide ideas for peak periods.
   d. For direct respose advertisers, be careful of weekday newspaper issues, since there are heavy grocery and retailing advertisements crowding the newspaper then.

▶ Marketers Should Become Familiar with the Opportunities of Telemarketing.

Almost 3 billion phone calls are made yearly to sell or serve prospective customers. A telemarketing program is simply a formalized and systematic way of using the phone, possibly in combination with computers and other advanced electronic devices. It can be useful for both household and business-to-business marketers.

Many successful marketing executives believe that the phone commands attention; there are few distractions from a phone call, compared with other persuasive channels. Telemarketing—both outgoing phone selling and taking incoming calls from service centers—can also be very efficient and economical. At one successful national commodity distributor, the company's 27-member exclusive in-house sales force uses telemarketing for such diverse functions as finding new customers, finding new territories, and maintaining positive customer relations. Sales personnel use a sophisticated interconnected telecommunication system that integrates computers and phone systems with the workforce. This allows people in the service centers, located throughout the United States, to communicate with each other by typing messages on the CRT terminals and integrating them with a good inventory system, interoffice mailing system, special call-distribution equipment, toll-free numbers, CRTs, and computer-generated sales reports. Their whole telemarketing process has been designed for both operations and sophisticated marketing research activities.

The telephone medium can allow a company to gauge consumers' immediate reactions to its offer or request. Many successful direct marketers also use the telephone for activating dead accounts, increasing the frequency rate of purchases, "trading up" the sale, taking orders,

cross-selling, prospecting, building traffic, and supplementing other marketing techniques.

In short, the overriding potential benefit of telephone marketing is that it gives quick and spontaneous verbal feedback. Not only can the recipient's current positive and negative reactions to propositions be judged but also the strengths and weaknesses of other parts of the marketing strategy. In his book, *Telemarketing for Business: A Guide to Building Your Own Telemarketing Operation,* Eugene Kordahl went even further. He noted that telemarketing gives the only true method of *systematically controlling* sales-related costs. Telemarketing can therefore reduce selling costs *while increasing sales.*

Despite the benefits of telemarketing, caution is still a virtue. There are numerous success stories, but there are also failures and disappointments, and in some organizations top executives are now quite negative about the virtues of telemarketing. Telemarketing thus needs careful planning and implementation. Early failures tax the patience of management while negating future support.

▶ Special People Are Needed to Make a Telecommunication Strategy Successful

For telemarketing, people need seven basic skills:

1. A strong pleasing voice
2. Sound manners, effective phone techniques, and articulate vocabulary
3. Outstanding listening skills so person picks up subtle clues and responds in an impromptu but positive way
4. Thorough understanding of products and industry practices (unless the people are mere order takers, in which case the job could be subcontracted to a specialized firm that handles incoming calls)
5. The ability to handle a variety of questions while stating the benefits of the proposition
6. Appreciation of the company's policies and procedures
7. A talent for making good sales presentations

Given the high frequency of taking or making calls, the staff also needs a strong constitution and perseverance. A number of rejections or discourteous responses on the other end of the line necessitates individ-

uals who can handle them in a positive manner and not take them personally.

It is not an easy task to find an effective and conciliatory communicator who possesses the aforementioned traits. And one myth must be debunked: A company's best outside salespeople will not necessarily make good telemarketers. They may even feel uneasy with the phone medium and seek the person-to-person contact of the field. Good phone techniques can be taught, but the student must have the knack, personality, and interest for this medium.

To succeed, telemarketing operation should be staffed with people committed to selling by phone. Standards and testing procedures for the prescribed skills are needed. The final interviewees should actually make and/or receive phone calls to and from a controlled group of callers, to see how they handle sensitive and difficult situations. Other marketing personnel should be included in the selection process, so they can interact with the telemarketing staff. Some field people feel that telephone personnel take business away from them or are an obstacle instead of a conduit for completing sales. The groups can do several activities together, to encourage cooperation and interdepartmental communication. Once good telemarketers are hired, they should be compensated well to avoid turnover problems. Telemarketing should not be a dumping ground, nor should the people be treated like second-class citizens.

Newly hired people should be given an orientation period, followed by solid and continuous training. Since the market environment changes so rapidly, an ongoing training program with periodic updates can give telemarketers a competitive edge.

▶ Telemarketers Should Use a Predetermined, Pretested Script

The telephone message should contain basic elements and steps. The message usually includes identification of the sponsor of the caller, a request for the identity of the person called, qualifying statements, and a spelling out of the purpose of the call. This purpose should clearly include the benefits to the person being called.

Since every organization has a different situation, it is not feasible to give specific scripts here. The company must analyze its own situation, identify its telemarketing objectives, and then study the people or organizations to be called. The major point is that telemarketers should have standardized forms and general outlines that will give them a

good idea of what to emphasize. They can make adjustments according to what is said on the other end of the line, but must cover major selling points. A pretested telephone message that embodies the basics may give additional confidence to callers while leading to a natural phone conversation.

For those who are serious about telemarketing and would like good practical advice on this topic, I recommend three books and one magazine: *Telemarketing for Business: A Guide to Building Your Own Telemarketing Operation,* by Eugene B. Kordahl; *Profitable Telephone Sales Operations,* by Robert C. Steckel; *Telephone Marketing* by Murray Roman; and *Telemarketing.*

19

Developing Guidelines for Successful Distribution

Marketing people are directly or indirectly involved with the actual movement of goods and the activities associated with this movement. Involvement entails both physical distribution and channels of distribution.

Physical distribution activities involve the equipment and facilities needed to get the right quantity of goods to the right place at the right time for the lowest possible cost, without sacrificing customer service requirements. Channels of distribution are the institutions, businesses, and people that comprise the supply process. In some cases a channel may be a direct flow from supplier to consumer; other channels may encompass all types of intermediaries who help by processing, assembling, taking title, handling physical movement, or marketing the goods. For most products in today's marketplace, the channel usually involves some type of middle-person—wholesaler, distributor, or retailer.

This chapter explores guidelines and suggestions for enhancing "place" decisions as related to physical distribution and channels of distribution. Place refers to making products available to consumers at the right time, location, and quantities. Physical distribution has emerged as a complicated, detailed, and specialized field in itself. Many organizations, in fact, have centralized this function and made it a specialized entity distinct from marketing. Because it has become so highly technical and sophisticated, this chapter covers only general issues.

Even if physical distribution is outside the marketing department or the department does not work directly with its distribution channel members, these members are vital wheels to the company's marketing strategies. They help in having the product available when the consumer wants it, which is a key purpose of the marketing program.

▶ A Company Cannot Afford to Have Distribution Functions Poorly Dispersed Among Manufacturing, Marketing, and Finance

Physical distribution must be regarded as a separate and positive force for achieving a competitive niche. Some executives assume that physical distribution should be under the marketing domain, while others expect it to be subordinate to another corporate activity, such as manufacturing. Another group—perhaps the majority—advocates a separate department for physical distribution and thus argues for equal billing with the other corporate activities. The structure chosen must depend on market targets, competition, the industry, and internal resources.

Following are seven requisites for a powerful physical distribution organization:

1. Responsibilities and authority for carrying out distribution activities are clearly defined and assigned specific people.
2. Top management provides support to the distribution function.
3. The structure provides smooth communication between other functional areas, such as marketing.
4. All policies and procedures for the distribution function are defined.
5. Physical distribution personnel have access to important information.
6. People in physical distribution have opportunities to serve on important staff committees, such as a corporate planning committee.
7. The chief manager of the department is a strong manager; the position is not used as a dumping ground for a weak person.

The best organization is one that permits sound integrative planning and control over all aspects of physical distribution, that allows the physical distribution operations to exist as one entity, and that has an objective mechanism to measure performance.

▶ A Total Systems Perspective Is Needed to Dramatize the Interrelationships and Interdependencies of the Parts of the Physical Distribution System and the Relationship of the System to Marketing Strategy

As noted, marketing and physical distribution people must depend on each other. For example, sales forecasting, market research, and the input of middlemen and the sales force aid in locating branches and warehouses, product/stock rotations, optimal inventory levels, efficient order processing procedures, and the best transportation carriers. On the other hand, physical distribution serves as a potential tool for marketing strategy by creating customer satisfaction at the lowest possible costs.

Physical distribution may include

- Inbound transportation and receiving
- Inventory management
- Packaging
- In-plant warehousing
- Shipping
- Outbound transportation
- Field warehousing
- Customer Service
- Order processing

Each component is essential to marketing strategy. Following are some recurring problems that are symptomatic of major problems with the physical distribution system:

- Goods damaged in transit
- Transporting orders to wrong locations
- Double orders sent due to poor recordkeeping
- Excessive order cycle times
- Delivery bottlenecks
- Thefts in transit
- Expensive carriers selected due to emergency delivery needs
- Inadequate or too much inventory stock
- Faulty billing or claims procedures
- Warehouses improperly sized
- Insufficient insurance

- Accepting and shipping orders regardless of weight or size
- Goods lost in warehouse
- High distribution expenditures (compared with industry norms)
- Large number of customer service complaints
- Large number of interwarehouse shipments

If these problems are common, the company may need a good management audit to identify the underlying problems and initiate corrective action. An evaluation of the physical distribution system is also prudent if the company is enacting major marketing strategy changes, adding a number of new products, or seeking new markets. Under these circumstances, many new questions and decisions transpire with the distribution system. In essence, the management team may crave new organizational positions, may consolidate physical distribution functions, and may emphasize total distribution expenses instead of the costs of performing each function.

▶ Management Must Examine and Dissect Total Physical Distribution Costs While Recognizing the Challenges of Cost Trade-offs Versus Levels of Customer Service

The overall objective is to pursue total system performance to avoid suboptimization. The costs will vary for different industries. They can range from 2 percent of sales to around 30 percent of sales, as in the food industry. The physical distribution area used to be popularly characterized as the last dark continent for lowering expenses. Today there is greater attention toward this function, since the lowering of expenses by a few percentage points can make significant contributions to profits.

To reduce expenses, it might be possible to

- Increase order processing operations
- Establish budgets and cost controls
- Arrange distribution expenses by major products, customers, or middlemen
- Reduce unnecessary inventory levels (e.g., "just-in-time" concept)
- Utilize new containerization and palletization concepts
- Employ latest technological innovations
- Computerize the warehouse system
- Perform efficiency studies

- Integrate marketing plans with physical distribution
- Improve communication and working relationships among marketing, manufacturing, and distribution
- Provide financial/staff support
- Modify policies/procedures for delivery and related customer transaction issues
- Create better packing to aid handling and storage
- Eliminate unprofitable channel members
- Introduce a reward system for improved efficiency
- Unbundle distribution activities and pinpoint direct costs
- Study competition's physical distribution system to copy strengths and avoid weaknesses
- Develop an MIS structure related to strategy and performance analysis for inventory, warehousing, unit loading, transportation, and customer service requirements

Perhaps the three costs that seem to be steadily increasing the most are transportation, warehousing, and inventory carrying costs. The increases are indicative of recent problems with government restraints, rising energy costs, union contracts, foreign competition, and the shortage in capital financial markets of reasonable interest rate loans for inventory. These issues will continue to strain physical distribution management capabilities.

Besides different efficiency opportunities, there are trade-off considerations. Reducing the cost of one distribution activity may actually make total distribution costs even higher. Some illustrations:

> Eliminating warehouses can increase transportation and inventory carrying costs.
> Lowering transportation expenses can increase lot quantity costs or warehousing needs.
> Reducing inventory might decrease customer service levels and thus result in lost sales.
> More customer demands might tax the order-processing function.

Airlines are quite sensitive to the total costs concept. Although they usually have higher rates than other carriers, in some cases their use is cheaper. Total costs analysis could show that even a few hours shorter travel time will save expenses in warehousing, rental insurance, taxes, and other areas.

▶ Selection of a Specific Mode of Transportation Is a Complex Decision

This is why many organizations use a traffic department or manager. They must carefully weigh all the factors that determine what type of carrier or combination of carriers to use. With government deregulation and its aftermath, executives are uncomfortably learning the significance of transportation decisions.

Even if daily logistical or transportation choices do not have to be made, knowing something about the more salient factors—flexibility, dependability, frequency, transit speed, and rate structure—is worthwhile. Each of the five major transportation modes—railroads, pipelines, waterways, trucking, and airways—have pros and cons and present trade-offs. For example, trucking may be more available and dependable but could have higher rates. The criteria considered most important will influence the selection of carriers. Decisions will also be influenced by the products being transported, the needs of the market targets and middlemen, and the strategic objectives of the company.

▶ The Greatest Potential for Improving Physical Distribution Is in Management Interrelationships

The historical diffusion of physical distribution activities to various departments has created sticky problems. For example, order processing or customer service may have been under marketing, while inventory control was the province of accounting or purchasing.

More accountability requirements or the consolidation of the physical distribution process will frighten some people. Executives may believe that they are losing part of their empire or are being asked to continually justify some decisions. Contradictory behavior and tumultuous misunderstandings could cause organizational chaos.

Smooth relationships and coordination must be developed and implemented, especially if the company is currently centralizing the physical distribution activities. A matrix organizational concept might even be necessary to get some tasks completed. Top management must recognize and redesign the unresolved issues.

▶ A Few Variables Influence Which Channel of Distribution System Is Chosen

Alternative channels are (1) going directly to customers (short channel), (2) employing various middlemen (medium to long channel), and/or (3)

using multiple distribution. Since channels are so dynamic, constant management attention and continuous decisions are required. Channel selection depends on these critical factors:

1. *Product characteristics.* If the price of the product per unit is low, if the product is a staple (household or drug product, for example), or if the product is standardized and/or requires little service, the channel of distribution is usually long (many middlemen). On the other hand, many industrial products have a short channel (often due to the many services needed by customers and the high price per unit of the product).

2. *Customers.* The preferences of customers often dictate the choice of a channel. Many larger customers—big industrial companies, retailers, wholesalers—like to go direct. They are willing to forgo the services provided by middlemen. Geographic distance may require more middlemen in the channel.

3. *Company characteristics.* Companies with enough financial, managerial, and physical resources may sell products and services with few middlemen. They have the capabilities to assume the functions of the middlemen. A firm with many different products can usually pool them and have a shorter channel. The more control management wants, the shorter the channel will be.

4. *Channel members.* In selecting a channel, a marketer tries to find channel members who can do the best job. The channel members selected should be able to get along with each other and allow each other to achieve organizational objectives.

5. *Environment.* Government, competition, and cultural customs can all influence the type of channel selected.

Sometimes different channels can be tested to discover which ones are the most profitable. Unique policies and procedures, however, may be needed to evaluate each type of channel.

▶ A Channel Manager May Be Needed

A company concludes that it needs a separate manager within the firm to establish channel strategies. Some companies have created a special slot in the organization, known as a channel, distribution, licensing, or dealer manager. These executives

- Identify channel problems
- Determine needs and likely responses of each channel member

- Improve relationships among channel members
- Develop and measure performance standards for each member
- Coordinate channel activities as they relate to manufacturing, engineering, financing, and/or marketing
- Play a major role in formulating channel strategies

In today's complicated environment, channel management is not a simple endeavor. The individuality of the channel members makes it hard to define a normative approach or even a set of rules that will work in every channel. What succeeds for one set of channel circumstances might prove disastrous in another. The best generalized rule is to first define the market target and then select and design the channel that meets the market needs while accomplishing the firm's objectives.

▶ The Amount of Market Exposure—Intensive, Selective, and Exclusive—Traditionally Depends on the Type of Goods Being Sold and the Market Being Targeted

Market availability has to be balanced with the required distribution costs to achieve the desired exposure. Intensive distribution involves placing products or services in as many outlets as possible. This strategy is usually apparent used for low unit-value goods with high repurchase rates and consumers who want convenience. Wide distribution is preferred for convenience-type goods and for food-related products, beverages, and office supplies. Traditionally, intensive distribution requires advertising support and a strong physical distribution apparatus. In many cases its complexities necessitate multiple channels and a variety of procedures.

Selective distribution involves limited market exposure through selection of a small number of outlets. The number of distribution points is carefully controlled to ensure good working relationships with the fewer channel members. Marketers of shopping goods, such as furniture, appliances, home furnishings, and expensive clothing, frequently adopt selective distribution strategies. Since only a few outlets in a given territory are chosen, the middlemen must demonstrate capabilities in marketing and service, supplier loyalty, financial strength, and reputation within the territory in question. Also, their concerns must be considered. Often they are actually business adversaries. They expect equitable treatment from the supplier and become quite upset if their opponents appear to be receiving more attention or preferential treatment.

In a selective distribution structure, a marketer could sell to both

national chains and small specialty retailers. The two have different needs and expectations. Furthermore, the markets they serve may be different, or there could be a transition period with retail sales. For example, the sales pattern could move from the specialty houses to national retail merchandisers.

Exclusive distribution offers an outlet exclusive territorial rights to a producer's goods and full protection from competition. This type of distribution is common in the marketing of items that dictate specialized selling efforts and usually a large investment or commitment by the channel member. There are exclusive distribution arrangements in the automotive, soft drink/beverage, brewery, and building contracting industries. This system has also been popular in franchising or contractual licensing agreements. The franchisee or licensee is traditionally given a protected territory in which to operate. The exclusive relationship is a tight marriage. Both parties are highly dependent on each other for succeeding in the marketplace.

A producer, franchisor, or licensor must avoid one common mistake—giving too large a territory and exclusive rights to marginal outlets. These could be distributors, retailers, sales agents, franchisees, or licensees. Sometimes large chunks of areas are allocated to outlets that lack the resources or expertise to develop the area. Marketers are then stuck with these businesses and poor sales penetration is often the outcome.

With exclusive distribution, a facilitator is sometimes essential for consolidating the channel members. Coca-Cola has served as a matchmaker by assisting sound bottlers to acquire weaker bottlers. Often the larger territory furnishes economies of scale and more marketing clout. Coca-Cola even arranges financial support for the bottlers. Their increased capacity and distribution efficiencies better prepare them for battles against bottlers from soft drink rivals like Pepsi-Cola.

Exclusive distribution requires very cooperative and smooth relations among channel members. Both parties can be extremely successful if they recognize the value of their relationship.

▶ **Marketers Should Decide Which Type of Marketing Strategy— Push, Pull, or a Combination —They Will Employ in Their Channel of Distribution**

The three alternatives can be explained as follows:

1. *Push.* The producer concentrates its marketing efforts on channel members. It tries to develop a high degree of loyalty among them. The middlemen then push the products to the consumer.

2. *Pull.* The producer aims aggressive promotion at the consumer. When demand has been stimulated, middlemen are forced to carry the product.

3. *Combination push/pull.* Many firms attempt to follow both strategies at the same time. This is possible if the firm has enough money allocated to the marketing budget.

The strength of a company's middlemen or of its advertising or personal selling program might determine which of the three it selects. A strong and loyal group of channel members can push the product through. Of course, profit incentives must be such as to encourage everyone to market the goods. On the other hand, promotion may be needed to support weaker middlemen or to sell around them. Competition may be very stiff. To acquire loyalty from both customers and middlemen, the company may pull with promotion.

Or, like a few other businesses, the company may take the expensive but aggressive approach of heavy promotion along with positive incentives and profit margins for channel members. This tactic requires a high gross margin and ample financial strength. Most organizations use a combination to some extent. But they cannot always afford a strong commitment to the combination approach. As a very general rule, household marketers prefer the pull strategy while industrial marketers prefer the push.

▶ The Company Needs Systematic Guidelines for Picking and Measuring How Well Potential Channel Members Can Fulfill Company Objectives

Management is constantly faced with selecting team members for different markets and products. In general terms, marketers want channel members who can

- Increase sales volume
- Keeps costs to a minimum
- Provide good market coverage
- Help with promotional support
- Spread goodwill
- Offer technical support/expertise
- Provide strong financial capabilities
- Give solid marketing and/or manufacturing support
- Possess sound managment skills within their own organization

Marketers can set up their own evaluation scheme to judge how well prospective members meet these and other criteria. The biggest mistake a company can make is to assume that once products are sold to another channel member, its responsibilities are completed. It must sell *through* these team members. Consumers can become angry with one channel member and then blame all the other firms involved.

▶ In Any Channel of Distribution, There Is a Channel Captain—One Dominant Business—That Can Greatly Influence the Decisions of the Other Members While Controlling the Overall Channel Operations

This captain will exercise control over common distribution decisions that affect the entire channel. The other members must appreciate the powerful position of the captain. They will sometimes have to modify their own strategies to comply with the captain's wishes and expectations. However, this leader should avoid a dictatorial attitude. The other members may resist his preferences. In the long run, this attitude will alienate everyone so that eventually they leave the self-centered channel captain and associated distribution channel. In his own interests the leader should find strategies that instill cooperation, understanding, and operating efficiency and marketing power among all the channel members. Since all members are interdependent, it behooves the channel captain to take a supportive role for the other members. Weaknesses should be identified and strong action taken to correct them.

At one time, wholesalers were channel captains. They bought goods and shipped them throughout the world. The goods were transported to retailers and far-reaching frontier/rural trading posts or general stores.

After manufacturing industrialization took place, the producers became powerful and decided on the marketing and logistical scheme for various channels. Eventually some retailers started to grow and emerged as economic and marketing giants. The term "countervailing power" came into being. The retailers counteracted the power of the manufacturers, which in a few cases had been dictatorial. Hence the retailers found new suppliers and in many instances built them into large producers. The manufacturers grew with the retailers.

Today the type of product, customer, competition, economic situation, and management decisions determine who is the channel captain. An uncertain milieu makes it hard to distinguish the true power base in certain channel systems.

In selecting channels, a company wants team members who appreciate their interdependence. Periodically there will be conflict among channel members. Each member will have different objectives and aspirations. A solid channel captain can minimize and regulate the degree of conflict. The marketing program will require negotiation, compromise, and empathy among channel members. The channel captain should be the leading force for enhancing channel cooperation.

Over the years, Whirlpool, a producer of appliances, has garnered the reputation of being a benevolent channel captain. A few other appliance manufacturers would flood their dealers with inventory, on the assumption that the dealers would have to be loyal to them because they had such a large stock to sell. However, even with favorable inventory financing, many dealers went broke or lost their devotion to the producers. The turnover sales ratio was too poor. Whirlpool, on the other hand, did not overstock its dealers. The captain also gave useful dealer seminars on marketing and management techniques to improve profitability. Whirlpool provided quality products, postsale service support, toll-free customer hot lines, and reasonable advance warnings on price changes that allowed dealers to advance order on old price sheets. Instead of being a hostage to the channel captain, these dealers felt like part of a team that was building a successful channel system.

▶ Sometimes Distrust and Destructive Behavior Develop Between Channel Members

Certain areas or decisions can plant the seeds of conflict among channel members. Examples are:

- Poor warranty or service support
- Bypassing of middlemen and communicating to customers without their knowledge
- Little territorial protection
- Cancellation and termination of channel agreements without ample justification
- Private branding versus national branding, each one cannabilizing sales for the other
- Interference in each other's operations and managerial prerogatives
- Giving more attention and interest to channel members' competition
- Lack of marketing support

- Placing of inventory burden on the other channel members
- Unfair pricing, discounts, or margins
- Inequitable dual distribution
- Complicated volume-discount offerings
- Taking customers away from channel members (e.g., moving to in-house national acounts)

A number of marketing tactics are available to overcome anarchy and a disruptive channel. These tactics can create a loyal channel unit out of channel members. Some of them are:

- Cooperative advertising allowances
- Liberal return policy
- Training sessions
- Financial incentives
- Marketing support via displays, labeling, and promotional supplies or materials
- Preticketing
- Inventory adjustments
- Favorable loans and credit support
- Management system support
- Exclusive contracts for territorial protection
- Missionary and detail people to help promotional efforts and set up displays
- Contests and sweepstakes for personnel of channel members
- Logistical support
- Higher profit margins
- Special deals, discounts, and price incentives
- Sharing of market information/technical advice and backup service
- Cooperative management information system
- Merchandising help plus setting up inventory
- Management consultation

These tactics motivate channel members. Each member is an independent business with specific needs and market concerns. The company must continually attempt to develop channel relations that encourage a cooperative mood whereby all members feel they are in the channel together. Above all, constant communication and reasonable compromise are needed among all of the members.

APPENDIX
Judging a Shopping Center for Locating or Relocating a Retail Business

"I don't care how good a store looks or how well priced the merchandise is. If that store isn't in a convenient location, it is not going to make money. Pure and simple."

                               Fred F. Canning, President, Walgreen Company

The guidelines and rules covered in this book are universal to all types of organizations. However, I feel that the shopping center/mall location issue is so important to numerous small retailers that it requires coverage. Hence this appendix.

Every new or established retailer must sooner or later evaluate the profitability of moving to a shopping center or staying in a center when the lease expires. Marketers know that every shopping center—large or small, regional or strip, enclosed mall or open/outside cluster—has a perceived personality and image among consumers. A poorly run center can have a bad impact on all the retailers in it. In fact, there have been cases of bankruptcy throughout an entire shopping center.

Assuming the shopping center is under a centralized management and leasing arrangement, a retailer should weigh certain factors in making the decision about locating in it.

▶ The Center Must Have Physical and Environmental Conditions that Make Consumer Shopping an Easy and Enjoyable Task

Good location, easy access, and ample parking enhance consumer traffic volume. Today's consumers are hedonistic when it comes to shopping. They expect a pleasurable experience, and the physical properties of a retail shopping center are a basic prerequisite.

A poorly run shopping center can hurt all the retailers in it. Such environmental concerns as cleanliness, safety, climate control, aesthetics, and other consumer amenities can affect the entire consumer behavior process.

▶ Managers of the Shopping Center Must Promote the Center Effectively

The landlord or the center's hired management team must be a shrewd merchandiser and have a flair for promotion. Effective promotional

strategy should be culminated with special events, exhibitions, sales themes, and community events that all create interest. The promotion should create excitement while building traffic to the retail center.

▶ The Shopping Center Must Not Be Top-Heavy with Administrative Support

A number of centers, especially malls, have gone bankrupt because too much money was spent on administrative personnel and overhead. The higher expenditures penalized the budget for promotion and special events. Obviously, enough money must be spent to attract good mall managers and a supportive staff, but money must not be wasted either.

▶ The Relationship Between Landlord and Tenants Must Be Smooth

Smaller retailers should make sure that the landlord has empathy for their unique problems and challenges. Sometimes a landlord will be so concerned with satisfying the larger anchor stores that he neglects the needs of smaller retailers.

The prospective tenant should avoid shopping center developers who are overly aggressive and slick in signing up tenants. Realistic business projections, market studies, rental fees, leasing terms, hidden charges, and a sound business plan must be provided. The developer must be stable, have a favorable reputation for building successful shopping centers, and have the financial strength to withstand the hidden surprises and expenditures that can easily besiege and inundate a developer. One sample question to address to the developer: Are there any pending lawsuits or previous litigation against the developer by the tenants?

▶ The Retailers in the Shopping Center Must Complement Each Other While Providing a Powerful Competitive Drive Against Other Retailing Clusters

The right blend of stores and consumer services, such as eating establishments, beauty salons, barbershops, and banks, must be available in the prospective shopping center. Some neighbors are undesirable: A massage parlor, an adult-rated bookstore, or a lounge may attract a seedy group of people.

The center should have large well-known retailers that create traffic while giving the center a favorable identity. These anchor stores should attract a market segment appropriate to the smaller stores.

Some developers are indifferent to the combination and type of tenants they sign up. They merely try to get as many tenants as possible. The developer should also have stringent rules and policies of limiting the amount of intracompetition within the shopping center itself. This is one of the most common complaints of my retailing friends.

Another common complaint is having to compete with a special sales theme event even though the retailer was assured that it would have no direct competition. For example, sellers of arts and crafts are given an opportunity to display their wares in the hallway of a store for a week or so, resulting in competition for an established hobby, gift, or card shop.

▶ The Shopping Center Should Give Support and Major Opportunities for Policy and Strategic Decisions that Can Be Effected by a Merchants' Association

An efficient association is able to develop a sound program for the shopping center while handling the complaints and concerns of individual retailers. A shopping center in which anchor stores hold all the association's power or in which the association is merely cosmetic should be shunned.

PART FIVE:
A CHANGING ENVIRONMENT AND BEING PREPARED

20

Succeeding in a State of Flux: Etc., Etc.

Marketing is a fascinating and never-ending story. Its many facets require continuous attention to intracompany and environmental changes. The uncertainties and volatility of the marketplace have been one of the major themes of this book. Various principles, rules, and guidelines have been presented for enhancing company strategies.

This chapter explores marketing strategies in relation to fluid business conditions. The suggestions it contains should inspire further thoughts on general issues in marketing. Every organization has experienced devastating periods. None is immune from misfortunes or sudden downturns in either business or individual product lines. Companies that have experienced such crises and survived include Sears, Coca-Cola, Kroger, Armco, Apple Computer, McDermott International, AT&T, Woolworth, Georgia-Pacific, Cummins, Walt Disney Productions, Chrysler, Uniroyal, Gould, Avon, and Procter and Gamble. Some organizations don't make it; they declare bankruptcy, reorganize, or simply dissolve.

Some people truly enjoy the chance to overturn a bleak situation and rescue the organization. Lee Iacocca is perhaps the best-known executive who turned around a company (Chrysler) teetering on the edge of bankruptcy. Other managers have established prosperous careers as turnaround specialists. They successfully formulate new programs or restructure old ones to save troubled companies, divisions, or product lines. Some organizations specialize in this process. For example, Re-

public Health, formed in 1982, specifically buys and turns around relatively weak hospitals, eventually making them into strong profit centers. Republic Health is now the fifth largest hospital management chain.

Many turnaround tactics surfaced during the early 1980s, a period that saw an unprecedented number of business failures and a transformation of the corporate and economic segments of our society. In retrospect, the business community learned from this ominous period. It is now better prepared for future commotions.

▶ A Turnaround Plan Should Embody Strategies for Correcting Immediate Problems While Instilling Credibility and Confidence into Stakeholders of the Organization

Everyone, including customers, must believe that the organization can retrench, revitalize itself, and return to successful profit levels. Without commitment to this belief, good employees, suppliers, shareholders, middlemen, and customers may abandon the organization.

The following are plausible tactics and strategies that might be incorporated into turnaround marketing and operational plans.

1. *Identify key problem areas.* Without creating time-consuming committee meetings and paper work, do have a few candid staff meetings that are free-flowing exchanges. Everyone should try to pinpoint the current strengths and weaknesses. What went wrong and why? A tight system must be developed that can control the downslide while helping to correct the current mess. A word of caution: The luxury of time for slow decisions about next maneuvers is absent. Frequently creditors, customers, and suppliers are leaving or pressuring the company. They want answers and action within a reasonable period. In fact, if the situation is desperate, the turnaround program may have to show results in weeks or at most months. Urgency is a constant lurking shadow.

2. *Establish a sound financial plan and control.* Cash flow must be analyzed more frequently. Analysis may even be needed on daily or weekly basis. To enhance cash position and working capital, penny-pinching strategies may have to be adopted, such as:

- Selling excessive inventory, equipment, or product lines at reduced prices
- Tightening accounts receivables or even factoring them out

- Paying only the most pressing items to keep company doors open, such as payroll, utilities, key suppliers, and the like
- Reducing short-term debt
- Selling off customer lists, patents, licenses, trademarks, or product lines
- Restricting credit business
- Tightening expense accounts, employee perks, salaries, or wages—the meat-ax approach
- Delaying disbursements and negotiating with creditors to explain the current situation
- Controlling purchasing, inventory mix, and inefficient assets that are draining cash
- Making sure employees comprehend the importance of improving the cash position

3. *Consolidate and prune various product lines.* Marginal products must go if they are losers. Greater concentration on "core" products is mandatory. Product development priorities should be given to those projects that fit into the new company mission, as defined by the turnaround plan, and that will provide favorable returns within a reasonable period. Product development budgets for tenuous, fluid, or unclear projects must be reduced or eliminated. On the other hand, product quality and service standards must be maintained, despite limited financial resources and the drive to cut costs. It might be possible to reposition current products to new markets to increase sales.

4. *Identify and give extra attention to key accounts and markets.* Marginal or costly business may have to be dropped. Future markets that will fit the new corporate mission must be identified and current and future competition be examined in light of the market target analysis.

5. *Direct marketing efforts to where the company has proprietary advantages and thus can demand better prices.* Make price cuts in selective areas, but avoid a price war. Explore feasibility of short-run price gimmicks, such as discounts, rebates, and contests.

6. *Consolidate distribution channels and see what can be done to improve merchandising and sales power.* Marginal channel members that drain resources and time must be dropped, as must feeble, incompetent, or uninterested members. Encourage cooperative marketing efforts and hunt for new ways to promote aggressively within the channel, such as dealer training programs and inventory incentives. Explore the feasibility of vertical integration.

7. *Aim advertising and sales promotion strategies to move existing business.* Offer additional incentives to reward selling efforts. Experiment with various image-building techniques that might counteract the negative reputation garnered during the downslide. Assign a healthy budget to the promotion mix. Amply reward and keep good people in promotion; they are now more important than ever. Drop weak salespeople and replace them with good professional people.

8. *Make a clear blueprint for the organization's strategic objectives and how it can achieve them.* Consider major strategic decisions on divesting, merging, closing facilities, restructuring capitalization, selling off assets, refurbishing / renovating, and diversifying or expanding into new businesses. These are complex decisions that take vision and steadfastness. Restructuring is time consuming and the results are not immediately transparent. The focus of the financial community is sometimes on short-term earnings. This viewpoint compounds the problem of credibility. It is hard to convince stakeholders that a turnaround plan is indeed working.

Finally, during a turnaround the whole corporate culture usually moves through a brutal renaissance and reformation. The possible resulting forces of "leaner/meaner," lower operating costs, shutdowns, salary freezes, staff reduction, and dislocation cause terrible bloodletting and discomfort. Top management should not sugarcoat the problems or downplay them in the beginning. In the final analysis, candor will save everyone valuable time and prevent future misunderstandings.

No-Growth/Mature Industries

In some industries marketers are faced with a no-growth proposition. The environment in these industries is stagnant and seems unglamorous, and marketing challenges are stiff. Market share must be taken away from the competition, career promotions seem slow, and the business appears mundane. Nevertheless, no-growth industries are commonplace—currently steel, education, public health, heavy machinery, food, beverages, aluminum, and copper—and there are methods for improving the situation.

▶ **In No-Growth Industries, Marketers Must Explore Strategies to Make the Organization More Productive While Aggressively Taking Business Away from the Competition**

Certain strategies to improve sales or enter new markets can be explored. Among them are the following:

1. Acknowledge previous errors that have placed the company in stodgy markets and see if organizational changes would allow it to be more market driven.
2. Explore joint ventures and mergers to capture economies of scale and synergistic opportunities (for example, in the steel industry).
3. Slash weak product lines and carve out a niche in highly profitable specialized markets.
4. Downsize the organization to reflect the no-growth environment.
5. See if productivity opportunities prevail and develop constructive methods for enhancing profit margins.
6. Make the management climate flexible so the company can react quickly to competitive changes that threaten current market share or profits. (Some textile and apparel firms are successfully following this strategy.)
7. Provide shorter lead times to fulfill customer needs.
8. Fine tune customer service, product quality, and terms of delivery to achieve customer allegiance.
9. Constantly seek new efficient methods in production, marketing, and distribution, to either achieve better customer devotion or lower costs.
10. Explore the benefits of vertical integration. For example, if the company already has a distribution network, the network might distribute lines of other companies as well.
11. Avoid mindless diversification and acquisition in hot growth industries: Does the firm have the experience or understand what to do with uncharted growth businesses?
12. Optimize integration between technology and customers. Even in an industry with low R&D expenditures, such integration has spin-off value on making matured products more competitive. It could provide new innovative concepts that might even turn the firm into a future growth industry.
13. Manage human resources wisely. Good management is critical, since promotions and upward career moves are sluggish. The job environment must provide challenges and career counseling to overcome boredom or indifference.

Uncontrollable Growth

A growing and emerging business is exciting for marketers. Promotions, bonuses, and professional accolades seem constant. But the fluctuating

market—with new competition, investment requirements, and consumer expectations—poses constant problems and risks.

▶ A Growing Organization Must Maintain Sensible Operational Controls with Existing Products and Businesses

A common marketing blunder is failing to pursue satisfactory operational procedures when expanding into new businesses or markets.

For example, the Pizza Time Theatre franchise, a pizza parlor with a video arcade room and singing robots, was at one time feverishly increasing, new stores opening constantly. Poor controls resulted in declining profit margins for older stores due to inferior food, poor service, and rising operating costs. The overall decline in the arcade business compounded the problem.

▶ In a High-Growth Business, Management Must Prevent Common Mistakes

The mistakes that managers of high-growth businesses commonly make are the following:

1. They forget that strategic windows (i.e., market opportunities match organizational resources) close abruptly in high-growth markets.

2. They respond too deliberately to new technological changes.

3. They build too many management layers, which results in a top-heavy firm.

4. They ignore the old-line businesses, which causes the cash cows to become dogs even though their future could still be bright.

5. They take on excessive debt with the assumption that there is no limit to growth (the oil service industry is full of examples). Highly leveraged firms are unable to cope effectively with sudden downturns.

6. They lose the reputation for good product quality because they are too preoccupied with moving goods out and increasing sales.

7. They focus on sales growth obsessively, allowing marginal expenditures to exceed marginal revenues; eventually profit margins turn sour.

8. They constantly introduce new products and models. Sometimes industry executives make glib announcements about new models soon to hit the marketplace. Consequently, customers postpone purchase of current lines and wait for the new improved products. Premature declarations hurt sales of current product lines, and sometimes they turn out to be false or the proposed products are delayed.

9. They falsely believe that new problems will be overcome by future sales.

10. They ignore the cultural climate and mystique that made the firm prosperous. They are unable to make the transition from a growing dynamic business to a larger but mature company.

11. They develop a "can't miss" attitude. Success can breed false security, and diversification becomes a problem.

In short, marketing in a high-growth industry is not a guaranteed success. Every manager wants a growth business, but even in such a business effective marketing management is needed.

Product Strategies for Consumers

Periodically, marketing people encounter situations in which they are unable to fulfill consumer demand for their goods and services. In the past—for example, the early 1970s—shortages occurred in such product areas as oil, gas, cotton, paper, cement, plastics, wood, steel, copper, aluminum, sugar, and silver. To truly serve customers, the proper role of marketing strategy must be determined during shortages.

▶ A Unique, Effective Marketing Strategy Must Be Formulated for Periods of Excessive Buyer Demand—Without a Decrease in Marketing

In periods of high demand, an error is made if the importance of marketing is deemphasized. Poor practices that limit demand can haunt marketers when their supply once again exceeds demand.

Previously, when there were shortages, a few marketers would adopt shortsighted strategies. They would:

- Lower the advertising budget
- Narrow the product mix
- Lay off key sales personnel

- Eliminate fairly good distributors
- Lower product quality
- Drop accounts with minimal performance
- Indiscriminately raise prices
- Cast aside marketing plans
- Forget about informing the public on the seller's true role

These marketers falsely believed that since their products were selling easily, the need for marketing had lessened. A more sensible strategy for a company is to protect and help its customers. They will then remain more loyal and continue to be profitable customers when shortages evaporate.

Marketing executives must convince top management that excessive buyer demand should not dictate a smaller marketing budget. Instead, reallocation of marketing funds is needed. The company's buyers need support and knowledge to handle the frustrating periods of supply shortages.

A strategic marketing management audit is a potential first task. The company may, for instance, explore the feasibility of mergers / acquisition, vertical or horizontal integration, or reassignments of personnel. The goal is to see what strategic changes can be executed to help buyers receive at least minimum levels for continuing operations.

Certain marketing objectives and tasks may be modified during shortages. The company may search for methods to increase supply or for new substitute sources, while making sure that everyone has a fair chance to buy reasonable quantities. (Some purchasers stockpile their inventory, which can hurt other buyers who lack adequate quantities to continue operations.) The company might help their customers to:

- Reduce customer waste
- Find alternative supplies
- Encourage marketing research for product ideas
- Change channels for quicker distribution
- Improve logistical support and delivery schedules
- Advocate intraindustry cooperation with noncompeting buyers for sharing the limited supplies
- Refrain from raising prices and profit margins
- Modify promotional efforts to accentuate conservation of company goods and services

The company may also have to educate the government and work with it. Occasionally, government intervention is a potential outcome

because the buying community complains about inadequate supply. There may even be complaints or accusations of unfair profit margins or price gouging.

During periods of high consumer demand, marketers must make a smooth change in their marketing strategies. They must keep in mind that the market shifts rapidly back and forth, and buyers have good memories. If they feel mistreated, they will refuse to do business with the shortsighted sellers again.

Inflation/Stagflation/Hyperinflation

Increasing prices combined with declining consumer purchasing power (inflation) causes uneasiness among marketers. Worry is compounded when high unemployment is associated with rising and then decreasing purchasing power (stagflation). The most extreme case, hyperinflation, results in people spending their wages immediately to avoid rapid price increases for needed goods and services. Any one of these three situations can tax a company in formulating effective marketing strategies. Further, inflation is a persistent and continuous anxiety for everyone.

▶ In Inflationary Times, Marketing Strategies Must Encompass Better Accounting Methods, Reasonable Price Changes, and Greater Efficiency in the Entire Marketing Program

A balance is needed between the cost of doing business and meeting customers' needs at fair prices.

First, the impact of inflation must be clearly identified in internal managerial accounting reports and in external financial statements. Accounting procedures must be adjusted to get a clearer picture of performance levels. If they are not, profits may be overstated, depreciation figures understated, and the future costs of replacement capital and of materials, manpower, machinery, and services underestimated. Returns on investment, equity, and assets must also be examined for inflationary impact. The whole inflationary climate calls for capable asset-allocation decisions concerning individual product lines, sales territories, market segments, and distribution units. Thus, inflation-accounting techniques are needed to make effective diagnostic analyses and then prescribe corrective actions.

Second, the pricing function must be carefully handled. Automatic price increases may alienate customers or cause them to do business elsewhere. Judicious pricing policies and procedures are mandatory. A successful pricing strategy should encompass:

- Monitoring the competition for price increases
- Knowing the elasticity of demand for company products
- Creating the ability to adjust prices quickly to accommodate to the inflationary environment
- Recognizing the impact of timing price changes
- Understanding other marketing options: unbundling products / services, differentiating products, tightening credit, decreasing quantity offered, segmenting markets more distinctly, lowering expected profit margins for certain marketing units
- Keeping flexibility and control in pricing strategies by using escalation clauses, final quotation pricing delays, rebates, and liberal discounts (these tactics give better control over unforeseen elements)
- Working with key groups, channel members, the sales force, advertising people, and so on to successfully implement price changes

Third, careful attention is needed to the costs side of doing business. Marketing productivity has already been discussed in an earlier chapter, and the discussion will not be repeated here. Suffice it to say that in inflationary times, executives must be extra sensitive to business costs. A firm cannot merely pass additional costs on to consumers in the form of higher prices. Household and business buyers adjust their purchasing practices: They become less wasteful, do more comparative shopping, and carefully look for value. They spend more time shopping for specials and bargains. Thus, price increases may cause loss of sales. This danger makes it critical to improve operations and reduce expenditures. These actions permit more leeway on final prices while possibly providing a competitive advantage.

Managing Dynamic Interdepartmental Conflicts

Management theory stresses departmental cooperation within an organization. Yet counterproductive and contradictory behavior often occurs in marketing and other departments.

Marketing people are concerned with both revenues and costs. Other departments, such as production or engineering, may be cost centers. Consequently, short-run conflicts can arise between marketing and the other functions. Executives from other departments want to know how a particular marketing course of action may affect their own costs. For example, a desire by marketing for higher inventory levels could increase production or physical distribution costs.

Another cause for disagreement is the role and scope of marketing in

creating change within the organization. Marketers are change agents who might disrupt the normal procedures or philosophy of conducting business. Their encouragement of change may polarize behavior and cause extreme positions.

In trying to meet consumer demands and interests, marketing people may disagree with other corporate functions. Personnel from other departments may be unaware of consumer preferences or believe that marketers have misinterpreted consumer wishes. Intermittently, nonmarketing professionals may feel that there is too much attention to sales revenue.

▶ Managerial Effort Must Be Applied to Change Relations from Conflict to Resolution to Cooperation

If a conflict exists between the marketing department and other departments, management can take certain actions to resolve it:

1. *Make a diagnostic audit.* Identify specific interdepartmental concerns that cause strife. Encourage candid discussion to clarify the exact problems.

2. *Use participative problem solving.* Encourage the marketing staff to work with other departments in identifying and fulfilling prospective customer's needs. Cooperative attitudes must be encouraged for overlapping functions. A marketing team composed of professional personnel from different areas might be developed to sell and service key accounts. Often key executives (e.g., from engineering, physical distribution, production, and postsale service) are indispensable in securing a major contract.

3. *Encourage communication.* Design formal joint meetings between selected marketing people and professionals from other functional areas to determine and solve subversive organizational conflicts. Appointing interdepartmental representatives who can facilitate the exchange of ideas and suggestions between departments is sometimes helpful. Marketing liaison people could then brief nonmarketing executives on consumer trends, competition, product specifications, market research data, and the like.

4. *Use manpower planning, development, and rotation.* More togetherness should be sanctioned. Evaluate prospective marketing people on how they would handle intergroup conflict. They should also appreciate ways to minimize future contradictory behavior. In some cases, job ro-

tation between departments might be feasible. For instance, some companies have rotated technical marketers and engineers. Both groups soon learn to promote technical products while recognizing the engineering limitations and strengths of their own departments.

5. *Practice continuous management development.* Formal and informal training sessions can indoctrinate company personnel with the challenges and issues of marketing. Greater empathy and exchange of ideas on possible strategies for individual departments and the total organization are healthy and help to improve intergroup conflicts.

6. *Arrange the organizational structure to meet strategic objectives.* Some firms have evolved from a functional to a matrix organization. This evolution can alter traditional departmental relationships and lines of authority. Product development or project teams, for instance, must complete tasks that are not structured through the normal organizational chart. Top management should arrange the web of relationships to meet the strategic company and departmental objectives. Top executives can also aid marketing people and those in other departments by emphasizing the serious need for cooperation.

▶ Intergroup Conflict Should Not Be Completely Eliminated; Instead It Should Be Controlled to Promote Positive Change

Complete harmony may not be achievable. There are situations in which individual departmental integrity must be maintained. Marketing and other departmental executives can be effective checks and balances for each other. In fact, managed and controlled conflict may promote positive changes. It may serve to reallocate unused assets, develop methods for better efficiency, discourage inept status quo decisions, increase innovative ideas, and decrease collusion among middle managers who are not aggressive enough.

Future Outlook: Finding a Better Forecasting Procedure

Marketers should not only learn to develop flourishing marketing strategies in a fluid environment but to anticipate and forecast future sales. Marketing people either perform the actual sales forecast, provide input for formulation of the final forecasted figures, or respond and adjust to the figures. (Which personnel have sales forecasting responsibility varies from firm to firm). Details of the number crunching involved in sales forecasting and the ramifications of the forecast are beyond the scope of this book. However, a few points are addressed to show what the sales forecasting process "ought to be."

▶ Final Sales Forecast Figures Have a Profound Impact on Corporate Decisions

Executives from various departments use sales estimates in making decisions. Sales forecast figures affect the firm's plans and actions in regulating production, determining inventory needs, budgeting various corporate units or departments, analyzing physical distribution requirements, controlling purchasing plans, forecasting cash flow, making capital budgeting decisions, identifying manpower and staffing needs, and evaluating actual performance levels.

All departments have a vital stake in the accuracy of forecast figures. If they are too high or too low, executives will soon be facing problems within their own corporate unit. For instance, poor forecasting could result in either excessive or inadequate inventories, costly production setups and retooling, overexpansion, a cash crunch, or an imbalance in the type and quantity of goods needed to fulfill strategic organizational objectives.

A number of nonmarketing professional organizations and associations now instruct their members on the art of sales forecasting. Some executives have felt that they were misled by forecasters and relied too heavily on the estimated figures. They based their decisions on these figures and were then unfairly blamed for the poor end results within their units.

▶ Sales Forecast Figures Are Only Estimates

Those who criticize forecasting results should realize that the figures are tools for aiding decision making rather than absolute assertions about the future. At the same time, forecasters must be candid about their estimate, and admit the margin of error.

The accuracy of forecasts varies by industry, product line, customers, and the business situation. It is especially difficult to predict sales for new businesses, products, or markets. International markets or volatile economic conditions can complicate the issue even further.

Forecasts should periodically be evaluated and adjusted to reflect environmental changes. This policy lets the company modify decisions so that they reflect evolving actualities as accurately as possible.

To lessen the risks of inaccuracy, some executives ask for two or three forecasts, which might embrace (1) a low and a high range or (2) an optimistic, a pessimistic, and a most likely set of figures. This mixture of figures enables users to make ball park decisions. The users feel more secure. In fact, a few organizations—especially in high-tech indus-

tries—have asked forecasters to predict the minimum number of a new product that the firm could sell. In the meantime, financial analysts compare the investment requirements with payoffs at various potential sales levels, and determine the minimum sales amount required to meet the desired financial objectives. If this minimum amount is greater than the forecasters' minimum (pessimistic) sales estimate, a go decision is made or adjustments are made, such as in financial expectations and costs, to match the minimum sales estimates and financial objectives.

▶ A Sales Forecaster Must Utilize Forecasting Techniques that Are Most Appropriate for the Prevailing Circumstances While Recognizing the Limitations and Advantages of Each

The forecaster must also select the methods that are best suited to the firm's level of resources and capabilities. Figure 20.1 summarizes the most popular forecasting techniques, their advantages and disadvantages, and when each is useful.

In deciding which techniques are best for the organization, the costs of each should be equated as nearly as possible with the benefits to be derived from its utilization. In addition, the degree of accuracy of previous forecasting methods should be studied. Past experience gives a good feeling for which techniques to select.

The techniques chosen must make the best use of available data. For example, past sales data and marketing variables that affect sales may create problems, respectively, in using time series and multiple regression techniques. The time available for doing a forecast will also influence selection of techniques. Certain methods, such as regression and model building, take time, and management may want the estimates much sooner. Last, the technical or quantitative requirements of some methods might preclude their use. The staff may lack the skills needed to follow through with sophisticated techniques.

It is good practice to use more than one technique, since all have some weaknesses. A number of executives strongly believe, however, that the need is not for improved forecasting methods but for better application of the techniques.

▶ Sales Forecasting Process Can Be Enhanced

There are various ways to enhance the sales forecasting procedure. Some are given in the following list:

Figure 20.1. Summary of eight popular sales forecasting techniques

Method/Explanation	Applications/Advantages/Disadvantages
Jury of executive opinion: Top executives give their own estimates. Figures may be adjusted and compromised to account for different viewpoints	Useful for total company sales Easy and quick No need for elaborate statistics Popular for strategic planning May be only alternative if available data inadequate Total picture seen, since executives have access to both macro and micro data Subjective in nature Popular among small and medium-sized companies The larger the organization, the more difficult to break down forecasts for individual products, markets, territories
Sales person estimates: Sales force or distributors provide sales estimations for their own territory. These may then be combined for a total company forecast	Salespeople closest to the marketplace Useful when market or competition is dynamic Can be overly optimistic or pessimistic Subjectivity hard to eliminate Common in industrial markets The fewer the number of customers for each sales person, the greater the potential for accuracy of the forecast (sales person should know customer buying plans quite well) Helpful for individual products, territories, or customer breakdowns Time consuming and could detract from actual sales efforts (i.e., selling time) Difficult to use for total company sales, since salespeople do not have all of the data Marginal for long-term trends Forecast will be low if used as a device for setting sales quotas
Moving average: Taking a weighted average of a number of sales points and dividing by the number of points	Ignores irregular, or extreme sales points. Enough sales points needed to make average meaningful Useful for stable product and marketplace environment Easy to use More helpful for immediate future than for long-term/strategic forecasts
Exponential smoothing: Like a weighted average in that more value (alpha factor) is given to more recent sales points (in a moving average, all sales points are given equal value)	Can make adjustments to recent seasonal factors Recent data may reflect the market more than earlier historical data Subjective due to placing a value on the alpha factor (the higher its value, the more weight given to recent periods) Does not account for trends Easy to figure and inexpensive Does not require a lot of historical data

Figure 20.1. Summary of eight popular sales forecasting techniques

Method/Explanation	Applications/Advantages/Disadvantages
Trend projections and time series analysis: Mathematical equation allows plotting of a trend line by means of which future sales can be projected	Past trends may not reflect changes, such as new competition, products, marketing strategy, or economic conditions Popular when environment is stable Fast, easy, and cheap to use Enough sales points must be available to project future sales Poor for measuring turning points Assumes previous sales patterns are consistent, complete, and logical
Correlation/regression: Quantitative method for studying relationship between sales (dependent variable) and one or more factors (independent variables) that explain or influence sales volume	Powerful analytical tool Requires determination of predictable independent variables Motivates user to see what factors might influence sales Complex and time consuming Now easier to use because of computer-packaged programs Illustrates causation and can predict turning points False correlation may prevail Weak related data must be eliminated Requires an on-going analysis to modify independent variables that are used.
Survey buyer intentions: Customers are asked what they plan to buy during the forecasted period and an estimation is made on the amount of the planned purchases	Useful for new products or markets Small number of customers makes implementation easier Requires customer cooperation and objectivity Customers may not be sure about purchases; what they say they will do and what they actually do may not agree Gathering data could be time-consuming and expensive Hard to identify who future customers might be The longer the time frame between the responses versus actual marketplace conditions, the less likely the accuracy Gives "feel" for the marketplace May spot new trends or turning points
Test marketing	See Chapter 9 on test marketing

- If possible, incorporate consumer plans and attitudes in the forecast.
- Obtain opinions from the sales force, especially if sales personnel know their customers well.
- Provide enough time, money, computer staff, and other staff to perform the job.

- Be flexible: Note changing conditions and permit revisions.
- Identify clearly who is responsible for the forecast function.
- Balance the contributions of both good management judgment and sound statistical and mathematical tools.
- Avoid using sales estimates as a sledgehammer for motivating and evaluting sales personnel, particularly when they are giving input to the sales forecast.
- Study the assumptions that were made for the forecast.
- Develop a useful sales data base that can be broken down by various components, for example, product lines, Standard Metropolitan Statistical Areas (SMSA), customers, and sales territories. These categories could be vital for bottom-up forecasting.
- Give an adequate amount of information, even the bad news, that could affect the sales estimates.
- Provide an environment that is supportive of managers who make decisions based on the sales projections.

Despite problems, just going through the mechanics of preparing a forecast can be beneficial. The process forces examination of strengths and weaknesses, causes improvement in management communication, and highlights the need to anticipate and to plan and coordinate future operations. It also serves as a conduit to thinking about the future while facilitating positive change.

In the planning and implementation stages of the forecasting process, forecasters and users interact with each other. The users can support the forecaster in formulating the challenges properly. This interaction gives users more confidence in the actual forecast produced and allows them to employ the figures effectively. On the other hand, forecasters work on meaningful tasks that interest management. This communication and cooperation create more encouragement for and excitement in the sales forecasting system, and it helps the firm successfully anticipate changes while developing contingency strategies to deal with actual outcomes.

21

Epilogue: Lessons to Be Learned

Marketing has become a highly creative, far-reaching, and technical field, and it is in a perpetual (and at times perplexing) fluid state. Given the numerous stakeholders of any organization, either for profit or nonprofit, marketing personnel must be inspired to propagate winning ideas and contribute to the well-being of the organization.

An organization is like a living organism; it has certain needs to survive. Marketing people are the change makers and agents in fulfilling its needs. Their goal is to satisfy consumers and society while still meeting the organization's profit objective or some other standard.

Becoming a prosperous marketer is not a simple endeavor. Even seasoned veterans are constantly learning. The field demands hard work, innovative effort, and willingness to take good calculated risks. It entails comprehensive planning and then action. I sincerely believe that the principles, procedures, tips, and recommendations in this book can help the reader succeed with marketing strategies. Some may have merely reinforced ideas; others may have led to a rethinking of marketing approaches, strategies, or upcoming decisions.

The pursuit of marketing efficiency and fruitful strategies is an exciting but meticulous endeavor. Finding out what is best entails a diagnostic analysis, followed by a prescriptive marketing program. Depending on circumstances, this book can lead to fine tuning or a major overhaul

of a marketing program. Successful application of these marketing ideas, rules, and principles is up to the reader. Remember: None of us may ever reach that elusive rainbow in our favorite fairy tale. But a rigorous search and desire for the ideal strategy will nonetheless enable us to be excellent marketers. GOOD LUCK ON YOUR APPLICATION OF THIS BOOK AND YOUR FUTURE MARKETING ENDEAVORS.

SELECTED BIBLIOGRAPHY

Abel, Derek, F., and John S. Hammond. *Strategic Marketing Planning*. Englewood Cliffs, NJ: Prentice-Hall, 1979.

Agency Sales, Irvine, Ca.: Manufacturers' Agents National Association.

Allen, M. G., "Strategic Problems Facing Today's Corporate Planner." Speech given at the Academy of Management, 36th Annual Meeting, Kansas City, Missouri, 1976.

Ansoff, Igor. *Corporate Strategy*. New York: McGraw-Hill, 1965.

Bartlett, Harold E. "Tips for Trouble-Free Scheduling," in a special report, "Trade Shows Where Prospects Call on You." *Sales & Marketing Management* (August 20, 1979).

Berg, Thomas. *Case Histories of Marketing Misfires*. Garden City, NY: Doubleday, 1970.

Cohen, William A. *Building a Mail Order Business*. New York: Wiley, 1982.

Comer, James. "The Computer: Personal Selling and Sales Management." *Journal of Marketing* (July 1975): 27–33.

Day, George, "Diagnosing the Product Portfolio." *Journal of Marketing* (April 1977): 29–38.

Deal, Terrance, and Allen Kennedy. *Corporate Culture*. Reading, MA: Addison-Wesley, 1982.

Direct Marketing, Garden City, NY: Direct Marketing Publisher.

Drucker, Peter. *The Practice of Management*. New York: Harper & Row, 1954.

Guidelines for Preparing More Effective Technical Proposals for the Navy Department. Washington, D.C.: No date given.

Hartley, Robert F. *Marketing Mistakes*. 3rd ed. New York: Wiley, 1986.

Hartley, Robert F. *Marketing Successes*. New York: Wiley, 1985.

Haspeslagh, Phillippe. "Portfolio Planning Uses and Limits." *Harvard Business Review* (January–February 1982): 58–73.

"How to Evaluate Your Trade Show," *Industrial Marketing* (October 1981).

Hughes, David. "Computerized Sales Management." *Harvard Business Review* (March–April 1983): 102–112.

Kordahl, Eugene. *Telemarketing for Business: A Guide to Building Your Own Telemarketing Operation.* Englewood Cliffs, NJ: Prentice-Hall, 1984.

Kotler, Philip. *Marketing Management Analysis, Planning and Control.* 5th ed. Englewood Cliffs, NJ: Prentice-Hall, 1984.

Kuswa, Webster. *Big Paybacks from Small Budget Advertising.* Chicago: The Darnell Corporation, 1982.

Levinson, Robert. *The Decentralized Company.* New York: AMACOM, 1983.

Levitt, Theodore, "Marketing Myopia." *Harvard Business Review* (September–October 1975).

McCall, Morgan, and Michael Lombardo. "What Makes a Top Executive?" *Psychology Today* (February 1983): 26–31.

McGuire, Patrick. *Evaluating New-Product Proposals.* New York: The Conference Board, 1973.

Mutter, John. "To Keep Costs Down, Watch the Details." *Sales & Marketing Management* (August 26, 1979).

Ogilvy, David. *Ogilvy on Advertising.* New York: Crown, 1983.

Peters, Thomas, and Robert Waterman, Jr. *In Search of Excellence: Lessons from America's Best-Run Companies.* New York: Harper & Row, 1982.

Ricks, David. *Big Business Blunders.* Homewood, IL: Dow Jones-Irwin, 1983.

Ries, Al, and Jack Trout. *Positioning: The Battle for Your Mind.* New York: McGraw-Hill, 1981.

Rogers, Everett. *The Diffusion of Innovations.* New York: Free Press, 1962.

Roman, Murray. *Telephone Marketing: How to Build Business by Telephone.* New York: McGraw-Hill, 1976.

Steckel, Robert C. *Profitable Telephone Sales Operations.* New York: ARCO, 1976.

Stone, Bob. *Successful Direct Marketing Methods.* Chicago: Crain Books, 1979.

"Survey of Buying Power," "Survey of Buying Power II," "Survey of Industrial Purchasing Power," and "Survey of Selling Costs" are published annually in *Sales and Marketing Management.* New York: Sales and Marketing Management Publishers.

Telemarketing Norwalk, CT. Technology Marketing Corporation

"The Product Portfolio," Perspective No. 66, Boston: The Boston Consulting Group, 1970.

Weinrauch, J. Donald, and William E. Piland. *Applied Marketing Principles.* Englewood Cliffs, NJ: Prentice-Hall, 1979.

Weinrauch, J. Donald, and Terri Langley, "Marketing Management's Utilization of Trade Shows: Confronting the Opportunities, Mistakes and Challenges." *1984 Academy of Marketing Science Proceedings* 7 (1984): 338–342.

Index

Advertising:
  advantages, 166–167
  budget, 169–170
  limiting costs, 173
  measuring results, 192–196
  misconceptions, 167–169
  mistakes, 169–171
  visual elements, 182–183
Advertising agency:
  functions of, 189–190
  selection process, 191–192
Advertising budget, 169–170, 171–173
Advertising copy:
  evaluation, 179–180
  headlines, 181–182
  humor, 181
  music, 180
  objectives, 174
  strategy, 178–180
Advertising effectiveness, 192–196
Advertising pretests, 194
Advertising post-tests, 194
Advertising slogan, 182
Advertising strategy, 197
Affordability method, 172
Agency Sales, 224
Aluminum Company of North America, 41
Amco, 281
American Express, 260
American Patent Law Association, 118
American Telephone & Telegraph, 102, 281
Annual marketing plan:
  do's and don'ts for preparing, 38–39
  major elements in, 35–36
  questions to ask, 35
  strategic *vs.*, 31
Apple computer, 93, 281
Audience profile, 244–245
Avon, 281

Base salary, 204
Bean, L. L., 260
Berg, Thomas I., 25
Bidding process:
  do's and don'ts, 161–162
  government jobs, 162
  guidelines, 162–163
Big Business Blunders, 25
Billboard, 178
Boston Consulting Group, 19, 105–106
Bottom-up, 257
Brainstorming sessions, planning aid, 37–38
Branding:
  caveats in, 121
  strategy, 119–121
Brand name, 119
Break-even, 46

313

314   INDEX

Brunswick, 41
Budgeting, 26, 61–62
  marketing research, 61–62
Burger King, 93
Business-to-business markets, 58–59
Business Marketing, 251
Business Periodical Index, 70
Business screen, 38

Campbell, 6, 120
Careers:
  national account management, 203–204
  personal selling, 199–201
  successful marketer, 15
Case Histories of Marketing Misfires, 25
Cash cows, 105–106
Cash flow, 152, 163–164, 292–293
Celebrities, in advertising, 184–186
Certification of foreign trade shows, 252
Channel captain, 283–284
Channel manager, 279–280
Channel members, 151–152, 283–285
Channels of distribution, 273, 278–285
Chase Manhattan, 260
Chrysler, 3, 4, 57, 291
C.I.F. (Cost-insurance-freight), 253
Coca-Cola, 7, 22, 120, 281
Coleco, 90
Columbia House Records, 260
Comer, James, 215
Competition:
  checklist, of questions about, 22
  direct marketing, 258
  product teardown, five steps, 18
  profile, 20
  questions, 22–23
  sales territories, 214
Competitive information, 18–22
Competitive parity approach, 171–172
Competitive profile, 20
Competitor weaknesses, 20–21
Conflict resolution, 301–302
Consumer adoption process, 96–98
Consumer discontentment, 139–140
Consumer loyalty, 232
Consumer movement, 140
  discontentment, 139–140
  ombudsman for, 142–143
  suggestions for dealing with, 141–143
Consumer panel, 193
Consumer panels, 75
Consumer protest, 139–142
Contests, 194–196
Contribution margin, 43–44, 250

Cooperative advertising:
  do's and don'ts, 188–189
  partnership between manufacturers and middlemen, 187–188
  uses, 186–187
Copyright protection, 118
Copywriter, 177–180
Corporate Culture, 3
Corporate mission, 32
Correlation, 305
Costs-per-order, 209
Costs trade-offs, 276–277
Coupons, 194
Creativity guidelines, 87
CRT terminals, 268
Cummins, 281
Customer lifestyle, 256–257
Customer service:
  audit, 133–134
  function, 131–132

Deal, Terrance, 3
Dealer brands, 120
Dean Witter Reynolds, 102
The Decentralized Company, 7
Department of the Navy, 162
Diffusion of innovation, 96–98
Digital Equipment, 204, 225
Directional policy matrix, 108
Direct mail:
  advantages and disadvantages, 178
  definition, 256–257
  image of, 263–264
  strategy tips, 264–268
Direct Marketing, 255
Direct marketing:
  definition, 256
  fulfillment, 262–263
  mail order, 263–268
  products for, 257–258
  prospect list, 260–261
  techniques, 257–258
Direct Marketing Association (DMA), 264
Direct response, 194–195
Disney, Walt, 281
Docutel, 102
Do's and Don'ts:
  bidding process evaluating, 161–162
  cooperative advertising enhancing, 188–189
  focus group interviews using, 74
  mistakes managing, 28
  plans preparing, 39–40
  product development developing, 99–100

productivity improving, 47
product management improving, 126–127
sales training program preparing, 216–219
test marketing forecasting, 82
warranty function improving, 137–139
Dr. Pepper, 21
Drucker, Peter, 3
DuPont, 10, 44

Eastern Airlines, 58
Ego-sensitive merchandise, 156
Emerson Electric, 41
Encyclopedia of Associations, 70
Entrepreneurs, 7
Evaluating New Product Proposals, 89
Exclusive distribution, 280–281
Exhibit Designers and Producers Associations, 244
Expense accounts, 207–208
Experience cost curve, 94
Experience curve, 44–45
Exponential smoothing, 305
Exposition Service Contractors Association, 244
Expressed warranty, 136
Extended warranty, 136
Exxon, 260

Family brands, 120
Federal Reserve Bulletin, 70
Focus groups:
  advantages and disadvantages, 73
  advertising strategy, 193–194
  do's and don'ts, 74
  moderator, 74–75
F.O.B. (Free-on-board), 253
Ford Motor Company, 18
Foreign sales exhibitions, 250–253
Functional costs, 42–43
Funk and Scott Index, 70

General Electric, 102, 107–108, 120, 260
General Foods, 10, 81
General Information Concerning Patents, 118
General Information Concerning Trademarks, 118
General Mills, 81
Generic brands, 120–121
Georgia-Pacific, 281
Gould, 58, 281
Government Printing Office, 118

Gross margin percent, 209
Guidelines for Preparing More Effective Technical Proposals for the Navy Department, 162

Hartley, Robert F., 25
Headlines, 181–182
Heinz, 120
Hospital Corporation of America, 102
Hughes, David, 215
Hyperinflation, 299

Iacocca, Lee, 291
IBM, 7, 212
Implied warranty, 136
Incremental costs, 44
Incremental revenue, 44
Individual brands, 120
Inflation, 299–300
Innovation, 6, 86–87. *See also* Product development
In Search of Excellence, 212
Intensive distribution, 280–281
Interdepartmental conflicts, 300–302
Intermediaries, 259
Intermediate consumers, 51, 58–59, 203
International business, 250–253
International Trade Administration, 252

J. C. Penney Company, 260
Johnson & Johnson, 10
Jury of Executive Opinion, 305

Kennedy, Allen, 3
Kordahl, Eugene, 269, 271
Kroger, 281

Leasing, 163–164
Levinson, Robert, 7
Levi Strauss, 7
Levitt, Theodore, 6
List broker, 260
Logo, 183–184
Longitudinal analysis, 75
Loss leaders, 157

McDermott International, 291
McDonald's, 93
McGuire, Patrick, 89
Magazine, 178
MANA (Manufacturers' Agent's National Association, 224
Management audit, 171, 226–227
Management by crisis, 28

Management information systems, 4, 8, 78
Manufacturers' representatives, 222–224
Markdowns, 153–154
Market account analysis, 213
Market exposure, 280–281
Marketing:
  audit, 10
  career, 15
  concept, 13
  costs, 42–43
  excellence, 3–11
Marketing Mistakes, 25
Marketing mistakes:
  budgeting, 26
  buyer behavior, 26
  communication program, 27
  do's and don'ts, managing, 28
  marketing intelligence system, 27
  marketplace trends, 25
  organization objectives, 27
  strategic planning, 26
"Marketing Myopia," 6
Marketing personnel:
  avoiding mistakes, 28
  responsibility, 25, 31
  successful traits, 13–15, 28
Marketing productivity:
  do's and don'ts, 47
  guidelines, 9–10
  questions to ask, 46–47
  significance, 41
Marketing research:
  conflict with management, 64–66, 68
  decision makers, 64–67, 71
  focus groups, 73–75
  objectives in, 68–70
  proposal, 75–78
  saving costs, 62–63
  secondary data, 70–71
  steps, 67–68
  strategic planning, 4
Marketing strategies:
  high growth business, 296–297
  inflationary times, 299–300
  no-growth conditions, 294–296
  shortages, 297–299
  turnarounds, 291–292
Market Research Corporation of America, 19
Market segmentation:
  basis, 52
  seven steps, 52–54
Market share approach, 171

Market share/market growth matrix, 105–107
Market target:
  demographics, 58
  overlooked subtleties, 59–60
  requirements, 54
  Standard Industrial Classification, 58–59
Media, 176–180
Media plan:
  advertising objectives, 174–176
  blunders, 170
  criteria for selection, 176–177
  types of media, 177–178
Middle managers, 41, 66
Middlemen, 231, 237–238, 278–280
Middlemen brands, 120
Moderator, focus groups, 74–75
Moody's, 71
Morris, Philip, 7, 21
Moving average, 305
Multifactor Portfolio Matrix, 107–108

National Account Management (NAM), 203–204, 225–226
National Association of Exposition Managers, 241, 243
National brands, 120
National Purchasing Diary Panel, 19
National Trade Show Association, 244
Natural costs, 42–43
NCR, 41
Neiman-Marcus, 260
Newspaper, 178
Nielsen, A. C., 19
No-growth environment, 294–296
Northwestern Mutual Life Insurance Company, 141

Oak Industry, 91
Objectives:
  advertising, 172, 174–176
  channel members, 282–283
  direct marketing, 262
  marketing research, 68–70
  planning, 32, 36–37
  pricing, 149–151
  sales promotion, 235–236
  trade shows, 243
  training, sales people, 216
Objective-task approach, 172
Olin, 225
Opportunity costs, 45–46

Order getter, 201–202
Order taker, 201–202
Organizational objectives, 5
Organization niche, 8
Osborne, 92
Outside sales force, 222–224

Packaging:
  benefits, 121
  channel concerns with, 122–123
  complaints and blunders, 121–122
  cost reduction, 123
  new products, 95
Past or predicted sales approach, 171
Patents, 92
  constraints and challenges, 116–117
Penetration strategy, 158–160
People Express, 58
Pepsi-Cola, 22, 281
Perceptual mapping, 55
Personal selling:
  audit, 226–227
  budgeting, 202–204
  career concerns of, 199–201
  compensation structure, 204–207
  evaluation, 208–212
  motivation, 204–207
  quotas, 210–212
  sales promotion, 238–239
  selection of personnel, 220
  territories, 213–215
  training, 215–220
Peters, Thomas, 212
Physical distribution:
  components, 275–276
  costs, 276–277
  management, 278
  transportation modes, 278
Physiological tests, 193
PIMS, 38, 111
Pizza Time, 296
Place, 273
Planning process:
  challenges and problems, 33–34
  excuses to avoid, 38–39
Portfolio analysis, planning aid, 37
Portfolio tests, 193
Positioning: The Battle for Your Mind, 56
Post-show promotion, 249
The Practice of Management, 3
Preshow promotion, 247–248
Pretest, 237
Price changes, 155–156

Price elasticity, 154–156
Price negotiations, 162–163
Price-off allowances, 232
Price promotions, 157–158
Price strategies, 232
Pricing decisions:
  information, 147–148
  mistakes, 146
  objectives, 150–151
  problems, 148
  product adjustments, 154
  skimming *vs.* penetration, 158–160
  steps to follow, 149–151
Primary data, 70–71, 147
Private brands, 120
Problem children, 106
Procter & Gamble, 123, 281
Product development:
  do's and don'ts, 99–100
  generalizations, 86–87
  mistakes to avoid, 98–99
Product life cycle, 109–111
  planning aid, 38
  pros and cons of use, 110–111
Product management:
  do's and don'ts, 126–127
  feasibility, 123–124
  organizational headaches of, 125–126
Product mix:
  decision making, 112–113
  direct marketing, 259–260
  discontinuance, of product, 113–114
  good product qualities, 127
  prime products, 293
  problem products, 128–129
  recycling opportunities in, 115–116
  sales territories, 214
Product performance:
  principles of, 102–103
  top management's role, 103–104
Product positioning, 21, 56
  advertising strategy for, 95–96
Product quality, 111
Product specifications, 111–112
Professional service firms, 3
Profitable Telephone Sales Operations, 271
Profit Impact of Marketing Strategies
  (PIMS), planning aid, 38
Promotional bias, 5
Promotional warranty, 136
Proposals, 75–78
  marketing research, 75–78
  new products, 88–90

318 INDEX

Prospect list, 260–262
Psychographics, 52
Pull, 282
Push, 281
Push/pull combination, 282

Qualitative research, 73

Radio, 178
Ralston Purina, 81
Reach, 174
Recycling waste, 115–116
Register of Copyrights, 118
Regression, 305
Republic Health, 292
Research design, 71
Retail location, 286–288
Reynolds, R. J., 10
Ricks, David A., 25
Ries, Al, 177
Rogers, Everett, 96
Roman, Murray, 271

Safeway Stores, 5
Sales agents, 222–224
Sales audits, 226–227
Sales compensation, 204–207
Sales per customer, 209
Sales exhibits, see Trade shows
Sales forecasting, 302–307
Sales & Marketing Management, 246, 254
Sales per order, 209
Sales person estimates, 305
Sales-to-potential ratio, 209
Sales promotion:
 audit, 236–237
 objectives, 235–236
 problems, 233–234
 purpose, 230
 strategies, 234–239
 trends, 232–233
 types, 229–232
Sales quotas, 210–212
Sales representatives, 222–224
Sales-to-sales quota, 209
Sales territories, 212–215
Sales training, 215
Scientific Atlanta, 91
Secondary data, 70–71, 147
Selective distribution, 280–281
Service personnel:
 contacting, 135
 issues, 132
 reward, 134–135
 training, 132–133
Sears, 57, 102, 135, 260, 291
Shopping center, 286–288
Shopping goods, 203
Singer, 104
Skimming strategy, 158–160
Smith Kline, 9
Smuckers, 120
Source & Perrier, 104
Southwestern Airlines, 7, 53
Specialty goods, 203
Spiegel, 260
Spin-off products, 116
Split tests, 196
Stagflation, 299
Standard Industrial Classification (SIC), 58
Standard Metropolitan Statistical Area (SMSA), 307
Statistical Abstract of the United States, 70
Steckel, Robert, 271
Stimulus, response effect, 195
Straight commission, 205
Straight salary, 205
Strategic marketing plan:
 annual *vs.*, 31
 benefits, 34–35
 bottom-up approach, 32
 do's and don'ts for preparing, 38–39
 major components, 32
Strategic planning, 5–6, 93–94, 104–109
Survey of buyer intentions, 90, 305
Survey of Buyer Power, 71
Survey of Buying Power, 71
Survey of Industrial Purchasing Power, 71
Survey of Selling Costs, 71

Tape club, 260
Target marketing, see Market segmentation
Taylor Wine, 7
Teardown, 18
Telemarketing, 268–271
Telemarketing for Business: A Guide to Building Your Own Telemarketing Operation, 269, 271
Telephone Marketing, 271
Television, 178
Territory potential, 213–215
Test marketing, 79–82
Texas Instruments, 3, 44
Texscan, 91
Time series, 305

Toll-free numbers, 195
Top management:
  marketing *vs.*, 3, 6, 9–11, 27–28, 32
  personal selling strategies, 203–204
  product development role, 85–86
  product mix decisions, 103–104
  strategic planning, 34–35
Total cost, 45
Total cost concept, 45
Total system, 275–276
Trade shows:
  advantages, 241–242
  budgeting, 245–247
  checklist, 251
  evaluation, 249–251
  mistakes, 242–243
  objectives, 243
  steps for planning, 243–250
Treasure hunts, 195
Trend projections, 305
Trout, Jack, 56
Turnaround specialists, 291–292
Turnaround strategies, 292–294
TWA, 58
20-80, 80-20 rule, 56–57

Uniroyal, 281
U.S. Department of Commerce, 252
U.S. Government Manual, 70
U.S. Patent and Trademark Office, 92

Vernon, Lillian, 260

Warranty:
  do's and don'ts, 137–139
  successful program, 137
  types, 136
Waterman, Robert, 212
Weinrauch, J. Donald, 63
Wendy's, 93
Westinghouse, 225
Whirlpool, 284
White Motor Company, 112
White Trucks, 225
Woolworth, F. W., 101, 281
Workload, 213

Xerox, 41